The Newlywed Cookbook

Robin Vitetta-Miller

Sourcebooks, Inc.®
Naperville, IL

This publication is designed to provide accurate and authoritative information in regard to the subject matter covered. It is sold with the understanding that the publisher is not engaged in rendering legal, accounting, or other professional service. If legal advice or other expert assistance is required, the services of a competent professional person should be sought.

—*From a Declaration of Principles Jointly Adopted by*
a Committee of the American Bar Association and
a Committee of Publishers and Associations

Published by Sourcebooks, Inc.
P.O. Box 4410
Naperville, IL 60567-4410
630.961.3900
Fax: 630.961.2168

Library of Congress Cataloging-in-Publication Data
   Vitetta-Miller, Robin, 1964-
     The Newlywed Cookbook / Robin Vitetta-Miller
         p.   cm.
     ISBN 1-57071-458-4 (alk. paper)
     1. Cookery   I. Title
     TX714.V58   1999
     641.5—dc21   99-16755
                                                   CIP

Printed and bound in the United States of America

BA   10 9 8 7 6 5 4 3 2

Table of Contents

Chicken, Turkey, Duck, and Game Birds

Beef, Pork, Veal, Venison, and Lamb

Seafood and Shellfish

Side Dishes, Salads, and Salsas

Desserts and Other Sweet Treats

Special Occasions

New Year's Eve

Acknowledgments

Where to begin? Thank you Darrin, my incredible husband, for tasting different concoctions every single day (even the stuff with mushrooms). You're my No. 1 taster and best friend. And, thank you my great friends and supportive parents—you were always willing to sample endless creations at dozens of tasting parties. Without your valuable input and priceless suggestions (some quite unique, I must admit), this book would not have been possible.

Introduction

Congratulations! Best wishes for a long and happy life together! Now, what's for dinner?

There's nothing more romantic than dinner for two, prepared at home and served over candlelight. But how realistic is that these days? The fact is, many couples consist of two working people and dinner isn't exactly a priority. That's a shame because some of life's funniest moments and fondest memories happen over a pot of simmering sauce.

Before the big day, I'm sure you enjoyed registering for lots of new toys at your favorite store. There you were, drooling over the multi-function blenders, heavy-duty mixers, coffee makers with the espresso/cappuccino options, and shimmering pots and pans. Now that your kitchen is stocked, what are you supposed to do with it?

I realize you can't be bothered with lengthy recipes, discouraging ingredient lists, and intimidating cooking techniques. If preparing the meal seems daunting, you're likely to skip it altogether. The result? The fabulous new cookware never gets used and you both survive on a diet of take-out pizza, Chinese food, and ready-made meals from the market.

Now for the good news, *The Newlywed Cookbook* can change all that. Perfect for couples and cooks of all levels, this collection of more than two hundred recipes features meals that are simple to prepare, yet unique in composition. You may recognize some of the dishes as meals you ate as a child. The rest were developed to give you countless, innovative solutions to the inevitable "What's for dinner?" question every night of the week. The selection is vast—from bread and pizza to pasta, chicken, beef, seafood, side dishes, desserts, and special occasions—and all the recipes were created with clarity and simplicity in mind. Although the meals are easy to prepare, they boast complex flavors, vibrant colors, and contrasting textures. Believe it or not, extraordinary meals require just a handful of ingredients.

It's time to christen those gifts. Ideally, each gadget, saucepan, and casserole dish would come with a fool-proof recipe. Since they don't, I've included a comprehensive guide at the back of this book called "Equipment." For example, learn how to use your stand mixer to make a perfect chocolate cake, your blender for creamy basil pesto, and your food processor for quick pastry dough.

On to the pantry. With our growing fascination for international ingredients and cross-cultural cuisine, aromatic herbs and exotic spices have become pantry staples. Knowing how and when to use them is critical. In "Herbs and Spices," you'll find a description of each herb or spice, its inherent flavor, and what sweet and/or savory dish it's most suited to.

What if I told you to make a slurry, whisk it into the coulis in the Bain-Marie, and then finish the dish with a chiffonade of basil? You're not off and running? You soon will be after you check out the "Cooking Terms" chapter. It's not advanced Latin, it's simply translating unfamiliar cooking terms into plain, workable English.

Party day is every day. The "Special Occasions" chapter includes fantastic ideas for menu planning, whether entertaining two or twenty-two. These special times include New Year's Eve, Valentine's Day, Thanksgiving, Christmas, One Year Anniversary, Sunday Brunch, Super Bowl Sunday, Picnic for Two, Breakfast in Bed, and When In-Laws Come for Dinner. The recipes for each occasion are extremely versatile, so feel free to use them anytime—Cinco de Mayo, Columbus Day, 4th of July, your best friend's birthday, election day, or whenever the urge to cook something fabulous strikes you.

Rip off those bows, tear away the wrapping paper, and get cooking…together.

Pizza and Bread

Deep Dish Pizzas

Add your favorite toppings to this basic recipe. I love broccoli and spinach, my husband—sausage and pepperoni. Understand why the recipe makes two **separate** *pizzas?*

1. To make the dough, place warm water in a large bowl and sprinkle in yeast. Let stand 5 minutes.

2. Add olive oil and salt. Add 2½ cups of the flour and mix until a manageable dough forms, adding remaining flour if necessary. Using the dough hook attachment on your mixer (or your hands), knead 2 minutes (or 5 minutes by hand), until dough is smooth and elastic. Place dough in a large bowl that has been coated with non-stick spray and turn to coat all sides. Cover with a dish towel and let rise in a warm place, free from draft, until doubled in bulk, about 1 hour.

3. Punch dough down with your fist and divide in half. Press dough into the bottom of two 9-inch round cake pans that have been coated with non-stick spray. Set aside for 20 minutes (for a thinner crust, top and bake right away to prevent the dough from rising again).

4. Preheat oven to 450° F.

5. In a small bowl, combine diced tomatoes, tomato paste, and oregano. Mix well. Top pizza dough with an even layer of mozzarella cheese. Top with tomato mixture and Parmesan cheese (and additional mozzarella cheese if desired).

6. Bake pizzas 15-20 minutes, or until edges are golden and begin to pull slightly away from the sides of pan. Cool slightly before slicing.

Preparation and rising time: 1½-2 hours
Cooking time: 15-20 minutes

Serves 2-4

Needed items
    large and small bowls
    mixer with dough hook
        attachment (optional)
    2 9-inch round cake pans

For the pizza dough:
    1 cup warm water (about 110° F)
    1 packet active dry yeast
    1 teaspoon olive oil
    ½ teaspoon salt
    2½-3 cups all-purpose flour
        non-stick cooking spray

For the topping:
    1 14½-ounce can diced tomatoes
    2 tablespoons tomato paste
    1 tablespoon dried oregano
    4 ounces grated mozzarella
        cheese (regular or part-skim), or
        more as desired
    2 tablespoons grated Parmesan
        cheese

Additional topping ideas:
    grilled vegetables and basil pesto
    wild mushrooms and gorgonzola
        cheese
    sundried tomatoes and
        caramelized onions
    smoked oysters and broccoli rabe
    sautéed spinach and ricotta cheese

Needed items
2 large bowls
mixer with dough hook
    attachment (optional)
large non-stick skillet
large baking sheet

For the dough:
1 cup warm water (about 110° F)
1 packet active dry yeast
1 teaspoon olive oil
1 teaspoon salt
2-2½ cups all-purpose flour
    non-stick cooking spray

For the filling:
2 teaspoons olive oil, divided
1 pound hot Italian turkey
    sausage, casing removed and
    crumbled
2 teaspoons dried oregano
2 teaspoons dried basil
¼ teaspoon ground black pepper
1 cup tomato sauce (canned
    or jarred)
6 ounces grated mozzarella
    cheese (regular or part-skim)
1 tablespoon grated Parmesan
    cheese

Calzones with Turkey Sausage and Mozzarella

To save time, you can use commercially-made, frozen bread dough. Thaw the dough as directed and pick up the recipe at step 3. And, since this recipe is fairly time-consuming, consider eating one calzone now and saving one for later (wrap the calzone in plastic wrap, then wrap it in foil and freeze for up to 2 months. To reheat, thaw completely and bake in a 350° F oven until hot, about 45 minutes).

1. To make the dough, place warm water in a large bowl and sprinkle in yeast. Let stand 5 minutes.

2. Add olive oil and salt. Add 2 cups of the flour and mix until a manageable dough forms, adding remaining flour if necessary. Using the dough hook attachment on your mixer (or your hands), knead 2 minutes (or 5 minutes by hand), until dough is smooth and elastic. Place dough in a large bowl that has been coated with non-stick spray and turn to coat all sides. Cover with a dish towel and let rise in a warm place, free from draft, until doubled in bulk, about 1 hour.

3. Meanwhile, to make the filling, heat 1 teaspoon of the oil in a large non-stick skillet over medium heat. Add turkey sausage and sauté until browned and cooked through, breaking up the meat as it cooks. Add oregano, basil, and pepper and mix well. Add tomato sauce and simmer 10 minutes. Remove from heat and set aside until ready to use.

4. Preheat oven to 500° F.

5. Punch dough down with your fist and divide in half. Transfer each half to a lightly floured surface and roll into two 10-inch circles. Divide sausage filling in half and spoon onto the center of each round. Spread mixture out, to within 1 inch of the edge. Divide mozzarella in half and arrange over sausage mixture. Lift one side of dough and fold over so that it meets the other side, forming a half moon. Pinch the edges together to seal.

6. Transfer calzones to a large baking sheet that has been coated with non-stick spray. Brush the top of each calzone with remaining teaspoon of olive oil and sprinkle the top with Parmesan cheese.

7. Bake 15 minutes, or until puffed up golden. Let stand 5 minutes before slicing.

Preparation and rising time: 1½ hours
Cooking time: 15 minutes

Serves 4-6

Caramelized Red Onion and Rosemary Focaccia

Focaccia is a semi-flat bread typically coated with olive oil and fresh herbs. The fact is, it's so popular these days, dinner rolls have become passé. You can top this basic dough with almost anything before baking—sautéed wild mushrooms, feta cheese, and fresh oregano, or sliced tomatoes and basil…experimenting is encouraged.

1. To make the dough, place warm water in a large bowl and sprinkle in yeast. Let stand 5 minutes.

2. Add olive oil and salt. Add 2½ cups of the flour and mix until blended. Using the dough hook attachment on your mixer (or your hands), mix ingredients together until a manageable dough forms, adding remaining flour if necessary. Knead 2 minutes with the dough hook (or 5 minutes by hand), until dough is smooth and elastic. Place dough in a large bowl that has been coated with non-stick spray and turn to coat all sides. Cover with a dish towel and let rise in a warm place, free from draft, until doubled in bulk, about 1 hour.

3. Punch dough down with your fist and divide in half. Press dough into the bottom of two 9-inch square or round cake pans that have been coated with non-stick spray. Set aside for 20 minutes (make the topping while you wait).

4. Preheat oven to 400° F.

5. To make the topping, heat oil in a large non-stick skillet over medium heat. Add onion and sugar and sauté 10 minutes, or until onions are tender and golden brown. Stir in rosemary, salt and pepper and remove from heat.

6. Top focaccia dough with onion mixture. Sprinkle the top with Parmesan cheese.

7. Bake 20-25 minutes, or until golden. Cool in pans on a wire rack 5 minutes before slicing. Serve warm or room temperature.

Preparation and rising time: 1½-2 hours   *Makes 2 focaccia (8 servings)*
Cooking time: 20-25 minutes

Needed items
 large bowls
 mixer with dough hook
  attachment (optional)
 large non-stick skillet
 2 9-inch square or round
  cake pans

For the dough:
 1 cup warm water (about 110° F)
 1 packet active dry yeast
 1 teaspoon olive oil
 1 teaspoon salt
 2½-3 cups all-purpose flour
  non-stick cooking spray

For the caramelized red onion and rosemary topping:
 2 teaspoons olive oil
 1 large red onion, halved and
  thinly sliced
 2 tablespoons granulated sugar
 2 tablespoons chopped fresh
  rosemary
 ½ teaspoon salt
 ¼ teaspoon ground black pepper
 2 tablespoons grated Parmesan
  cheese

Needed items
    2 large bowls
    mixer with dough hook
        attachment (optional)
    blender or food processor
    small skillet
    8-inch loaf pan
    wire rack

For the dough:
    ¾ cup warm water (about 110° F)
    1 packet active dry yeast
    2 teaspoons olive oil
    ½ teaspoon salt
    1½-2 cups all-purpose flour
    1 egg white
        non-stick cooking spray

For the pesto filling:
    1 cup tightly packed fresh
        basil leaves
    ¼ cup sour cream (regular
        or nonfat)
    ¼ cup grated Parmesan cheese
    3 tablespoons olive oil
    2 tablespoons lightly toasted
        pine nuts*
    2 garlic cloves, peeled
    ½ teaspoon salt

Rolled Basil-Pesto Bread

As you cut into this bread, wonderful green spirals appear in every slice. Serve this basil-infused bread with a big bowl of pasta smothered in tomato sauce.

1. To make the dough, place warm water in a large bowl and sprinkle in yeast. Let stand 5 minutes.

2. Add olive oil and salt. Add 1½ cups of the flour and mix until blended. Using the dough hook attachment on your mixer (or your hands), mix ingredients together until a manageable dough forms, adding remaining flour if necessary. Knead 2 minutes with the dough hook (or 5 minutes by hand), until dough is smooth and elastic. Place dough in a large bowl that has been coated with non-stick spray and turn to coat all sides. Cover with a dish towel and let rise in a warm place, free from draft, until doubled in bulk, about 1 hour.

3. Meanwhile, to make the pesto, combine all ingredients in a blender or food processor fitted with the metal blade. Process until smooth and thick. Set aside until ready to use.

4. Punch dough down with your fist and remove from bowl. Transfer dough to a lightly floured surface and roll into an 8x12-inch rectangle. Spread pesto over top, to within ½ inch of edges. Starting with the shorter end, roll dough up tightly, jellyroll fashion. Transfer dough to an 8-inch loaf pan that has been coated with non-stick spray. Cover with a dish towel and let rise in a warm place, free from draft, for 45 minutes.

5. Preheat oven to 375° F.

6. Brush the top of the bread with egg white and bake 40 minutes, or until top is golden brown and loaf has pulled slightly away from the sides of pan. Cool in pan, on a wire rack, 10 minutes. Remove bread from pan and cool completely.

Preparation and rising time: 2 hours   *Makes 1 loaf (8 servings)*
Cooking time: 40 minutes

* Toast pine nuts by heating in a small skillet over medium heat until golden, shaking the pan frequently (it should take about 3-5 minutes).

French Bread

Making bread from scratch may seem too difficult or time-consuming, especially when dozens of wonderful bread varieties are available at your local market. I enjoy making bread—kneading the dough, watching it rise, and then basking in the incredible aroma as it bakes up to a warm, golden brown. I suggest you try it once, to see what I mean.

Note: French bread is characterized by its crispy crust—achieved by brushing the dough with an egg white before baking. For a softer crust—an Italian-style bread—skip the egg white and bake as directed. For a buttery crust, brush the baked bread with melted butter as soon as it comes out of the oven.

Needed items
2 large bowls
mixer with dough hook
    attachment (optional)
baking sheet
wire rack

1¼ cups warm water (about 110° F)
  1 packet active dry yeast
  2 teaspoons olive oil
  1 teaspoon salt
3-3½ cups all-purpose flour
  1 egg white
    non-stick cooking spray

1. Place warm water in a large bowl and sprinkle in yeast. Let stand 5 minutes.

2. Add olive oil and salt. Add 3 cups of the flour and mix until blended. Using the dough hook attachment on your mixer (or your hands), mix ingredients together until a manageable dough forms, adding remaining flour if necessary. Knead 2 minutes with the dough hook (or 5 minutes by hand), until dough is smooth and elastic. Place dough in a large bowl that has been coated with non-stick spray and turn to coat all sides. Cover with a dish towel and let rise in a warm place, free from draft, until doubled in bulk, about 1 hour.

3. Punch dough down with your fist and remove from bowl. Transfer dough to a lightly floured surface and roll into an 8x12-inch rectangle. Starting with the longer end, roll dough up tightly, jellyroll fashion. Pinch the ends together to seal. Place dough on a baking sheet that has been coated with non-stick spray. Cover with a dish towel and let rise in a warm place, free from draft, for 45 minutes.

4. Preheat oven to 425° F.

5. Brush the top of the dough with egg white and make several diagonal slices (about ⅛-inch deep) across the top.

6. Bake 30 minutes, or until top is golden brown and bread sounds hollow when tapped. Cool on a wire rack slightly before slicing.

Preparation and rising time: 2 hours
Cooking time: 30 minutes
Makes 1 loaf (8 servings)

Needed items
  2 large bowls
  mixer with dough hook
       attachment (optional)
  8-inch loaf pan
  wire rack

  1¼ cups warm milk (about 110° F)
  1   packet active dry yeast
  ⅓   cup honey
  1   tablespoon butter, melted
  1   teaspoon salt
  3-3½ cups whole wheat flour
       non-stick cooking spray

Honey Wheat Bread

A perfect blend of honey and wheat. This wholesome, hearty bread is great for sandwiches and breakfast toast, and pairs well with all types of salads, soups, and stews.

1. Place warm milk in a large bowl and sprinkle in yeast. Let stand 5 minutes.

2. Add honey, butter, and salt. Add 3 cups of the flour and mix until blended. Using the dough hook attachment on your mixer (or your hands), mix ingredients together until a manageable dough forms, adding remaining flour if necessary. Knead 2 minutes with the dough hook (or 5 minutes by hand), until dough is smooth and elastic. Place dough in a large bowl that has been coated with non-stick spray and turn to coat all sides. Cover with a dish towel and let rise in a warm place, free from draft, until doubled in bulk, about 1 hour.

3. Punch dough down with your fist and remove from bowl. Transfer dough to a lightly floured surface and roll into an 8x12-inch rectangle. Starting with the shorter end, roll dough up tightly, jellyroll fashion. Place in an 8-inch loaf pan that has been coated with non-stick spray. Cover with a dish towel and let rise in a warm place, free from draft, for 45 minutes.

4. Preheat oven to 375° F.

5. Bake bread 40 minutes, or until top is golden brown and loaf has pulled slightly away from the sides of pan. Cool in pan, on a wire rack, 10 minutes. Remove bread from pan and cool completely.

Preparation and rising time: 2 hours
Cooking time: 40 minutes

Makes 1 loaf (8 servings)

Super Moist Banana Bread

I've made this bread dozens of times, and I still can't believe how easy it is, or how much banana flavor it has. For the best results, use over-ripe bananas.

1. Preheat oven to 350° F.

2. In a medium bowl, combine flour, sugar, baking powder, baking soda, and salt. Mix well with a fork and set aside.

3. In a large bowl or food processor fitted with the metal blade, mash bananas until mushy. Add milk, egg, and vanilla and mix or process until blended.

4. Add dry ingredients to banana mixture and mix or process until just blended. Pour batter into an 8-inch loaf pan that has been coated with non-stick spray.

5. Bake 1 hour, or until a knife or wooden pick inserted near the center comes out almost clean (little bits clinging to the knife or wooden pick mean the bread's still moist). Cool in pan, on a wire rack, 10 minutes. Remove bread from pan and cool completely.

Preparation time: 15 minutes
Cooking time: 1 hour

Makes 1 loaf (8 servings)

Needed items
medium bowl
large bowl or food processor
8-inch loaf pan
wire rack

2 cups all-purpose flour
¾ cup granulated sugar
2 teaspoons baking powder
½ teaspoon baking soda
½ teaspoon salt
4 large over-ripe bananas
¼ cup milk (regular or nonfat)
1 egg
1 teaspoon vanilla extract
   non-stick cooking spray

Needed items
  large and small mixing bowls
  8-inch loaf pan
  wire rack

2½ cups all-purpose flour
¾   cup rolled oats (regular or
      quick cooking)
2   teaspoons baking powder
1   teaspoon baking soda
½   teaspoon salt
2   cups buttermilk
2   egg whites
      non-stick cooking spray

Oat-Buttermilk Quick Bread

Quick bread is called "quick" because, unlike yeast breads, there's no long "rising" period. I love this bread—it's hearty enough to hold up to any soup or stew, yet light enough for a great turkey sandwich. For a sweeter version, replace ½ cup of the buttermilk with maple syrup or honey.

1. Preheat oven to 350° F.

2. In a large bowl, combine flour, oats, baking powder, baking soda, and salt. Mix well with a fork, make a well in the center and set aside.

3. Whisk together buttermilk and egg whites in small bowl. Fold mixture into dry ingredients until just blended. Pour batter into an 8-inch loaf pan that has been coated with non-stick spray.

4. Bake 50-55 minutes, or until a knife inserted near the center comes out almost clean. Cool in pan, on a wire rack, 10 minutes. Remove bread from pan and cool completely.

Preparation time: 15 minutes
Cooking time: 50-55 minutes

Makes 1 loaf (8 servings)

Pumpkin-Orange Spice Loaf

Need a great gift idea for the holidays? Bake the batter in miniature loaf pans, wrap the loaves in colored cellophane and garnish with a decorative bow.

1. Preheat oven to 350° F.

2. In a large bowl, combine flour, baking powder, cinnamon, baking soda, cloves, salt, and ginger. Mix well and set aside.

3. In a medium bowl, whisk together pumpkin, milk, orange juice, egg, and orange zest and set aside.

4. In a large mixing bowl, beat together butter and sugar until light and fluffy. Gradually add flour and pumpkin mixtures, alternating each, beginning and ending with flour mixture. Blend until smooth. Pour batter into an 8-inch loaf pan that has been coated with non-stick spray.

5. Bake 1 hour, or until a wooden pick inserted near center comes out clean. Cool in pan, on a wire rack, 10 minutes. Remove bread from pan and cool completely.

Preparation time: 15 minutes
Cooking time: 1 hour

Makes 1 loaf (8 servings)

Needed items
large and medium bowls
mixer
8-inch loaf pan
wire rack

- 1¾ cups all-purpose flour
- 2 teaspoons baking powder
- 1½ teaspoons ground cinnamon
- ½ teaspoon baking soda
- ½ teaspoon ground cloves
- ½ teaspoon salt
- ¼ teaspoon ground ginger
- 1 cup canned pumpkin (not pie filling)
- ½ cup milk (regular or nonfat)
- ¼ cup orange juice
- 1 egg
- 1 tablespoon grated orange zest
- 4 tablespoons butter or margarine, softened
- 1 cup granulated sugar
  non-stick cooking spray

Needed items
  large and medium mixing bowls
  8-inch loaf pan
  wire rack

  2 cups all-purpose flour
  2 teaspoons baking powder
  1½ teaspoons ground cinnamon
  ½ teaspoon baking soda
  ¼ teaspoon allspice
  ¼ teaspoon ground cloves
  ¼ teaspoon salt
  4 Granny Smith apples (about 2
       pounds), peeled and grated
  ¾ cup packed light brown sugar
  2 tablespoons fresh lemon juice
  2 tablespoons butter or
       margarine, melted
  1 egg, lightly beaten
  1 teaspoon vanilla extract
     non-stick cooking spray

Apple Spice Bread

For bread with a crunch, fold in 1 cup chopped walnuts or pecans before baking.

Note: The apples will brown quickly after they're grated. To prevent discoloration, add the lemon juice and toss to coat.

1. Preheat oven to 350° F.

2. In a large bowl, combine flour, baking powder, cinnamon, baking soda, allspice, cloves, and salt. Mix together with a fork, make a well in the center and set aside.

3. In a medium bowl, combine apples, brown sugar, lemon juice, butter, egg, and vanilla. Mix well and fold mixture into dry ingredients until just blended. Transfer batter to an 8-inch loaf pan that has been coated with non-stick spray.

4. Bake 1 hour, or until a knife or wooden pick inserted near the center comes out almost clean (little bits clinging to the knife mean the bread's still moist). Cool in pan, on a wire rack, 10 minutes. Remove bread from pan and cool completely.

Preparation time: 15 minutes
Cooking time: 1 hour

Makes 1 loaf (8 servings)

Buttermilk-Chive Biscuits

Quick and easy biscuits that puff up to a perfect golden brown. Mix the dough just before baking because once baking powder and baking soda meet the "wet" ingredients—buttermilk and melted butter—their rising qualities kick in.

Note: If you want to make the biscuits in advance, they freeze pretty well. Just arrange uncooked biscuits on a baking sheet, cover with plastic wrap and freeze for up to 10 days. Thaw at room temperature and bake as directed.

1. Preheat oven to 425° F.

2. In a large bowl or food processor fitted with the metal blade, combine flour, baking powder, baking soda, and salt.

3. In a small bowl, whisk together buttermilk, chives, and butter. Add mixture to dry ingredients and mix together (with your hands) or process until a manageable dough forms.

4. Transfer dough to a lightly floured surface and knead 1 minute. Roll dough out to ½-inch thickness and, using a biscuit cutter or upside-down glass, cut 8 biscuits (about 3 inches in diameter). Transfer biscuits to a baking sheet that has been coated with non-stick spray.

5. Bake 10-12 minutes, or until puffed up and golden. Serve warm.

Preparation time: 20 minutes
Cooking time: 10-12 minutes

Makes 8 biscuits

Needed items
  large mixing bowl or food
      processor
  small mixing bowl
  biscuit cutter or upside-down glass
  baking sheet

  1½ cups all-purpose flour
  1½ teaspoons baking powder
  ½   teaspoon baking soda
  ½   teaspoon salt
  ½   cup, plus 2 tablespoons
      buttermilk
  2   tablespoons minced fresh
      chives
  1   tablespoon butter or margarine,
      melted
      non-stick cooking spray

Pasta and Risotto

Spinach Lasagna

I've tested dozens of lasagna recipes and no two are alike—or quite right. The vegetable or spinach lasagnas are thin and watery, and the meat lasagnas are heavy and greasy. Not this one—the trick is lots of ricotta cheese and squeezing all the liquid from the spinach.

1. Preheat oven to 350° F.

2. In large stockpot, cook lasagna noodles according to package directions. Drain and set aside.

3. Meanwhile, in a medium saucepan, combine onion, tomatoes, basil, Italian seasoning, and red pepper flakes. Bring to a boil, reduce heat, and simmer until thickened, about 10 minutes. Remove from heat and set aside.

4. In a large bowl, combine ricotta, spinach, half of the mozzarella, egg, pepper, and nutmeg. Mix well.

5. Arrange 4 lasagna noodles in the bottom of a 13x9-inch lasagna pan that has been coated with non-stick spray, overlapping the noodles slightly to cover the bottom. Spoon half of the spinach and cheese mixture over top and top with ⅓ of the tomato mixture. Top with 4 more noodles, remaining cheese mixture, and ⅓ of the tomato sauce. Top with remaining 4 noodles. Spoon remaining tomato sauce over top and cover the surface with remaining mozzarella and Parmesan cheese.

6. Cover with foil and bake 45 minutes. Uncover and bake 15 more minutes, or until top is golden and bubbly. Let stand 5 minutes before slicing.

Preparation time: 20 minutes
Cooking time: 1 hour

Serves 4

Needed items
large stockpot
medium saucepan
large bowl
13 x 9-inch lasagna pan
aluminum foil

12	uncooked lasagna noodles
1	small onion, chopped (about ½ cup)
1	28-ounce can diced tomatoes
2	teaspoons dried basil
1	teaspoon Italian seasoning
¼	teaspoon red pepper flakes
1	28-ounce container ricotta cheese (regular or part-skim)
1	10-ounce package frozen chopped spinach, thawed and drained
8	ounces grated mozzarella cheese (regular or part-skim), divided
1	egg
½	teaspoon ground black pepper
¼	teaspoon ground nutmeg
¼	cup grated Parmesan or Romano cheese
	non-stick cooking spray

Needed items
  large stockpot
  large bowl
  13 x 9-inch lasagna pan
  small skillet
  aluminum foil

12 uncooked lasagna noodles
 2 pounds ricotta cheese (regular
      or part-skim)
 4 ounces grated sharp white
      cheddar cheese (regular or
      reduced fat)
 4 ounces grated Monterey Jack
      cheese (regular or reduced fat)
 1 medium Spanish onion, minced
      (about 1 cup)
 ¼ cup lightly toasted pine nuts,
      finely chopped*
 1 egg
 1 tablespoon Dijon mustard
 ½ teaspoon garlic powder
 ½ teaspoon salt
 ¼ teaspoon white pepper
 4 ounces grated mozzarella
      cheese (regular or part-skim)
 3 tablespoons grated Parmesan
      cheese
      non-stick cooking spray

White Lasagna with Five Cheeses

Who says lasagna has to be red? Sautéed wild mushrooms make a nice addition to the filling, if you feel inclined.

1. Preheat oven to 350° F.

2. In large stockpot, cook lasagna noodles according to package directions. Drain and set aside.

3. Meanwhile, in a large bowl, combine ricotta, cheddar, and Monterey Jack cheeses, onion, pine nuts, egg, mustard, garlic powder, salt, and pepper. Mix well.

4. Arrange 4 lasagna noodles in the bottom of a 13x9-inch lasagna pan that has been coated with non-stick spray, overlapping the noodles slightly to cover the bottom. Top with half of the cheese mixture. Top with 4 more noodles and remaining cheese mixture. Arrange remaining 4 noodles on top of cheese mixture and top with mozzarella and Parmesan cheeses.

5. Cover with foil and bake 45 minutes. Uncover and bake 15 more minutes, or until top is golden and bubbly. Let stand 5 minutes before slicing.

Preparation time: 20 minutes   *Serves 4*
Cooking time: 1 hour

 * Toast pine nuts by heating in a small skillet over medium heat until
    golden, shaking the pan frequently (it should take about 3-5 minutes).

Shells with Roasted Vegetables

By folding roasted vegetables into pasta, this dish is like a spruced-up Italian antipasto.

Note: Parmigiano-Reggiano is one of the most important cheeses in the Italian kitchen—well worth the extra cost. The good news is, because of its powerful flavor, a little goes a long way.

1. Preheat oven to 450° F.
2. In a large bowl, combine eggplant, artichoke hearts, olive oil, thyme, and rosemary. Toss to coat vegetables with oil and herbs. Arrange vegetables on a large baking sheet that has been coated with non-stick spray. Roast 20 minutes, or until golden brown and tender, turning halfway through cooking. Remove vegetables from oven and set aside.
3. Meanwhile, in a large stockpot, cook pasta according to package directions, drain and transfer to a large bowl. Stir in roasted vegetables (eggplant and artichoke hearts) and roasted red peppers.
4. Whisk together chicken broth, vinegar, mustard, salt, and pepper. Pour mixture over pasta and toss to coat.
5. Spoon mixture into shallow bowls and sprinkle Parmigiano-Reggiano cheese on top.

Preparation and cooking time: 30 minutes   *Serves 4*

Needed items
large bowls
large baking sheet
large stockpot

2 small eggplants (about ½ pound each), quartered lengthwise and cut into 1-inch cubes
1 14-ounce can artichoke hearts in water, drained and quartered
2 tablespoons olive oil
2 tablespoons chopped fresh thyme, or 1 teaspoon dried
2 tablespoons chopped fresh rosemary, or 1 teaspoon dried
1 pound uncooked medium or large (not jumbo) pasta shells
1 7-ounce jar roasted red peppers in water, drained and chopped
½ cup chicken broth
¼ cup balsamic vinegar
1 tablespoon Dijon mustard
½ teaspoon salt
½ teaspoon ground black pepper
4 tablespoons grated Parmigiano-Reggiano cheese
non-stick cooking spray

Needed items
   large stockpot
   large bowl
   large non-stick skillet

1 pound uncooked penne pasta
2 teaspoons olive oil
1 large yellow onion, quartered
    and thinly sliced
2 garlic cloves, minced
1 tablespoon granulated sugar
3 medium zucchini (about 1½
    pounds), quartered lengthwise
    and cut into 1-inch cubes
1 tablespoon chopped fresh
    rosemary, or 1 teaspoon dried
1 tablespoon chopped fresh
    oregano, or 1 teaspoon dried
½ teaspoon salt
¼ teaspoon ground black pepper
2 cups chicken broth
1 tablespoon cornstarch
½ cup crumbled feta cheese

Penne with Caramelized Onions, Herbed Zucchini, and Feta

A light pasta dish, infused with the flavors of aromatic herbs. Feel free to load up your cart at the farmer's market and substitute fresh, seasonal vegetables for the zucchini.

1. In a large stockpot, cook penne according to package directions. Drain, transfer to a large bowl, and cover with foil to keep warm.

2. Meanwhile, heat oil in a large non-stick skillet over medium heat. Add onion, garlic, and sugar and sauté 10 minutes, or until onions are golden brown and tender. Stir in zucchini, rosemary, oregano, salt, and pepper and sauté until zucchini is golden and tender, about 3-4 minutes.

3. Dissolve cornstarch in chicken broth and add to skillet. Simmer 1 minute, or until sauce thickens. Pour sauce over cooked penne, add feta cheese, and toss to combine.

Preparation and cooking time: 20-30 minutes　　　　　　　*Serves 4*

Needed items
   large stockpot
   large bowl
   large skillet
   aluminum foil

1 pound uncooked linguine
2 teaspoons olive or vegetable oil
1 small onion, chopped (about
    ½ cup)
2 garlic cloves, minced
1 pound sweet Italian turkey
    sausage, casing removed
1 teaspoon dried basil
¼ teaspoon salt
¼ teaspoon ground black pepper
1 28-ounce can crushed tomatoes
    grated Parmesan cheese

Linguine with Sweet Sausage

I like to use Italian turkey sausage, it has the same incredible flavor as pork, but produces a lighter sauce.

1. In a large stockpot, cook pasta according to package directions. Drain, transfer to a large bowl, and cover with foil to keep warm.

2. Meanwhile, heat oil in a large skillet over medium heat. Add onion and garlic and sauté 2 minutes. Add sausage and sauté until browned and cooked through, breaking up the meat as it cooks. Add basil, salt, and pepper and stir to coat. Add tomatoes and bring mixture to a boil. Reduce heat and simmer 10 minutes.

3. Pour mixture over cooked pasta and toss to combine. Serve with grated Parmesan cheese on the side.

Preparation and cooking time: 20 minutes　　　　　　　*Serves 4*

Pasta e Fagioli

Affectionately referred to as "pasta fazool" in my house. Excellent soup and hearty pasta meal. Serve with a chunk of sourdough bread for dunking.

Note: Pasta and beans absorb liquid over time. If you plan to make the dish ahead of time (or store leftovers) add a little chicken broth before reheating if necessary.

1. Heat oil in a large stockpot over medium heat. Add onion and garlic and sauté until tender and transparent, about 3 minutes. Add chicken broth, tomatoes, beans, salt, and pepper. Bring mixture to a boil, reduce heat, cover and simmer 10-15 minutes.

2. Meanwhile, cook ditalini in medium saucepan according to package directions. Drain and add to bean mixture. Simmer 5 minutes to heat through.

3. Ladle soup into bowls and top with Parmesan cheese.

Preparation and cooking time: 20 minutes   *Serves 4*

Needed items
   large stockpot
   medium saucepan

   2   teaspoons olive oil
   1   small onion, chopped (about ½ cup)
   2   garlic cloves, minced
   3   cups chicken broth
   1   28-ounce can crushed tomatoes
   2   19-ounce cans white kidney (cannellini) beans, rinsed and drained
   ½   teaspoon salt
   ½   teaspoon ground black pepper
   1   pound uncooked ditalini pasta (pasta shaped liked little tubes)
   ¼   cup grated Parmesan cheese

Linguine with Roasted Garlic-Basil Pesto

This super-easy pesto can be made nonfat by using nonfat sour cream and nonfat milk. The result is a pesto cream with intense roasted garlic and basil flavors. Serve it with any pasta variety, chicken, shellfish, or as a spread for sourdough bread.

1. Preheat oven to 400° F.

2. Slice off the top ¼-inch of the garlic head to reveal the cloves. Wrap head in foil and roast 45 minutes, or until soft. Loosen foil and let cool. When cool enough to handle, squeeze cloves from head and transfer to a blender. Add sour cream, basil, milk, Parmesan, salt, and pepper. Process until smooth. Set aside until ready to use.

3. In large stockpot, cook linguine according to package directions. Drain and while still warm, toss with prepared pesto.

Preparation and cooking time: 50 minutes   *Serves 4*

Needed items
   blender
   large stockpot
   aluminum foil

   ½   head garlic
   1   8-ounce container sour cream (regular or nonfat)
   1½   cups tightly packed fresh basil leaves
   ¼   cup milk (regular or nonfat)
   2   tablespoons grated Parmesan cheese
   ½   teaspoon salt
   ¼   teaspoon ground black pepper
   1   pound uncooked linguine

Needed items
- large stockpot
- large bowl
- small saucepan
- 4-quart casserole dish

1   pound uncooked elbow
    macaroni
½   cup sour cream (regular
    or nonfat)
1   12-ounce can evaporated skim
    milk (or nonfat milk)
6   ounces grated sharp cheddar
    cheese (about 1½ cups)
2   ounces grated Swiss cheese
    (about ½ cup)
2   tablespoons Dijon mustard
½   teaspoon ground black pepper
¼   teaspoon salt
⅛   teaspoon ground nutmeg
1-2 drops hot sauce (optional)
2   tablespoons plain dry bread
    crumbs
2   tablespoons grated Parmesan
    cheese

Mac 'n Cheese

A great post-dentist dinner. Super creamy, really cheesy, with hints of mustard and nutmeg.

1. Preheat oven to 350° F.
2. In large stockpot, cook pasta according to package directions. Drain and transfer to a large bowl. While pasta is still hot, stir in sour cream, and set aside.
3. Scald milk by heating in a small saucepan over medium heat until tiny bubbles just appear around the edges.
4. Add cheddar and Swiss cheeses, mustard, pepper, salt, nutmeg, and hot sauce and simmer until cheese melts, stirring constantly.
5. Fold cheese mixture into pasta and transfer mixture to a 4-quart casserole dish.
6. Mix together bread crumbs and Parmesan cheese and sprinkle mixture over pasta.
7. Bake, uncovered 30 minutes, or until top is golden.

Preparation time: 15 minutes
Cooking time: 30 minutes

Serves 4

Bowties with Roasted Sweet Potatoes and Caramelized Fennel

Sweet potatoes with pasta? You'll love this sensational blend of tender pasta with anise-flavored fennel and sugary sweet potatoes.

1. Preheat oven to 375° F.

2. In a large bowl, combine sweet potatoes, rosemary, and olive oil. Toss to coat and transfer potatoes to a large baking sheet that has been coated with non-stick spray.

3. Bake 25 minutes, or until tender and golden.

4. Meanwhile, in a large stockpot, cook pasta according to package directions. Drain and cover with foil to keep warm.

5. Melt butter in a large non-stick skillet over medium heat. Add fennel and sugar and sauté 10 minutes, or until tender and golden brown.

6. Whisk together chicken broth, milk, and flour. Gradually add to skillet and simmer 3 minutes, or until mixture thickens, stirring constantly. Stir in roasted sweet potatoes, Parmesan, parsley, salt, and pepper and heat through. Spoon sauce over pasta and toss to combine.

Preparation and cooking time: 45 minutes

Serves 4

Needed items
  large bowl
  large baking sheet
  large stockpot
  large non-stick skillet
  aluminum foil

2 large sweet potatoes, peeled and cut into 1-inch cubes
1 tablespoon chopped fresh rosemary, or 1 teaspoon dried
2 teaspoons olive oil
12 ounces uncooked bowtie (farfalle) pasta
1 tablespoon butter or margarine
1 fennel bulb, sliced crosswise into ¼-inch thick slices
1 tablespoon granulated sugar
1 cup chicken broth
1 cup milk (regular or nonfat)
1 tablespoon all-purpose flour
2 tablespoons grated Parmesan cheese
2 tablespoons chopped fresh Italian parsley
½ teaspoon salt
¼ teaspoon ground black pepper
  non-stick cooking spray

Needed items
 large stockpot
 medium and large bowls
 large non-stick skillet
 aluminum foil

 8 ounces uncooked somen
   noodles
 1 cup chicken broth
 2 eggs
 1 tablespoon soy sauce
 1 tablespoon creamy peanut
   butter
 1-2 teaspoons chile or other
   hot sauce
 2 teaspoons dark sesame oil
 1 red bell pepper, seeded
   and diced
 1 teaspoon minced fresh ginger
 1 garlic clove, minced
 ¼ cup dry-roasted salted peanuts,
   coarsely chopped
 2 tablespoons chopped green
   onions

Thai Noodles with Peanuts (Pad Thai)

This traditional Thai dish is a snap to prepare, and the subtle sweetness from the peanut butter balances both the saltiness of the soy sauce and the heat of the chile sauce.

Note: Substitute angelhair or capellini pasta for the somen noodles, if desired.

1. In a large stockpot, cook noodles according to package directions. Drain, transfer to a large bowl, and cover with foil to keep warm.

2. Meanwhile, in a medium bowl, whisk together chicken broth, eggs, soy sauce, peanut butter, and chile sauce. Set aside until ready to use.

3. Heat oil in a large non-stick skillet over medium heat. Add red pepper, ginger, and garlic and sauté 2 minutes. Transfer red pepper mixture to noodles and toss to combine.

4. Return skillet to heat and add chicken broth mixture. Simmer until eggs are cooked and still moist, about 2-3 minutes (mixture will be lumpy), stirring constantly with a wooden spoon. Stir mixture into noodles and mix well.

5. Divide noodle mixture evenly between 2 dinner plates and top each portion with peanuts and green onions.

Preparation and cooking time: 15-20 minutes   *Serves 2*

Penne with Andouille and Parmesan

Andouille is a cured, garlic sausage infused with herbs and spices. It can be eaten cold, or added to soups, stews, and main dishes. In this dish, its distinct flavor creates a robust sauce for penne.

Note: In order to create a Parmesan-rich broth, it's important to add a piece of Parmesan rind to the simmering liquid. Just slice a piece from the end of a wedge of Parmesan and reserve the rest of the block for grating.

1. In a large stockpot, cook penne according to package directions. Drain, transfer to a large bowl, and cover with foil to keep warm.

2. Meanwhile, heat oil in a large skillet over medium heat. Add shallot and sauté 2 minutes. Add andouille and sauté 5 minutes, or until golden brown on all sides. Add chicken broth, vermouth, Parmesan rind, bay leaves, salt, and pepper and bring mixture to a boil. Reduce heat and simmer 10 minutes.

3. Discard rind and bay leaves. Pour mixture over cooked penne, add grated Parmesan and parsley and toss to combine.

Preparation and cooking time: 15-20 minutes   *Serves 4*

Needed items
   large stockpot
   large bowl
   large skillet
   aluminum foil

12 ounces uncooked penne pasta
2 teaspoons olive or vegetable oil
1 shallot, minced
2 links (about ¾ pound total) andouille sausage, halved lengthwise and sliced crosswise into ¼-inch thick pieces
1½ cups chicken broth
½ cup vermouth or dry white wine
1 3-inch piece Parmesan cheese rind
2 bay leaves
¼ teaspoon salt
¼ teaspoon ground black pepper
¼ cup grated Parmesan cheese
2 tablespoons chopped fresh Italian parsley

Needed items
large stockpot
large bowl
large skillet
aluminum foil

5   ripe beefsteak tomatoes (about 3 pounds)
12 ounces uncooked spinach fettucine (or any spinach pasta)
2   teaspoons olive oil
1   small onion, chopped (about ½ cup)
2   garlic cloves, minced
1   teaspoon dried oregano
½   teaspoon salt
¼   teaspoon crushed red pepper flakes
¼   cup tightly packed fresh basil leaves, chopped
2   tablespoons grated Parmesan cheese

Spinach Fettucine with Fresh Tomatoes

There's no match for this refreshingly light tomato sauce, one made with ripe, juicy summer tomatoes. You can serve the sauce over grilled chicken or fish, too.

1. Bring a large pot of water to a boil.

2. Cut large X's (just enough to break the skin) on both ends of each tomato. Immerse tomatoes in boiling water for 15 seconds. Remove tomatoes with a slotted spoon (reserve boiling water for pasta) and when cool enough to handle, peel away outer skin and discard. Slice each tomato in half crosswise and squeeze out seeds. Chop tomatoes into ¼-inch pieces and set aside.

3. Cook fettucine (in reserved water) according to package directions. Drain, transfer to a large bowl, and cover with foil to keep warm.

4. Meanwhile, to make the sauce, heat oil in a large skillet over medium heat. Add onion and garlic and sauté 2 minutes. Add oregano, salt, and red pepper flakes and toss to coat. Add tomatoes and simmer 10 minutes, or until sauce is thick and tomatoes are broken down. Remove from heat and stir in basil. Pour sauce over spinach fettucine and toss to combine.

5. Divide pasta evenly among four dinner plates and top with Parmesan cheese.

Preparation and cooking time: 25-30 minutes   *Serves 4*

Linguine with White Clam Sauce

Typically thought of as a heavy, oil-based dish, this lighter white clam sauce relies on chicken broth and white wine to create a mouth-watering sauce that tastes just as rich and sinful as the original.

1. In a large stockpot, cook linguine according to package directions. Drain, transfer to a large bowl, and cover with foil to keep warm.

2. Meanwhile, heat oil in a large non-stick skillet over medium heat. Add onion and garlic and sauté 2 minutes, or until tender. Add clams and sauté 2 minutes. Add oregano, salt, and pepper and stir to coat. Add clam juice, chicken broth, and wine and bring mixture to a boil. Reduce heat and simmer 5 minutes. Stir in Parmesan and simmer 1 minute, or until cheese melts.

3. Pour clam sauce over linguine and toss to combine. Garnish with fresh parsley if desired.

Preparation and cooking time: 25 minutes   *Serves 4*

Needed items
large stockpot
large bowl
large non-stick skillet
aluminum foil

12 ounces uncooked linguine
2 teaspoons olive oil
1 small onion chopped (about ½ cup)
2 garlic cloves, minced
2 10-ounce cans whole baby clams, drained
1 teaspoon dried oregano
¼ teaspoon salt
¼ teaspoon ground black pepper
8 ounces bottled clam juice
½ cup chicken broth
½ cup dry white wine or vermouth
¼ cup grated Parmesan or Romano cheese
¼ cup fresh Italian parsley leaves, chopped (optional)

Needed items
  large saucepan
  large stockpot
  large bowl

2 teaspoons olive oil
1 small onion, chopped (about
   ½ cup)
2 carrots, peeled and chopped
2 garlic cloves, minced
1 pound lean ground beef
   or turkey
1 teaspoon dried basil
1 teaspoon dried oregano
½ teaspoon salt
¼ teaspoon crush red pepper
   flakes
1 28-ounce can crushed tomatoes
1 cup beef broth
2 tablespoons tomato paste
1 pound uncooked spaghetti
2 tablespoons grated Parmesan
   cheese

Spaghetti Bolognese

This famous meat sauce was first created in Bologna, Italy, hence the name Bolognese. In Italy, the hearty sauce is traditionally served over fresh, homemade tagliatelle—a slightly wider fettucine-type pasta. In this country, it's almost always served over spaghetti, but you can ladle it over any pasta shape, including cheese ravioli and tortellini. If you have the time, the longer the sauce cooks, the better and deeper the flavor.

1. Heat oil in a large saucepan over medium heat. Add onion, carrots, and garlic and sauté 2 minutes. Add beef and sauté until browned and cooked through, breaking up the meat as it cooks. Add basil, oregano, salt, and red pepper flakes and stir to coat. Add tomatoes, beef broth, and tomato paste and bring mixture to a boil. Reduce heat, partially cover, and simmer 20 minutes (and up to 1 hour).

3. Meanwhile, in a large stockpot, cook pasta according to package directions. Drain and transfer to a large bowl. Pour meat sauce over pasta and toss to combine.

4. Spoon pasta and sauce into shallow bowls and top with Parmesan cheese.

Preparation and cooking time:
30 minutes (and up to 1 hour if desired)

Serves 4

Bowtie Primavera in a Pink Sauce

The great thing about this dish is its versatility—you can use whatever vegetables you want, making it the perfect "clean out the vegetable drawer" dinner.

1. In a large stockpot, cook pasta according to package directions. Drain, transfer to a large bowl, and cover with foil to keep warm.

2. Meanwhile, heat olive oil in a large saucepan over medium heat. Add onion, garlic, and leek and sauté 3 minutes, or until tender. Add basil, oregano, salt, and pepper and stir to coat. Stir in diced tomatoes and chicken broth, bring mixture to a boil, reduce heat, and simmer 5 minutes. Stir in broccoli, cauliflower, carrots, and frozen peas. Cover and simmer 4-5 minutes, or until vegetables are tender-crisp. Remove from heat and stir in sour cream. Pour mixture over cooked pasta and toss to combine.

3. Divide pasta mixture among four dinner plates and top with Parmesan cheese.

Preparation and cooking time: 25 minutes   *Serves 4*

Needed items
  large stockpot
  large bowl
  large saucepan
  aluminum foil

12 ounces uncooked bowtie
      (farfalle) pasta
2 teaspoons olive oil
1 small onion, chopped (about
      ½ cup)
2 garlic cloves, minced
1 leek, green portion discarded,
      white portion halved, rinsed,
      and chopped
1½ teaspoons dried basil
1 teaspoon dried oregano
¼ teaspoon salt
¼ teaspoon ground black pepper
1 28-ounce can diced tomatoes
½ cup chicken broth
3 cups broccoli florets
2 cups cauliflower florets
½ cup chopped carrots
½ cup frozen green peas
1 cup sour cream (regular or
      nonfat)
¼ cup grated Parmesan cheese

Needed items
  medium saucepan
  large stockpot
  shallow dishes
  large non-stick skillet
  4-quart casserole dish
  aluminum foil

 1 28-ounce can diced tomatoes
 1 8-ounce can tomato sauce
 2 tablespoons tomato paste
 1 small onion, chopped (about
      ½ cup)
 1 teaspoon dried oregano
 1 teaspoon dried basil
 ¼ teaspoon ground black pepper
12 ounces uncooked Mafalda
      pasta (mini lasagna), or any
      spiral pasta
 ½ cup all-purpose flour
 ½ teaspoon salt
 1 egg
 2 tablespoons milk (regular or
      nonfat)
 2 small white eggplants
      (about ½ pound each), sliced
      crosswise into ¼-inch thick
      slices
 ½ cup Italian-style dry
      breadcrumbs
 2 teaspoons olive oil
 ½ cup grated mozzarella cheese
      (regular or part-skim)
 1 tablespoon grated Parmesan
      cheese

Eggplant Parmesan Casserole

Eggplant Parmesan takes on a new meaning in this dish—tender, golden eggplant slices, nestled between layers of savory tomato sauce and tender pasta.

1. Preheat oven to 350° F.

2. In a medium saucepan, combine diced tomatoes, tomato sauce, tomato paste, onion, oregano, basil, and pepper. Set the pan over medium heat and bring to a boil. Reduce heat, cover, and simmer 20 minutes.

3. Meanwhile, in a large stockpot, cook pasta according to package directions. Drain and cover with foil to keep warm.

4. Combine flour and salt in a shallow dish. Whisk together egg and milk in another shallow dish. Dip eggplant slices into flour mixture and then into egg mixture. Dip in breadcrumbs and turn to coat both sides.

5. Heat oil in a large non-stick skillet over medium heat. Add eggplant slices (in batches to prevent crowding) and sauté 2 minutes per side, or until golden.

6. To assemble casserole, spoon ½ cup of the tomato sauce in the bottom of a 4-quart casserole dish. Top with half of the cooked pasta. Arrange half of the eggplant slices on top and spoon over half of the remaining tomato sauce. Repeat layers with remaining pasta, eggplant slices and sauce. Sprinkle mozzarella and Parmesan cheeses over top.

7. Cover with foil and bake 30 minutes. Uncover and bake 30 more minutes, or until top is golden and bubbly.

Preparation time: 20 minutes
Cooking time: 1 hour

Serves 4

Rigatoni with Wild Mushrooms

A robust meal with deep, earthy flavors. You can add any variety of mushrooms to this dish, so please "go wild" (with or without the mushrooms).

1. Preheat oven to 350° F.

2. In a large stockpot, cook pasta according to package directions. Drain and, while still warm, stir in ricotta cheese.

3. Meanwhile, heat oil in a large non-stick skillet over medium heat. Add onion and garlic and sauté 2 minutes. Add mushrooms and sauté 4 minutes, or until tender and releasing juice. Add tomatoes, red pepper flakes, and oregano and simmer 5 minutes. Remove from heat and stir in basil.

4. Spoon ½ cup of the tomato mixture into the bottom of a 4-quart casserole dish. Top with half of the rigatoni mixture. Top with half of the remaining tomato sauce and all of the remaining rigatoni. Spoon over remaining tomato sauce and top with Parmesan cheese.

5. Cover with foil and bake 30 minutes. Uncover and bake 5 more minutes, or until Parmesan is golden brown.

Preparation time: 20 minutes
Cooking time: 35 minutes

Serves 4

Needed items
large stockpot
large non-stick skillet
4-quart casserole dish
aluminum foil

1 pound uncooked rigatoni
1 cup ricotta cheese (regular or part-skim)
2 teaspoons olive oil
1 small onion, diced (about ½ cup)
2 garlic cloves, minced
3 portobello mushrooms (about 1 pound), stems discarded, caps sliced into 1-inch pieces
1 28-ounce can crushed tomatoes
½ teaspoon crushed red pepper flakes
1 teaspoon dried oregano
½ cup tightly packed fresh basil leaves, chopped
¼ cup grated Parmesan cheese

Needed items
large stockpot
large bowl
small saucepan
aluminum foil

1 pound uncooked rigatoni
1 cup milk (regular or nonfat)
2 cups sour cream (regular or nonfat)
½ cup crumbled Gorgonzola or blue cheese
¼ teaspoon salt
¼ teaspoon ground black pepper
2 tablespoons minced fresh sage

Creamy Rigatoni with Gorgonzola

Gorgonzola is a classic Italian, blue-veined cheese available in two strengths—"dolce" or sweet gorgonzola, and "piccante" a sharper gorgonzola variety. Either will work in this dish, and because they both melt easily, the result is a rich, creamy sauce with a distinct blue cheese flavor.

1. In a large stockpot, cook pasta according to package directions. Drain, transfer to a large bowl, and cover with foil to keep warm.
2. Meanwhile, scald milk in a small saucepan by heating over medium heat until bubbles just appear around the edges. Reduce heat to low and whisk in sour cream. Stir in Gorgonzola, salt, and pepper and stir until cheese melts. Remove from heat and stir in sage.
3. Pour cheese mixture over cooked pasta and toss to combine.

Preparation and cooking time: 15-20 minutes   *Serves 4*

Needed items
large stockpot
large bowl
large skillet
aluminum foil

12 ounces uncooked fusilli pasta
2 teaspoons olive or vegetable oil
1 small onion, minced (about ½ cup)
2 garlic cloves, minced
½ cup pitted, oil-cured black olives, chopped
3 tablespoons drained capers
2 teaspoons anchovy paste
¼ teaspoon salt
¼ teaspoon crushed red pepper flakes
1 14½-ounce can crushed tomatoes
½ cup dry red wine

Fusilli Puttanesca

Puttanesca sauce is a spicy blend of olives, capers, and anchovies. Because of its exciting, zesty flavor, it was aptly named after "streetwalkers" or "ladies of the night." Makes for interesting dinner conversation.

1. In a large stockpot, cook fusilli according to package directions. Drain, transfer to a large bowl, and cover with foil to keep warm.
2. Meanwhile, heat oil in a large skillet over medium heat. Add onion and garlic and sauté 2 minutes. Add olives, capers, anchovy paste, salt, and red pepper flakes and stir to coat. Add tomatoes and wine and bring mixture to a boil. Reduce heat and simmer 5 minutes.
3. Pour mixture over cooked fusilli and toss to combine.

Preparation and cooking time: 20 minutes   *Serves 4*

Spaghetti Carbonara

Carbonara is a classic Italian sauce made with eggs and pancetta (Italian-style bacon cured with salt, black pepper, and spices). Pancetta is not smoked, it is moist and mild (much milder than smoked bacon). The curing process creates an incomparable blend of flavors, making an excellent base for this pasta sauce (suffice to say, substitute bacon only when necessary).

1. In a large stockpot, cook pasta according to package directions. Drain and set aside.
2. Meanwhile, heat oil in a large saucepan over medium heat. Add pancetta and garlic and sauté until pancetta is crisp and fat is cooked off, about 5 minutes. Add cooked spaghetti and toss to combine.
3. In a medium bowl, whisk together milk, cheese, eggs, and pepper. Add mixture to spaghetti and cook 1 minute to heat through (do not over-cook or eggs will scramble). Transfer mixture to dinner plates and serve hot.

Preparation and cooking time: 20 minutes　　　　　　*Serves 4*

Needed items
large stockpot
large saucepan
medium bowl

12	ounces uncooked spaghetti
2	teaspoons olive or vegetable oil
¼	pound pancetta, minced
2	garlic cloves, minced
2	cups milk (regular or nonfat)
¼	cup grated Parmesan or Romano cheese
2	eggs
¼	teaspoon ground black pepper

Chinese Noodles with Ginger and Vegetables

Chinese noodles are just as versatile as traditional American and Italian-style pastas. They tend to cook up soft, while absorbing the flavors of broths, sauces, herbs, and spices.

Note: Chinese egg noodles—often sold as "mein"—resemble spaghetti or fettucine.

1. In large stockpot, cook egg noodles according to package directions. Drain, transfer to a large bowl, and cover with foil to keep warm.
2. Meanwhile, heat oil in a large non-stick skillet over medium heat. Add carrots, sugar snap peas, ginger, garlic, and soy sauce and sauté 3-4 minutes, or until vegetables are tender-crisp. Dissolve cornstarch in chicken broth and add to skillet with the green onions. Simmer 1 minute, or until sauce thickens.
3. Pour sauce over cooked noodles and toss to combine.

Preparation and cooking time: 15-20 minutes　　　　　*Serves 2*

Needed items
large stockpot
large bowl
large non-stick skillet

½	pound Chinese egg noodles
2	teaspoons dark sesame oil
2	carrots, peeled and cut into matchstick-size pieces
1	cup sugar snap peas, ends trimmed
1	tablespoon minced fresh ginger
1	garlic clove, minced
1	tablespoon soy sauce
1	tablespoon cornstarch
2	cups chicken broth
½	cup chopped green onions

Needed items
    medium saucepan
    large stockpot
    large bowl
    aluminum foil

  2 teaspoons olive or vegetable oil
  1 small onion, chopped (about
        ½ cup)
  2 garlic cloves, minced
  ½ cup sliced sundried tomatoes
        (packed without oil)
  1 teaspoon dried oregano
  ½ teaspoon crushed red pepper
        flakes
  ½ teaspoon salt
  1 28-ounce can diced tomatoes
  ¼ cup dry red wine
  ¼ cup water
  12 ounces uncooked black pasta
        (any shape)
  ¼ cup tightly packed fresh basil
        leaves, chopped

Black (Squid Ink) Noodles with Spicy Tomato Ragout

Squid ink pasta has a firm texture and subtle seafood taste, making it the perfect base for this spicy tomato sauce—a sauce that's deepened with sweet, sundried tomatoes. This interesting black pasta can also be tossed with olive oil, garlic, and fresh parsley for a unique meal in minutes.

1. Heat oil in a medium saucepan over medium heat. Add onion and garlic and sauté 2 minutes. Add sundried tomatoes and sauté 1 minute. Add oregano, red pepper flakes, and salt and stir to coat. Add diced tomatoes, wine, and water, and bring mixture to a boil. Reduce heat, cover, and simmer 20 minutes (and up to 1 hour).

2. Meanwhile, in a large stockpot, cook pasta according to package directions. Drain, transfer to a large bowl, and cover with foil to keep warm.

3. Remove tomato mixture from heat and stir in basil. Spoon sauce over pasta and toss to combine.

Preparation and cooking time: 25 minutes   *Serves 4*

Stuffed Shells with Mustard Greens

Most stuffed shell recipes use spinach or just plain cheese. In this version, mustard greens add a fresh, slightly bitter flavor to a classic dish. You can substitute kale or collard greens for the mustard greens, if desired.

Note: This dish can be prepared in advance and refrigerated for up to 3 days (or frozen for up to one month) before baking. Thaw frozen stuffed shells completely before baking.

1. Preheat oven to 350° F.

2. In a large stockpot, cook shells according to package directions. Drain and set aside.

3. Meanwhile, in a medium saucepan, combine tomatoes, wine, tomato paste, oregano, and basil. Set pan over medium-high heat and bring mixture to a boil. Reduce heat, cover, and simmer 5 minutes.

4. In a large bowl, combine ricotta, half of the mozzarella, mustard greens, onion powder, salt, pepper, garlic powder, and nutmeg. Mix well. Stuff cheese mixture into cooked shells and arrange side-by-side in a shallow baking dish that has been coated with non-stick spray. Pour tomato sauce over top. Top with remaining mozzarella and Parmesan cheese.

5. Cover with foil and bake 45 minutes. Uncover and bake 10 more minutes, or until cheese is golden and bubbly.

Preparation time: 15 minutes
Cooking time: 55 minutes

Serves 4

Needed items
- large stockpot
- medium saucepan
- large bowl
- shallow baking dish
- aluminum foil

12	ounces uncooked jumbo pasta shells
1	28-ounce can diced tomatoes
½	cup dry red wine
2	tablespoons tomato paste
1	teaspoon dried oregano
1	teaspoon dried basil
1	15-ounce container ricotta cheese (regular or part-skim)
8	ounces grated mozzarella cheese (regular or part-skim), divided
1	10-ounce package frozen, chopped mustard greens, thawed and drained
½	teaspoon onion powder
½	teaspoon salt
¼	teaspoon ground black pepper
¼	teaspoon garlic powder
¼	teaspoon ground nutmeg
¼	cup grated Parmesan cheese non-stick cooking spray

Needed items
  medium saucepan
  large stockpot
  medium bowl
  4-quart casserole dish
  aluminum foil

  2   teaspoons olive or vegetable oil
  2   shallots, minced
  2   garlic cloves, minced
  1   28-ounce can diced tomatoes
  ½   cup dry red wine
  1   teaspoon dried thyme
  1   teaspoon dried rosemary
  ½   teaspoon ground black pepper
  1   pound uncooked ziti noodles
  1   15-ounce container ricotta
      cheese (regular or part-skim)
  8   ounces grated mozzarella
      cheese (regular or part-skim),
      divided
  ¼   teaspoon ground nutmeg
  ¼   cup grated Parmesan or
      Romano cheese

Baked Ziti

This is a great party dish—everyone loves it. You can make the dish ahead of time and refrigerate or freeze it until party day. Thaw frozen ziti completely before baking.

1. Preheat oven to 350° F.

2. Heat oil in a medium saucepan over medium heat. Add shallots and garlic and sauté 2 minutes. Add tomatoes, red wine, thyme, rosemary, and pepper and bring mixture to a boil. Reduce heat and simmer 10 minutes.

3. Meanwhile, in a large stockpot, cook pasta according to package directions. Drain and set aside.

4. In a medium bowl, combine ricotta, half of the mozzarella cheese, and nutmeg and mix well.

5. Spoon ½ cup of the tomato sauce in the bottom of a 4-quart casserole dish. Top with half of the cooked ziti. Top with half of the cheese mixture and half of the remaining tomato sauce. Layer remaining ziti on top and top with remaining cheese mixture and remaining tomato sauce. Sprinkle remaining mozzarella and Parmesan cheese on top.

6. Cover with foil and bake 30 minutes. Uncover and bake 15 more minutes, or until cheese is golden and bubbly.

Preparation time: 20 minutes
Cooking time: 45 minutes

Serves 4

Wild Mushroom Risotto

The secret to perfect risotto is the gradual addition of liquid (not like traditional rice, where you add the liquid all at once) and constant stirring. As the short grains of rice slowly absorb liquid, they create a thick, creamy sauce. In this dish, it's a sauce that's deepened with the warm, earthy flavors of wild mushrooms.

1. In a small bowl, combine porcini mushrooms and warm water and let stand 15 minutes.

2. Meanwhile, heat oil in a large saucepan over medium heat. Add onion and garlic and sauté 2 minutes. Add sliced wild mushrooms and sauté 4 minutes, or until tender and releasing juice.

3. Strain porcini mushrooms through a paper towel-lined sieve, reserving soaking liquid. Mince porcinis and add to the saucepan with the thyme, salt, and pepper. Add rice and stir to coat.

4. Add reserved soaking liquid and simmer until liquid is absorbed.

5. Add ½ cup broth and simmer until liquid is absorbed. Add remaining broth, ½ cup at a time, waiting until liquid is absorbed before adding the next ½ cup (risotto takes about 20 minutes to cook from the time the first liquid is added).

6. Add sherry and simmer until liquid is absorbed. Spoon risotto into shallow bowls and serve hot.

Preparation and cooking time: 30-35 minutes

Serves 4 as a main course, 6 as an appetizer or side dish

Needed items
  small bowl
  large saucepan
  fine sieve

½ ounce dried porcini mushrooms
½ cup warm water
2 teaspoons olive or vegetable oil
1 small onion, chopped (about ½ cup)
2 garlic cloves, minced
1 pound wild mushrooms (any combination of Shiitake, cremini, oyster, portobello, black trumpet, etc.), stems discarded, caps chopped into ½-inch pieces
2½ teaspoons dried thyme
½ teaspoon salt
½ teaspoon ground black pepper
1 pound uncooked Arborio (short grain) rice
4 cups beef or chicken broth
½ cup sherry wine

Needed items
  large saucepan

  2 teaspoons olive or vegetable oil
  2 shallots, minced
  2 garlic cloves, minced
1½ cups uncooked Arborio (short
     grain) rice
  5 cups chicken broth
  1 pound cooked lobster meat, cut
     into 1-inch pieces
  2 cups fresh cob corn (about
     4 ears)
  ¼ cup chopped fresh Italian
     parsley
  2 tablespoons grated Parmesan or
     Romano cheese
  2 tablespoons sherry wine
  ½ teaspoon salt
  ¼ teaspoon ground black pepper

Lobster-Corn Risotto

An excellent combination—the rich taste of lobster balanced with the sweetness of corn. Sherry is added at the end to bring out the different flavors, while adding a fresh taste of its own.

Note: If desired, you can substitute chicken or shrimp for the lobster and frozen corn for the fresh.

1. Heat oil in a large saucepan over medium heat. Add shallots and garlic and sauté 2 minutes. Add rice and cook 3 minutes, or until translucent, stirring constantly.

2. Add ½ cup of the chicken broth and simmer until liquid is absorbed, stirring constantly. Add remaining chicken broth, ½ cup at a time, waiting until liquid is absorbed before adding the next ½ cup (risotto takes about 20 minutes to cook from the time the first liquid is added).

3. Fold in lobster and remaining ingredients. Simmer 2 minutes to heat through. Spoon risotto into shallow bowls and serve hot.

Preparation and cooking time: 30-35 minutes   *Serves 4*

Chicken, Turkey, Duck, and Game Birds

Tarragon-Crusted Chicken with Braised Baby Vegetables

This one-pan dish sounds much harder to make than it is. Baby vegetables are nestled under chicken breasts in a roasting pan, and the whole thing is popped in the oven. As the meal cooks, the vegetables take on a sweet, roasted flavor, and the chicken (infused with the anise-flavor of tarragon) cooks up to a perfect golden brown.

1. Preheat oven to 400° F.
2. Rinse chicken breasts and pat dry. Coat both sides with tarragon, salt, and pepper and set aside.
3. In a shallow roasting pan, combine onions, carrots, cherry tomatoes, Brussels sprouts, corn, chicken broth, thyme, and pepper and toss to coat. Arrange chicken on top of vegetables in roasting pan.
4. Bake 35-40 minutes, or until chicken is cooked through (juices will run clear when meat is pierced with a fork) and vegetables are tender.

Preparation time: 5-10 minutes
Cooking time: 35-40 minutes

Serves 4

Needed items
  shallow roasting pan

For the tarragon-crusted chicken:
  2 whole skinless chicken breasts (with bone), halved
  ¼ cup chopped fresh tarragon
  ½ teaspoon salt
  ¼ teaspoon ground black pepper

For the braised baby vegetables:
  2 cups frozen pearl onions, thawed
  1 cup baby carrots
  8 cherry tomatoes
  1 cup Brussels sprouts, rinsed and trimmed
  1 15-ounce jar baby corn, drained
  ½ cup chicken broth
  1 teaspoon dried thyme
  ¼ teaspoon ground black pepper

Needed items
    baking sheet
    zip-top bag

¼ cup all-purpose flour
½ teaspoon garlic powder
½ teaspoon onion powder
½ teaspoon mustard powder
½ teaspoon paprika
½ teaspoon dried thyme
½ teaspoon salt
½ teaspoon ground black pepper
1 whole skinless chicken breast
    (with bone), halved
1 teaspoon olive or vegetable oil
    non-stick cooking spray

Oven-Baked "Fried" Chicken

There's no need to break out the deep-fat fryer for this dish. Get the fried food taste without actually smothering the chicken in oil. After you've tried this dish, experiment with different spices in the flour mixture, such as chili powder, cumin, Bay seasoning, and oregano.

1. Preheat oven to 400° F.
2. Combine flour, garlic powder, onion powder, mustard powder, paprika, thyme, salt, and pepper in zip-top bag and shake to combine. Add chicken, seal the bag and shake to coat chicken with flour mixture. Remove chicken from bag and discard flour mixture. Place chicken on a baking sheet that has been coated with non-stick spray and drizzle oil over top.
3. Bake 35-40 minutes, or until golden brown and cooked through (juices will run clear when meat is pierced with a fork).

Preparation time: 5-10 minutes   *Serves 2*
Cooking time: 35-40 minutes

Needed items
    large non-stick skillet

2 teaspoons peanut or
    vegetable oil
1 pound skinless, boneless
    chicken breasts, cut into
    1-inch pieces
1 8¼-ounce can crushed
    pineapple in unsweetened
    pineapple juice
¼ cup apricot preserves
¼ cup Hoisin sauce
¼ teaspoon ground black pepper

Sweet-n-Sour Chicken

I like to use Hoisin sauce for its combination of flavors—garlic, ginger, soy sauce, and spices. It has incredible character and eliminates the need for lots of extra ingredients in one recipe. Serve the chicken with pasta or rice on the side, using the extra sweet-n-sour sauce as a topping.

1. Heat oil in a large non-stick skillet over medium heat. Add chicken and sauté 4 minutes, or until golden brown on all sides.
2. Add pineapple, apricot preserves, Hoisin sauce, and pepper and simmer 5-7 minutes, or until chicken is cooked through and sauce thickens and reduces.

Preparation and cooking time: 20 minutes   *Serves 2*

Tandoori Chicken

Indian cooks often marinate chicken in yogurt and spices before throwing it into the tandoor, an intensely hot, charcoal-fire oven. The acid in the yogurt tenderizes the meat while the spices add a distinct flavor. Don't worry, you don't need a tandoor for this dish, just a very hot oven!

1. In a small bowl, whisk together yogurt, cumin, turmeric, garlic powder, salt, ginger, coriander, and cinnamon. Transfer to a shallow dish, add chicken and turn to coat both sides. Cover with plastic wrap and refrigerate 20 minutes (and up to 24 hours).

2. Preheat oven to 400° F.

3. Transfer chicken to a shallow roasting pan and bake 35-40 minutes, or until golden brown and cooked through (juices will run clear when meat is pierced with a fork).

Preparation time: 25 minutes
Cooking time: 35-40 minutes

Serves 2

Needed items
  small bowl
  shallow dish
  shallow roasting pan
  plastic wrap

  ½ cup plain yogurt (regular or nonfat)
  1 teaspoon ground cumin
  ½ teaspoon turmeric
  ½ teaspoon garlic powder
  ½ teaspoon salt
  ¼ teaspoon ground ginger
  ¼ teaspoon ground coriander
  ⅛ teaspoon ground cinnamon
  1 whole skinless chicken breast (with bone), halved

Chicken and Black Bean Enchiladas

This is a great way to use up leftover, cooked chicken. Or, skip the chicken altogether and you've got vegetarian enchiladas in a snap!

1. Preheat oven to 400° F.

2. In a blender or food processor fitted with the metal blade, combine beans, chili powder, cumin, and jalapeños. Process until almost smooth. Spoon an equal amount of the mixture onto the center of each tortilla. Divide chicken evenly over bean mixture. Roll up tortillas, fold in the ends, and place side-by-side in the bottom of a shallow baking dish that has been coated with non-stick spray. Top with salsa, grated cheese, and green onions.

3. Cover with foil and bake 20 minutes. Uncover and bake 10 more minutes, or until cheese is golden and bubbly.

Preparation time: 20 minutes
Cooking time: 30 minutes

Serves 6 (or 4 with leftovers—
they freeze very well!

Needed items
  blender or food processor
  shallow baking dish
  aluminum foil

  2 15-ounce cans black beans, drained
  2 teaspoons chili powder
  1 teaspoon ground cumin
  1 tablespoon diced pickled jalapeños, or one small fresh jalapeño pepper, seeded and minced
  1 pound cooked skinless, boneless chicken breasts, cut into strips
  6 8-inch flour tortillas
  1 cup mild, medium or hot salsa
  4 ounces grated Monterey Jack cheese (regular or reduced-fat)
  ½ cup chopped green onions
  non-stick cooking spray

Needed items
 blender
 shallow roasting pan
 large zip-top bag

4 garlic cloves, peeled
¼ cup fresh lemon juice
2 tablespoons molasses
2 teaspoons Worcestershire sauce
2 pounds skinless chicken thighs
¼ teaspoon salt
¼ teaspoon ground black pepper
 non-stick cooking spray

Garlic-Lemon Chicken Thighs

The powerful blend of molasses, lemon juice, and garlic makes an ideal glaze for chicken. You can also try the marinade with pork, shellfish, and hearty, firm-fleshed fish, such as swordfish, tuna, and monkfish.

1. In a blender, combine garlic, lemon juice, molasses, and Worcestershire sauce. Purée until smooth. Transfer marinade to a large zip-top bag and add chicken thighs. Seal and shake gently to coat chicken with mixture. Refrigerate 20 minutes (and up to 24 hours).

2. Preheat oven to 425° F.

3. Remove chicken from bag, reserving marinade, and arrange thighs in a shallow roasting pan that has been coated with non-stick spray. Pour over remaining marinade and sprinkle with salt and pepper.

4. Bake 25-30 minutes, or until chicken is cooked through (juices will run clear when meat is pierced with a fork), spooning marinade over chicken halfway through cooking time.

Preparation time: 30 minutes
Cooking time: 25-30 minutes

Serves 4

Layered Mexican Chicken with Corn Tortillas

As you cut into this dish, you plunge through chicken in a Mexican-style cream and cheese sauce to reach a layer of tender corn tortillas. Mexican lasagna?

1. Preheat oven to 350° F.

2. Place chicken in medium saucepan and pour over enough cold water to cover. Set pan over medium-high heat and bring to a boil. Reduce heat and simmer 10 minutes, or until chicken is cooked through. Drain and when cool enough to handle, cut chicken into 1-inch pieces.

3. Transfer chicken to a large bowl and add sour cream, 1¼ cups of the shredded cheese, salsa, chiles, cumin, and pepper. Mix well and set aside.

4. Arrange half of the tortillas in the bottom of an 11x7-inch baking dish that has been coated with non-stick spray, overlapping the pieces to cover the surface. Top with half of the chicken mixture and smooth over with the back of a spoon to even the top. Layer remaining tortillas over top, and spoon over remaining chicken mixture. Top with remaining ¾ cup of cheese and chopped cilantro.

5. Cover with foil and bake 30 minutes. Uncover and bake 30 more minutes, or until top is golden and bubbly. Let stand 5 minutes before serving.

Preparation time: 15 minutes
Cooking time: 1 hour

Serves 4

Needed items
  medium saucepan
  large bowl
  11 x 7-inch baking dish
  aluminum foil

1 pound skinless, boneless chicken breasts
2 cups sour cream (regular or nonfat)
2 cups Mexican-style shredded cheese blend (regular or reduced-fat), divided
½ cup mild, medium, or hot salsa
1 4-ounce can chopped green chiles
1½ teaspoons ground cumin
¼ teaspoon ground black pepper
8 6-inch corn tortillas, cut into 2-inch pieces
2 tablespoons chopped fresh cilantro
  non-stick cooking spray

Needed items
shallow baking dish
large non-stick skillet
fine sieve

3 tablespoons all-purpose flour
½ teaspoon salt
¼ teaspoon ground black pepper
1 whole skinless, boneless
   chicken breast, halved
1 tablespoon olive oil
1 cup chicken broth
½ cup vermouth or dry
   white wine
1 shallot, chopped
10 whole black peppercorns
6 sprigs fresh thyme, or
   1 teaspoon dried
1 tablespoon honey
1 tablespoon Dijon mustard
12 thin asparagus spears, ends
   trimmed

Dijon Chicken with Asparagus

Dijon mustard and fresh asparagus have a natural affinity—pairing them accentuates the wonderful flavor each one has to offer. The chicken just basks in the ensemble.

1. In a shallow baking dish, combine flour, salt, and pepper. Add chicken and turn to coat both sides.

2. Heat oil in a large non-stick skillet over medium heat. Add chicken and sauté 2-3 minutes per side, or until golden. Remove chicken from skillet and set aside.

3. To the same skillet, add chicken broth, vermouth, shallot, peppercorns, and thyme. Bring mixture to a boil, reduce heat, cover, and simmer 10 minutes.

4. Strain liquid through a fine sieve to remove solids and return liquid to pan. Whisk in honey and mustard. Return chicken to pan and simmer 10 minutes, uncovered, until cooked through. Remove chicken with a slotted spoon, reserving liquid in pan, and transfer to a serving platter or two dinner plates.

5. Add asparagus to pan and simmer 3 minutes, or until tender-crisp. Arrange asparagus next to chicken and spoon sauce over top.

Preparation and cooking time: 30 minutes   *Serves 2*

Chicken Fried Rice

This is a great recipe for leftover, cooked chicken, or any leftover meat such as pork, shrimp, or beef. Just add the cooked meat when you add the rice and pick up at step 2. For a vegetarian version, skip the meat and add a variety of mixed vegetables instead.

1. Heat oil in a medium saucepan over medium heat. Add onion and garlic and sauté 2 minutes. Add chicken and sauté 5 minutes, or until golden and cooked through, stirring frequently. Add rice and sauté 2 minutes, or until translucent. Add soy sauce and stir to coat.

2. Add chicken broth, salt, and pepper and bring mixture to a boil. Reduce heat, cover, and simmer 20 minutes, or until liquid is absorbed.

3. Stir in peas and green onions and heat through.

Preparation and cooking time: 30-35 minutes   Serves 2

Needed items
  medium saucepan

  2   teaspoons dark sesame oil
  1   small onion, chopped (about ½ cup)
  2   garlic cloves, minced
  1   pound skinless, boneless chicken breasts, cut into 1-inch pieces
  1   cup Basmati or long grain white rice
  1   tablespoon soy sauce
  2¼ cups chicken broth or water
  ½   teaspoon salt
  ¼   teaspoon ground black pepper
  ½   cup frozen green peas
  ¼   cup chopped green onions

Cajun Chicken with Cornbread Dressing

"Dressing" is actually stuffing that's not stuffed into anything. In this dish, the cornbread mixture serves as a "bed" for tangy, Creole-crusted chicken breasts.

1. Preheat oven to 400° F.

2. In a medium bowl, combine stuffing mix, onion, green pepper, oregano, ½ teaspoon of the salt, and black pepper. Toss to combine. Add chicken broth and mix well. Press mixture into the bottom of an 11x7-inch baking dish that has been coated with non-stick spray. Set aside.

3. Rinse chicken and pat dry. Season both sides of chicken with remaining ½ teaspoon salt and Creole seasoning and arrange halves on top of stuffing.

4. Bake 35-40 minutes, or until chicken is cooked through (juices will run clear when meat is pierced with a fork).

Preparation time: 10 minutes   Serves 4
Cooking time: 35-40 minutes

Needed items
  medium bowl
  11 x 7-inch baking dish

  3   cups cubed cornbread stuffing mix
  1   small onion, chopped (about ½ cup)
  1   green bell pepper, seeded and chopped
  2   teaspoons dried oregano
  1   teaspoon salt, divided
  ¼   teaspoon ground black pepper
  1   cup chicken broth
  2   whole skinless chicken breasts (with bone), halved
  2   tablespoons Creole or Cajun seasoning*
      non-stick cooking spray

  *   Available in the spice section of most supermarkets.

Needed items
large oven-proof skillet

2 teaspoons olive or vegetable oil
1 cup sliced fresh mushrooms
1 whole skinless, boneless
chicken breast, halved
¼ teaspoon salt
¼ teaspoon ground black pepper
1¼ cups beef broth, divided
½ cup Marsala wine
½ teaspoon dried thyme
1 tablespoon cornstarch
½ cup grated Monterey Jack
cheese (regular or reduced-fat)

Chicken Marsala with Jack Cheese

Marsala is typically a veal dish made with Marsala wine and mushrooms. This chicken version is spruced up with melted Monterey Jack cheese. Serve the dish with rice or pasta on the side to soak up the thick, rich gravy.

1. Heat oil in a large oven-proof skillet over medium heat. Add mushrooms and sauté 5 minutes, or until tender and releasing juice. Remove mushrooms with a slotted spoon and set aside.

2. Season both sides of chicken with salt and pepper. Place chicken in hot skillet (with reserved mushroom juice) and sauté 2-3 minutes per side, or until golden.

3. Return mushrooms to pan and add 1 cup of the beef broth, Marsala wine, and thyme. Simmer, uncovered, 10 minutes, or until chicken is tender and cooked through.

4. Preheat broiler.

5. Dissolve cornstarch in remaining ¼ cup of beef broth and add to pan. Simmer 1 minute, or until sauce thickens. Top chicken breast halves with grated Monterey Jack cheese and place skillet under the broiler.

6. Broil 2-3 minutes, or until cheese is golden.

Preparation and cooking time: 25-30 minutes   *Serves 2*

Chicken Curry with Lemongrass and Figs

Indian, Persian, and Turkish cooks often incorporate fresh and dried fruit in their savory dishes. The addition of lemongrass adds a little twist—a subtle Thai influence. If you can't find fresh lemongrass, substitute the bottled variety or use 1 teaspoon grated lemon zest. Serve the chicken and sauce over sticky rice or thin noodles for a complete meal.

1. Heat oil in a large non-stick skillet over medium heat. Add onion, garlic, lemongrass, and ginger and sauté 3 minutes. Add chicken and sauté 2-3 minutes, or until golden brown on all sides.

2. Add curry powder, coriander, salt, and pepper and stir to coat. Add chicken broth and figs and bring to a boil. Reduce heat and simmer 10 minutes, or until chicken is cooked through and liquid is reduced.

3. Remove from heat and stir in sour cream and cilantro.

Preparation and cooking time: 20 minutes   *Serves 4*

Needed items
large non-stick skillet

- 2 teaspoons olive or vegetable oil
- 1 small onion, chopped (about ½ cup)
- 2 garlic cloves, minced
- 1 stalk lemongrass, coarse top discarded and tender bottom minced (about 2 teaspoons)
- 1 teaspoon minced fresh ginger
- 1 pound skinless, boneless chicken breasts, cut into 1-inch pieces
- 2 teaspoons curry powder
- ½ teaspoon ground coriander
- ½ teaspoon salt
- ¼ teaspoon ground black pepper
- 1½ cups chicken broth
- 8 dried Mission figs, chopped
- ½ cup sour cream (regular or nonfat)
- ¼ cup packed fresh cilantro leaves, chopped

Needed items
roasting pan
medium and small bowls
small skillet

1   large Spanish onion, halved
    and sliced
2   red bell peppers, quartered and
    seeded
1   tablespoon chili powder
1   teaspoon ground coriander
½   teaspoon ground cinnamon
½   teaspoon garlic powder
½   teaspoon salt
½   teaspoon cayenne pepper
2   teaspoons olive oil
2   whole skinless chicken breasts
    (with bone), halved
¼   cup tightly packed fresh basil
    leaves, chopped
2   tablespoons pine nuts, lightly
    toasted*
1   tablespoon balsamic vinegar

Spicy Roast Chicken with Caramelized Onion and Red Pepper Relish

The time it takes to read the title of this dish may actually take longer than the preparation. The spice blend that forms the chicken's crust pairs beautifully with the sweetness of the caramelized onions and red bell peppers.

1. Preheat oven to 400° F.
2. Arrange onion and red peppers in the bottom of a roasting pan and set aside.
3. In a small bowl, combine chili powder, coriander, cinnamon, garlic powder, salt, and cayenne. Add olive oil and mix well with a fork. Rinse chicken and pat dry. Rub chili mixture all over both sides of chicken breasts.
4. Arrange chicken, meat side up, on top of onions and peppers in roasting pan.
5. Roast 35-40 minutes, or until chicken is cooked through (juices will run clear when meat is pierced with a fork). Transfer chicken to serving platter and set aside.
6. Peel away skin from red peppers and chop peppers and onion into small dice. Transfer to a medium bowl and toss with basil, pine nuts, and vinegar. Serve mixture along side roasted chicken.

Preparation time: 10-15 minutes   *Serves 4*
Cooking time: 35-40 minutes

*   Toast pine nuts by heating in a small skillet over medium heat until golden, shaking the pan frequently (it should take about 3-5 minutes).

Roast Chicken with Apples, Sweet Onions, and Dried Fruit

Roasting a chicken is easier than you think. Just plunk the bird in a roasting pan, arrange the apples, onions, and dried fruit around the bottom, pop that baby in the oven, and let it go.

1. Preheat oven to 450° F.
2. Rinse chicken inside and out and pat dry. Coat the chicken all over with rosemary, thyme, salt, and pepper. Transfer chicken to a shallow roasting pan and arrange apples, onion, and prunes around chicken, covering the bottom of the pan. Pour chicken broth over apples, onion, and prunes. Insert a meat thermometer deep into the thickest part of the thigh next to the body, not touching the bone.
3. Place chicken in oven and immediately reduce oven temperature to 325° F. Roast 20 minutes per pound, or until until thermometer reads 180°-185° F, basting every 30 minutes after the first 30 minutes of cooking. Let chicken stand 10 minutes before carving. Serve carved chicken with apples, onion, and prunes on the side.

Preparation time: 10 minutes
Cooking time: 2-2½ hours

Serves 4

Needed items
roasting pan
meat thermometer

1 6- to 7-pound roasting chicken, giblets removed and discarded
2 tablespoons chopped fresh rosemary, or 1 teaspoon dried
2 tablespoons chopped fresh thyme, or 1 teaspoon dried
½ teaspoon salt
½ teaspoon ground black pepper
2 Mackintosh or Winesap apples, cored and cut into thick slices
1 large red onion, cut into 2-inch pieces
1 cup pitted prunes
½ cup chicken broth

Needed items
    shallow baking dish
    large non-stick skillet or stove-top
        grill pan
    plastic wrap

¼   cup soy sauce
¼   cup red wine vinegar
2   tablespoons light corn syrup
½   teaspoon hot sauce (or more
        to taste)
¼   teaspoon ground black pepper
1   pound skinless, boneless
        chicken breasts, cut into
        thin strips
1   green bell pepper, seeded and
        cut into thin strips
1   red bell pepper, seeded and cut
        into thin strips
1   large onion, halved and sliced
8   6-inch flour tortillas
1   large beefsteak tomato, diced
½   cup sour cream (regular or
        nonfat)

Chicken Fajitas

For a truly authentic Mexican meal, serve the fajitas with refried beans and guacamole. And, when you're ready for a different version, substitute strips of beef or whole shrimp for the chicken. Vegetarian fajitas (with red, yellow, orange, and green bell peppers) are pretty awesome too.

1. In a shallow baking dish, whisk together soy sauce, vinegar, corn syrup, hot sauce, and pepper. Add chicken, bell peppers, and onion and toss to coat. Cover with plastic wrap and refrigerate 20 minutes (and up to 24 hours).

2. Set a large non-stick skillet (or stove-top grill pan) over medium heat. Add chicken and vegetables, with the marinade, and sauté 5-7 minutes, or until chicken is cooked through and vegetables are tender-crisp. Transfer chicken and vegetables to a serving platter, reserving marinade in skillet. Simmer marinade 5 more minutes, or until reduced and thickened.

3. Meanwhile, warm tortillas according to package directions.

4. Pour thickened sauce over chicken and vegetables and serve with warmed tortillas, diced tomato, and sour cream.

Preparation and cooking time: 35 minutes   *Serves 4*

Pesto-Crusted Chicken Breasts

To save time, you can make the pesto in advance and refrigerate it for up to 3 days. You can also marinate the chicken in the pesto for up to 24 hours.

1. Preheat oven to 400° F.
2. In a blender, combine basil, pine nuts, Parmesan, garlic, water, olive oil, salt, and pepper. Process until smooth.
3. Rinse chicken and pat dry. Pour basil mixture all over both sides of chicken and place in a shallow roasting pan that has been coated with non-stick spray.
4. Bake 35-40 minutes, or until cooked through (juices will run clear when meat is pierced with a fork).

Preparation time: 10 minutes
Cooking time: 35-40 minutes

Serves 2

* Toast pine nuts by heating in a small skillet over medium heat until golden, shaking the pan frequently (it should take about 3-5 minutes).

Needed items
  blender
  shallow roasting pan
  small skillet

1 cup tightly packed fresh basil leaves
2 tablespoons pine nuts, lightly toasted*
2 tablespoons grated Parmesan cheese
1 garlic clove, peeled
¼ cup water
1 tablespoon olive oil
½ teaspoon salt
¼ teaspoon ground black pepper
1 whole skinless chicken breast (with bone), halved
  non-stick cooking spray

Needed items
large saucepan

2 teaspoons olive or vegetable oil
1 small onion, chopped (about
    ½ cup)
2 celery stalks, chopped
2 carrots, peeled and chopped
½ pound skinless, boneless
    chicken breasts, cut into
    1-inch pieces
2 bay leaves
1 teaspoon dried thyme
½ teaspoon salt
¼ teaspoon ground black pepper
¼ teaspoon ground sage
5 cups chicken broth
6 ounces uncooked broad or
    extra broad egg noodles
2 tablespoons chopped fresh
    Italian parsley

Chicken Noodle Stew

A hearty meal that can easily be made with turkey, cooked ham, or a variety of vegetables.

1. Heat oil in a large saucepan over medium heat. Add onion, celery, and carrots and sauté 2 minutes. Add chicken pieces and sauté 5-7 minutes, or until golden brown on all sides. Add bay leaves, thyme, salt, pepper, and sage and stir to coat. Add chicken broth and bring mixture to a boil. Reduce heat, partially cover, and simmer 10 minutes.

2. Return mixture to a boil and add egg noodles. Cook 10 minutes, or until egg noodles are just tender.

3. Remove from heat, discard bay leaves and stir in fresh parsley.

Preparation and cooking time: 30 minutes   *Serves 2*

Almond-Crusted Drumsticks

The interesting blend of cornflakes cereal and almonds creates a nutty, crisp crust for the chicken. If desired, use the coating on skinless chicken breasts instead.

1. Preheat oven to 400° F.
2. Rinse chicken drumsticks and pat dry. In a shallow dish, combine flour, salt, and pepper. Add drumsticks and turn to coat all sides.
3. In shallow bowl, combine honey, mustard, and garlic powder and set aside. Combine cornflakes and almonds in a food processor fitted with the metal blade and process until mixture resembles coarse crumbs. Transfer to a shallow dish. Roll flour-coated drumsticks in honey mixture and then into cornflake mixture. Turn to coat all sides.
4. Transfer drumsticks to a baking sheet that has been coated with non-stick spray.
5. Bake 35-40 minutes, or until crust is golden brown and chicken is cooked through (juices will run clear when chicken leg is pierced with a fork).

Preparation time: 15 minutes
Cooking time: 35-40 minutes

Serves 4

Needed items
  shallow dishes
  shallow bowl
  food processor
  baking sheet

8 skinless chicken drumsticks
¼ cup all-purpose flour
½ teaspoon salt
¼ teaspoon pepper
¼ cup honey
1 tablespoon Dijon mustard
¼ teaspoon garlic powder
2 cups cornflakes cereal
½ cup sliced almonds
  non-stick cooking spray

Needed items
large bowl
large, oven-proof skillet or shallow
baking dish

1 pound skinless, boneless
   chicken breasts, cut into
   2-inch pieces
1 red bell pepper, seeded and cut
   into 1-inch pieces
1 acorn squash (about 1½
   pounds), peeled (with a sharp
   paring knife), halved,
   seeded, and flesh cut into
   1-inch pieces
4 garlic cloves, minced
3 tablespoons balsamic vinegar
2 tablespoons fresh lemon juice
1 tablespoon chopped fresh
   rosemary, or 1 teaspoon dried
2 teaspoons olive oil
½ teaspoon grated lemon zest
½ teaspoon salt
½ teaspoon ground black pepper
   non-stick cooking spray

Balsamic Glazed Chicken with Acorn Squash

Balsamic vinegar is definitely a kitchen staple—excellent for salads, pestos, marinades, glazes, and as a finishing touch for a variety of sauces. In this dish, as the chicken cooks, the balsamic vinegar reduces and intensifies, the vinegar flavor is cooked off, and the result is a savory-sweet coating for both the chicken and the acorn squash.

1. Preheat oven to 400° F.
2. Combine all ingredients in a large bowl and toss to combine. Transfer mixture to a large, oven-proof skillet (or shallow baking dish) that has been coated with non-stick spray.
3. Bake, uncovered, 45 minutes, or until chicken is cooked through and squash is tender.

Preparation time: 10 minutes
Cooking time: 45 minutes

Serves 4

Chicken Lo Mein

"Lo mein" simply means sautéed noodles. Chinese egg noodles are traditional, but any spaghetti-type noodle will work. And, it's not a crime to add your favorite vegetables to the dish.

1. In a large stockpot, cook noodles according to package directions. Drain, transfer to a large bowl, and cover with foil to keep warm.

2. Meanwhile, heat oil in a large non-stick skillet over medium heat. Add garlic, ginger, and celery and sauté 2 minutes. Add chicken and sauté 5 minutes, or until golden brown and cooked through, stirring frequently. Add snap peas and carrots and sauté 2 minutes.

3. Dissolve cornstarch in chicken broth and add to the skillet with the soy sauce, salt, and red pepper flakes. Simmer 1 minute, or until sauce thickens, stirring constantly.

4. Pour mixture over cooked noodles, add green onions, and toss to combine.

Preparation and cooking time: 25-30 minutes

Serves 2

Needed items
large stockpot
large bowl
large non-stick skillet
aluminum foil

1 8-ounce package uncooked Chinese egg noodles
2 teaspoons dark sesame oil
1 garlic clove, minced
1 teaspoon minced fresh ginger
2 celery stalks, chopped
½ pound skinless, boneless chicken breasts, cut into 1-inch pieces
½ cup sugar snap peas, ends trimmed
½ cup sliced carrots
1 tablespoon cornstarch
1 cup chicken broth
3 tablespoons soy sauce
½ teaspoon salt
¼ teaspoon crushed red pepper flakes
¼ cup chopped green onions

Needed items
small bowl
shallow baking dish
shallow roasting pan
plastic wrap

3 tablespoons red or white wine
vinegar
1 teaspoon granulated sugar
1 teaspoon ground allspice
1 teaspoon ground cloves
1 teaspoon dried basil
1 teaspoon dried thyme
½ teaspoon habañero sauce (or
any hot sauce)
½ teaspoon salt
¼ teaspoon ground black pepper
1 whole skinless chicken breast
(with bone), halved
non-stick cooking spray

Jamaican Jerk Chicken

"Jerk" seasoning is a vinegary, spicy marinade made with dried herbs and habañero peppers (chile peppers that are 5 times hotter than jalapeños!). I use habañero sauce in this recipe, but any hot chile sauce will do. Jerk flavors taste great on grilled pork and shrimp, too. Real jerks are not invited to dinner.

1. In a small bowl, whisk together vinegar, sugar, allspice, cloves, basil, thyme, habañero sauce, salt, and pepper. Set aside.

2. Rinse chicken and pat dry. Place in a shallow baking dish and pour over jerk marinade. Turn to coat chicken all over with marinade. Cover with plastic wrap and refrigerate 20 minutes (and up to 24 hours).

3. Preheat oven to 400° F.

4. Remove chicken from marinade (reserve marinade) and place in a shallow roasting pan that has been coated with non-stick spray. Pour over reserved marinade.

5. Bake 35-40 minutes, or until cooked through (juices will run clear when meat is pierced with a fork).

Preparation time: 30 minutes
Cooking time: 35-40 minutes

Serves 2

Rolled Chicken with Spinach and Blue Cheese

The chicken in this dish is pounded flat, stuffed with a savory blend of spinach and blue cheese, and then rolled up and cooked. As you cut each roll crosswise, wonderful green spirals appear in every slice.

1. Place each chicken breast half between two pieces of plastic wrap and pound until ¼-inch thick (use the flat side of a meat mallet, the bottom of a heavy skillet, or a rolling pin). Set aside.

2. Heat 2 teaspoons of the oil in a large non-stick skillet over medium heat. Add garlic and sauté 2 minutes. Add spinach and cook 2 minutes, or until liquid evaporates. Remove from heat and stir in ricotta, blue cheese, ¼ teaspoon of the salt, and nutmeg. Spread spinach mixture evenly over each piece of chicken. Starting from the shorter end, roll up chicken, jellyroll fashion, and secure the rolls with wooden picks.

3. In a shallow dish, combine flour, remaining ½ teaspoon salt and black pepper. Roll chicken rolls in flour mixture to coat all sides.

4. Heat remaining 2 teaspoons of oil in the same non-stick skillet over medium heat. Add chicken rolls and sauté 4 minutes, or until golden brown on all sides. Add tomatoes, oregano, basil, and red pepper flakes. Bring to a boil, reduce heat and simmer 10 minutes, or until chicken is cooked through.

5. Remove wooden picks from chicken, transfer rolls to a serving platter and spoon sauce over top.

Preparation and cooking time: 30 minutes   *Serves 4*

Needed items
  large non-stick skillet
  shallow dish
  plastic wrap
  wooden picks

2 whole skinless, boneless chicken breasts, halved
4 teaspoons olive oil, divided
2 garlic cloves, minced
1 10-ounce package frozen chopped spinach, thawed and drained
¼ cup ricotta cheese (regular or part-skim)
2 tablespoons crumbled blue cheese
¾ teaspoon salt, divided
⅛ teaspoon ground nutmeg
¼ cup all-purpose flour
¼ teaspoon ground black pepper
1 14½-ounce can diced tomatoes
1 teaspoon dried oregano
1 teaspoon dried basil
¼ teaspoon crushed red pepper flakes

Needed items
small saucepan
shallow dish
large oven-proof skillet
aluminum foil

1   14½-ounce can crushed
        tomatoes
3   tablespoons tomato paste
1   teaspoon dried basil
1   teaspoon dried oregano
3   tablespoons all-purpose flour
½   teaspoon salt
¼   teaspoon ground black pepper
1   whole skinless, boneless
        chicken breast, halved
1   egg, lightly beaten
¼   cup Italian-style dry bread
        crumbs
2   teaspoons olive oil
½   cup grated mozzarella cheese
        (regular or part-skim)
1   tablespoon grated Parmesan
        cheese

Chicken Parmesan

There's enough tomato sauce in this recipe to smother the chicken and a side dish of pasta. Serve a mixed green salad on the side and you've got a complete meal.

1. Preheat oven to 400° F.

2. In a small saucepan, combine tomatoes, tomato paste, basil, and oregano. Bring mixture to a boil, reduce heat, and simmer 10 minutes.

3. Meanwhile, in a shallow dish, combine flour, salt, and pepper. Add chicken breast halves and turn to coat both sides. Dip flour-coated chicken into egg and then into bread crumbs.

4. Heat oil in a large oven-proof skillet over medium heat. Add chicken breast halves and sauté 2-3 minutes per side, or until golden brown. Top each chicken breast half with ½ cup of the tomato mixture. Top with mozzarella and Parmesan cheese.

5. Cover with foil and bake 15 minutes. Uncover and bake 5 more minutes, or until chicken is cooked through and cheese is golden and bubbly. Serve chicken with extra sauce on the side.

Preparation time: 30 minutes
Cooking time: 20 minutes

Serves 2

Chicken Cacciatore

Cacciatore is Italian for "hunter's style," apropos for a dish with unlimited variations, all depending on the availability of fresh ingredients. Sometimes hunters used rabbit, sometimes chicken, occasionally mushrooms and bell peppers, but almost always tomatoes. The dish is traditionally served with polenta, but rice and pasta make ideal side dishes, too (just make sure you serve the chicken with something to soak up the savory sauce).

1. Heat oil in a large saucepan over medium heat. Add onion, garlic, bell pepper, mushrooms, and jalapeño and sauté 4-5 minutes, or until vegetables are tender and mushrooms are releasing juice. Add chicken and sauté 5 minutes, or until golden brown on all sides. Add basil, curry powder, salt, and pepper and stir to coat.

2. Add tomatoes, chicken broth, and red wine. Bring mixture to a boil, reduce heat, partially cover, and simmer 20 minutes.

3. Divide rice among four individual bowls and spoon chicken mixture over top. Garnish with fresh parsley if desired.

Preparation and cooking time: 45 minutes   *Serves 4*

Needed items
large saucepan

- 2 teaspoons olive or vegetable oil
- 1 small onion, chopped (about ½ cup)
- 2 garlic cloves, minced
- 1 green bell pepper, seeded and diced
- 1 cup sliced fresh mushrooms
- 1 small jalapeño pepper, seeded and minced
- 1 pound skinless, boneless chicken breasts, cut into 2-inch pieces
- 2 teaspoons dried basil
- 1½ teaspoons curry powder
- ½ teaspoon salt
- ¼ teaspoon ground black pepper
- 1 14½-ounce can diced tomatoes
- 1 cup chicken broth
- ½ cup dry red wine
- 4 cups cooked white rice
- ¼ cup fresh Italian parsley leaves, chopped (optional)

Needed items
  small bowl
  large non-stick skillet
  2-quart casserole dish
  large bowl or food processor
  rolling pin

For the filling:
  4 tablespoons all-purpose flour
  2½ teaspoons dried thyme
  ½ teaspoon salt
  ½ teaspoon ground black pepper
  2 teaspoons olive or vegetable oil
  1 small onion, chopped (about
       ½ cup)
  1 pound skinless, boneless
       chicken breasts, cut into
       1-inch pieces
  2 cups chicken broth
  1 Idaho potato, peeled and cut
       into ½-inch cubes
  1 tablespoon Dijon mustard
  ⅓ cup frozen corn kernels
  ⅓ cup frozen green peas
  3 tablespoons sherry wine

For the crust:
  1 cup all-purpose flour
  1 teaspoon baking powder
  ½ teaspoon salt
  1 tablespoon butter, chilled and
       cut up
  ¼ cup water
  1 egg, lightly beaten

Chicken Pot Pie

Nothing says "comfort food" like a hearty chicken pot pie. Homemade versions are always the best. Add your own personal touch by including any beloved vegetables and fresh herbs.

Note: You can substitute one 11-ounce can of refrigerated biscuit dough for the crust (knead the dough to form one solid mass and proceed as directed).

1. Preheat oven to 450° F.

2. To make the filling, in a small bowl, combine 4 tablespoons flour, thyme, salt, and pepper. Mix well with a fork and set aside.

3. Heat oil in a large non-stick skillet over medium heat. Add onion and sauté 2 minutes. Add chicken and sauté 5 minutes, or until golden brown on all sides. Add flour mixture and stir to coat chicken and onion. Add chicken broth, potato, and Dijon mustard and bring mixture to a boil. Reduce heat and simmer 10 minutes. Stir in corn, peas, and sherry and simmer 1 minute. Remove from heat and transfer mixture to a clean 2-quart casserole dish.

4. Meanwhile, to make the crust, in a large bowl or food processor fitted with the metal blade, combine flour, baking powder, and salt. Add butter and mix together with your fingers or process until mixture resembles coarse meal. Add water and mix or process until a manageable dough forms. Transfer dough to a lightly floured surface and knead 1 minute, or until smooth. Roll dough into a circle that is 1-inch larger than the diameter of your 2-quart casserole dish. Place dough on top of chicken mixture and pinch the edges to seal the dough to the dish. Brush the top with beaten egg and prick the surface with a sharp knife to allow steam to escape during cooking.

5. Bake 12-15 minutes, or until crust is puffed up and golden.

Preparation time: 20-25 minutes
Cooking time: 12-15 minutes

Serves 4

Turkey Chop Suey

Chop Suey is actually a Chinese dish in which vegetables and pork, chicken, or seafood are stir-fried together and served over steamed rice. Chow Mein is a similar dish served over fried noodles. This is neither. In fact, the mixture of ground turkey, pasta, and tomatoes is more reminiscent of an Italian meal. The truth is, my mother called it "Chop Suey," so the name stays!

Note: You can substitute ground beef, pork, or chicken for turkey, if desired.

1. Preheat oven to 350° F.

2. In a large stockpot, cook macaroni according to package directions. Drain, transfer to a large bowl, and set aside.

3. Meanwhile, heat oil in a large non-stick skillet over medium heat. Add onion and celery and sauté 2 minutes. Add ground turkey and sauté 5 minutes, or until cooked through, breaking up the meat as it cooks. Add basil, salt, and pepper and stir to coat. Stir mixture into cooked pasta. Stir in crushed tomatoes, tomato sauce, and milk.

4. Transfer mixture to a 4-quart casserole dish that has been coated with non-stick spray. Top with bread crumbs and Parmesan cheese.

5. Cover with foil and bake 30 minutes. Uncover and bake 15 more minutes, or until top is golden.

Preparation time: 20 minutes
Cooking time: 45 minutes

Serves 4

Needed items
  large stockpot
  large bowl
  large non-stick skillet
  4-quart casserole dish
  aluminum foil

12 ounces uncooked elbow macaroni
 2 teaspoons olive or vegetable oil
 1 small onion, chopped (about ½ cup)
 2 celery stalks, chopped
 1 pound ground turkey breast
1½ teaspoons dried basil
 ½ teaspoon salt
 ¼ teaspoon ground black pepper
 1 28-ounce can crushed tomatoes
 1 8-ounce can tomato sauce
 ½ cup milk (regular or nonfat)
 2 tablespoons Italian-style dry bread crumbs
 2 tablespoons grated Parmesan cheese
    non-stick cooking spray

Needed items
    large stockpot
    large bowl
    large non-stick skillet
    4-quart casserole dish
    aluminum foil

12 ounces uncooked broad or
       extra broad egg noodles
1½ cups sour cream (regular or
       nonfat)
 4 ounces grated mozzarella
       cheese, about 1 cup (regular
       or part-skim)
 2 teaspoons olive or vegetable oil
 1 small onion, chopped (about
       ½ cup)
 1 cup sliced fresh mushrooms
 1 pound skinless, boneless turkey
       breast, cut into 1-inch pieces
1½ teaspoons dried thyme
 1 teaspoon dried oregano
 ¾ teaspoon salt
 ¼ teaspoon ground black pepper
 1 cup chicken broth
 ½ cup vermouth or dry white
       wine
 ½ cup frozen green peas
 ¼ cup Italian-style dry bread
       crumbs
 2 tablespoons grated Parmesan
       cheese

Turkey Tetrazzini

This is a great way to use up leftover Thanksgiving turkey. Just add cooked, shredded turkey where the recipe calls for cut-up turkey breast.

1. Preheat oven to 350° F.

2. In a large stockpot, cook pasta according to package directions. Drain and transfer to a large bowl. Stir in sour cream and mozzarella and set aside.

3. Meanwhile, heat oil in a large non-stick skillet over medium heat. Add onion and mushrooms and sauté 5 minutes, or until onion is tender and mushrooms are releasing juice. Add turkey and sauté 5 minutes, or until golden brown on all sides. Add thyme, oregano, salt, and pepper and stir to coat.

4. Add chicken broth and vermouth and bring mixture to a boil. Reduce heat and simmer 10 minutes. Remove from heat and stir in green peas. Add turkey mixture to pasta and toss to combine. Transfer mixture to a 4-quart casserole dish and sprinkle the top with bread crumbs and Parmesan cheese.

5. Cover with foil and bake 30 minutes. Uncover and bake 15 more minutes, or until top is golden.

Preparation time: 25 minutes
Cooking time: 45 minutes

Serves 4

Moroccan Turkey Salad

In Northern Africa, slow cooking is the traditional way to prepare meals. Longer cooking times amplify the flavor of spices and dried fruits, and each mouthful is infused with the rich, deep flavor of the dish. I realize you may not have tons of extra time, so this dish can be prepared in just minutes. For a hearty lunch or dinner, stuff the salad into pita pockets or spoon it over couscous.

1. Preheat oven to 400° F.
2. Sprinkle both sides of turkey with salt and pepper and place on a baking sheet that has been coated with non-stick spray.
3. Bake 30-35 minutes, or until golden brown and cooked through. When cool enough to handle, cut into 1-inch pieces and set aside.
4. In a medium bowl, whisk together sour cream, vinegar, cumin, mustard, turmeric, coriander, and cayenne pepper. Fold in turkey, celery, and green onions. Serve warm or chilled.

Preparation and cooking time: 45 minutes   *Serves 4*

Needed items
baking sheet
medium bowl

1   pound skinless, boneless turkey breast
½   teaspoon salt
¼   teaspoon ground black pepper
1   cup sour cream (regular or nonfat)
2   teaspoons cider vinegar
2   teaspoons ground cumin
½   teaspoon ground mustard
½   teaspoon ground turmeric
½   teaspoon ground coriander
⅛   teaspoon cayenne pepper
2   celery stalks, chopped
2   tablespoons chopped green onions
    non-stick cooking spray

Needed items
 shallow dish
 large non-stick skillet
 aluminum foil
 plastic wrap

1 tablespoon Chinese Five Spice
   powder
1 tablespoon soy sauce
½ teaspoon salt
¼ teaspoon ground black pepper
2 boneless duck breasts (about
   ¾ pound each)
1 tablespoon peanut or
   vegetable oil
4 carrots, peeled and cut into
   thin, matchstick-size strips
2 garlic cloves, minced
1 tablespoon minced fresh ginger
1 stalk lemongrass, coarse top
   discarded and tender
   bottom minced (about 2
   teaspoons), or 1 teaspoon
   grated lemon zest

Peking Duck

Unlike chicken and turkey (with white-meat breasts and dark-meat legs), duck meat is entirely dark. The breast is tender and very lean and is best served rare to medium-rare. The crispy skin lends a wonderful shine and flavor to the dish, but feel free to discard it after cooking.

1. In a shallow dish, whisk together Chinese Five Spice powder, soy sauce, salt, and pepper. Add duck breasts and turn to coat both sides. Cover with plastic wrap and refrigerate 30 minutes (and up to 24 hours).

2. Heat oil in a large non-stick skillet over medium heat. Add carrots, garlic, ginger, and lemongrass and sauté 1 minute. Add duck breasts, skin-side down, and sauté 4 minutes. Flip and sauté until browned on the outside and medium-rare in the middle, about 3-4 more minutes. Remove from heat, cover with foil, and let stand 5 minutes.

3. Transfer duck to a serving platter, arrange vegetables along-side and serve immediately (you can also slice duck crosswise into ¼-inch thick slices before serving).

Preparation and cooking time: 45 minutes　　　　　　　*Serves 4*

Cornish Hens with Honey-Mustard Glaze and Pine Nut-Rice Stuffing

Cornish hens taste similar to chicken, and each 1-1¼-pound bird is the perfect amount for one person.

1. Preheat oven to 450° F.
2. Rinse hens inside and out and pat dry. Season the hens, inside and out, with ½ teaspoon of the salt and ¼ teaspoon of the pepper. Set aside while you prepare the glaze and rice stuffing.
3. In a small bowl, whisk together honey and Dijon mustard. Set aside.
4. To make the stuffing, heat oil in a medium saucepan over medium heat. Add onion and garlic and sauté 2 minutes. Add rice, oregano, remaining ½ teaspoon salt, and ¼ teaspoon pepper and stir to coat. Add chicken broth and pine nuts and bring mixture to a boil. Reduce heat, cover, and simmer 20 minutes, or until rice is tender and liquid is absorbed.
5. Remove from heat and spoon rice mixture loosely into cavity of hens. Transfer hens to a roasting pan.
6. Place hens in oven and immediately reduce oven temperature to 350° F. Bake 45 minutes to 1 hour, or until juices from thigh run clear when pierced with a fork, basting every 15 minutes with the honey-mustard glaze.

Preparation time: 30 minutes
Cooking time: 45-60 minutes

Serves 2

* Toast pine nuts by heating in a small skillet over medium heat until golden, shaking the pan frequently (it should take about 3-5 minutes).

Needed items
  small bowl
  medium saucepan
  roasting pan
  small skillet

2 Cornish game hens, about 1-1¼ pounds each, giblets removed and discarded
1 teaspoon salt, divided
½ teaspoon ground black pepper, divided

For the honey-mustard glaze:
¼ cup honey
4 teaspoons Dijon mustard

For the pine nut-rice stuffing:
2 teaspoons olive oil
1 small onion, minced (about ½ cup)
2 garlic cloves, minced
½ cup uncooked long grain white or Basmati rice
½ teaspoon dried oregano
1 cup chicken broth
¼ cup toasted pine nuts*, coarsely chopped

Beef, Pork, Veal, Venison, and Lamb

Wild Mushroom Stuffed Steaks

Great transformation for traditional steak and mushrooms. How so? The mushrooms are wild, and they're stuffed inside, rather than spooned over top. Not rocket science, just different.

1. Combine dried mushrooms and warm water in a small bowl and let stand 15 minutes. Drain mushrooms through a paper towel-lined sieve, reserving liquid, and chop into small pieces.

2. In a medium saucepan, combine chopped porcinis, reserved soaking liquid, beef broth, rice, thyme, and ground black pepper. Set pan over medium-high heat and bring mixture to a boil. Reduce heat, cover, and simmer 15-20 minutes, or until rice is tender and liquid is absorbed.

3. Meanwhile, using a sharp knife, slice pockets into steaks by slicing horizontally into the side, and almost through to the other side. Season the outside with cracked black pepper and salt. Stuff rice mixture into steak pockets and seal shut with wooden picks.

4. Heat oil in a large non-stick skillet over medium heat. Add steaks and sauté 4 minutes per side, until browned. Add wine to the skillet, cover and simmer 5 minutes, until steaks are tender and cooked through (stuffed steaks take less time to cook through than ordinary steaks, so keep an eye on them). Remove wooden picks before serving.

Preparation and cooking time: 45-55 minutes　　　　　　*Serves 4*

Needed items
small bowl
fine sieve
medium saucepan
large non-stick skillet
wooden picks

½ ounce dried porcini mushrooms
½ cup warm water
¾ cup beef broth
½ cup long grain white rice
1 teaspoon dried thyme
¼ teaspoon ground black pepper
4 4-ounce eye round or tenderloin beef steaks (about 1-inch thick), trimmed of fat
1½ teaspoons cracked black pepper
½ teaspoon salt
2 teaspoons olive or vegetable oil
½ cup dry red wine

Needed items
    meat mallet or heavy skillet
    large zip-top bag

1   pound flank steak, trimmed
        of fat
2   tablespoons peppercorn
        mélange
½   cup dry red wine
2   teaspoons Worcestershire sauce
2   garlic cloves, minced

Grilled Flank Steak with Peppercorn Mélange

Peppercorn mélange is a mixture of four different peppercorns, black, green, white, and pink. The blend of flavors—rich and spicy from the black, mild and fresh from the green, hot and gingery from the white, and ripe and sweet from the pink—make an excellent coating for this tender cut of meat. Peppercorn mélange is sold in the spice section with the other peppercorns.

1. Score flank steak by making ⅛-inch deep slices, crosswise, on both sides of steak.
2. Place peppercorns in a large zip-top bag and mash with the flat side of a meat mallet or the bottom of a heavy skillet until crushed. Add wine, Worcestershire sauce, and garlic to bag. Add steak and press peppercorns into both sides. Refrigerate 20 minutes (and up to 24 hours).
3. Preheat grill or broiler.
4. Remove steak from marinade and press in any peppercorns that have fallen off.
5. Grill or broil 4-5 minutes per side for medium-rare meat. Transfer steak to cutting board and let stand 10 minutes. When ready to serve, slice the steak diagonally, across the grain, into thin slices.

Preparation and cooking time: 35-40 minutes   *Serves 4*

Horseradish-Crusted Filet Mignon

This coating is incredible! As the filet cooks, the horseradish lends its fiery taste to the meat while forming a golden brown, crispy crust. You can prepare the filet mignon up to twenty-four hours in advance and refrigerate it until ready to roast.

1. Preheat oven to 425° F.
2. In a small bowl, combine horseradish, basil, thyme, garlic powder, salt, and pepper. Press mixture into both sides of filet mignons. Transfer meat to a shallow roasting pan that has been coated with non-stick spray.
3. Roast 20-25 minutes, or until brown on the outside and just pink in the middle.
4. Remove from oven, cover pan with foil, and let stand 10 minutes. (For flank steak, after 10 minutes, transfer meat to a cutting board and slice steak diagonally, across the grain, into thin slices).

Preparation time: 15 minutes
Cooking time: 20-25 minutes

Serves 4

Needed items
small bowl
shallow roasting pan
aluminum foil

⅓ cup drained prepared horseradish
1 teaspoon dried basil
1 teaspoon dried thyme
¼ teaspoon garlic powder
¼ teaspoon salt
¼ teaspoon ground black pepper
4 4-ounce filet mignons (or 1-pound flank steak)
non-stick cooking spray

Needed items
 medium saucepan
 large wok or non-stick skillet

For the Yellow Rice:
 2 teaspoons olive or peanut oil
 1 cup uncooked long grain
  white rice
 1 teaspoon turmeric
 2 cups chicken broth or water
 ½ teaspoon salt
 ¼ teaspoon ground black pepper

For the Sesame Beef:
 2 teaspoons dark sesame oil
 1 small red onion, halved
  and sliced
 2 garlic cloves, minced
 1 tablespoon minced fresh ginger
 1 pound beef tenderloin or top
  round steak, sliced crosswise
  into thin strips
 1 yellow bell pepper, seeded and
  sliced into thin strips
 1 tablespoon raw sesame seeds
 1 bunch bok choy, washed, outer
  leaves and ends removed,
  sliced into thin strips
 2 tablespoons soy sauce
 ¼ teaspoon ground black pepper
 1 tablespoon cornstarch
 ½ cup beef broth

Stir-Fried Sesame Beef with Yellow Rice

Stir fries are great last-minute meals because they're ready in minutes. This adaptable dish can be made with any combination of chicken, pork, shrimp, and vegetables. If you don't have a wok, any large skillet will do.

1. To make the yellow rice, heat oil in a medium saucepan over medium heat. Add rice and sauté 2 minutes, or until translucent, stirring constantly. Add turmeric and stir to coat. Add chicken broth, salt, and pepper and bring mixture to a boil. Reduce heat, cover, and simmer 20 minutes, or until rice is tender and liquid is absorbed.

2. Meanwhile, to make the sesame beef, heat oil in a large wok or non-stick skillet over medium heat. Add onion, garlic, and ginger and sauté 2 minutes. Add beef, bell pepper, and sesame seeds and sauté 5 minutes, or until beef is browned on all sides, stirring frequently. Stir in bok choy, soy sauce, and pepper and sauté 1 minute, or until bok choy just begins to wilt.

3. Dissolve cornstarch in beef broth and add to beef mixture. Simmer 1 minute, until sauce thickens to the consistency of gravy, stirring constantly.

4. To serve, spoon rice into shallow bowls and spoon beef mixture over top.

Preparation and cooking time: 30 minutes   *Serves 4*

Beef Pinwheels

Rolling up curly-edged lasagna noodles gives them a whole new look—and quite an impressive presentation. It's too easy to look so grand.

Note: The cooking time may seem long, but it's necessary to fully cook the meat. Don't start this recipe when you want dinner in 15 minutes!

1. Preheat oven to 375° F.
2. In a large stockpot, cook lasagna noodles according to package directions. Drain and lay out on a smooth, clean surface.
3. In a large bowl, combine sirloin, bread crumbs, egg, oregano, garlic powder, and pepper and mix well. Divide mixture into eight even portions and spread out on cooked lasagna noodles. Starting from one end, roll up noodles into tight pinwheels. Arrange pinwheels side-by-side (curly edge side up) in a small casserole dish, allowing them to crowd next to each other. Sprinkle the top with Parmesan cheese.
4. Cover with foil and bake 45 minutes. Uncover and bake 30 more minutes, or until top is golden.

Preparation time: 20 minutes
Cooking time: 1 hour 15 minutes

Serves 4

Needed items
large stockpot
large bowl
small casserole dish
aluminum foil

8 uncooked curly edge lasagna noodles
1 pound ground sirloin or lean ground beef
⅓ cup Italian-style dry bread crumbs
1 egg
1 teaspoon dried oregano
½ teaspoon garlic powder
½ teaspoon ground black pepper
2 tablespoons grated Parmesan cheese

Needed items
large bowl
8-inch loaf pan

1½ pounds meat blend (ground
   sirloin, veal and pork), or all
   lean ground beef
½ cup minced onion
½ cup Italian-style dry bread
   crumbs
¼ cup chopped fresh Italian
   parsley
1 teaspoon dried oregano
1 egg
½ teaspoon salt
¼ teaspoon ground black pepper
2 tablespoons ketchup
2 tablespoons Dijon mustard

Best-Ever Meatloaf

For a little surprise in the center, press half of the meat mixture into the loaf pan, top with a layer of grated cheddar or mozzarella cheese and then press remaining meat mixture on top. You can also sneak a birthday gift in there, but it might be a little messy to unwrap.

1. Preheat oven to 375° F.
2. In a large bowl, combine meat blend, onion, bread crumbs, parsley, oregano, egg, salt, and pepper. Mix well with a wooden spoon (or your hands).
3. Press mixture into an 8-inch loaf pan. Whisk together ketchup and mustard and spread mixture over prepared meatloaf.
4. Bake 1 hour, or until top is golden and loaf has pulled slightly away from the sides of the pan. Let stand 10 minutes before slicing.

Preparation time: 15 minutes   *Serves 4*
Cooking time: 1 hour

Needed items
large non-stick skillet
aluminum foil

2 teaspoons olive or vegetable oil
1 small onion, thinly sliced
1 tablespoon granulated sugar
½ pound thinly sliced steak
2 teaspoons Worcestershire sauce
¼ teaspoon salt
¼ teaspoon ground black pepper
2 steak rolls
½ cup grated cheddar cheese
   (regular or reduced-fat)

Cheese Steaks with Fried Onions

Serve with Sweet Potato Bay Fries for the perfect, fast-food dinner in the comfort of your own home.

1. Preheat oven to 350° F.
2. Heat oil in a large non-stick skillet over medium heat. Add onion and sugar and sauté 10 minutes, or until onions are tender and golden brown. Remove onions from pan with a slotted spoon and set aside.
3. Add steak to the skillet and sauté 4 minutes, or until browned and cooked through. Add Worcestershire sauce, salt, and pepper and cook until liquid is absorbed.
4. Slice rolls in half lengthwise. Divide steak evenly between rolls and top with onion slices and grated cheddar. Wrap cheese steaks in foil, transfer to the oven, and bake 15 minutes, or until cheese melts and rolls are warm.

Preparation and cooking time: 30 minutes   *Serves 2*

Sloppy Joes

These sandwiches are a hit every time I serve them—some things never change.
The list of ingredients may look long, but many items are pantry staples (if not,
they will be). Trust me, the combination of flavors is perfect. When I've tried
this recipe without one thing or another, it's just not the same.

1. In a large saucepan over medium heat, sauté ground beef until
   completely browned, breaking up the meat as it cooks. Remove
   from skillet, drain away any fat, and set aside.
2. Heat oil in the same pan over medium heat. Add onion, celery, and
   bell pepper and sauté 4 minutes, or until tender. Return beef to pan
   and add chili powder, basil, salt, pepper, and cayenne. Stir to coat
   beef and vegetables with herbs and spices. Add crushed tomatoes,
   ketchup, and mustard and mix well. Bring mixture to a boil, reduce
   heat, cover, and simmer 30 minutes, stirring occasionally.
3. Stir in corn and simmer 2 minutes to heat through. Spoon mixture
   onto rolls and serve hot.

Preparation and cooking time: 45 minutes   *Serves 4*

Needed items
large saucepan

- 1 pound lean ground beef or ground turkey
- 2 teaspoons olive or vegetable oil
- 1 small onion, chopped (about ½ cup)
- 2 celery stalks, chopped
- 1 green bell pepper, seeded and chopped
- 1 tablespoon chili powder
- 2 teaspoons dried basil
- ½ teaspoon salt
- ½ teaspoon ground black pepper
- ⅛ teaspoon cayenne pepper
- 1 14½-ounce can crushed tomatoes
- ½ cup ketchup
- 1 tablespoon Dijon mustard
- 1 cup frozen corn kernels
- 4 large Kaiser rolls, halved crosswise

Beef Stroganoff

A time-honored classic spruced up with wild mushrooms. This recipe can be
doubled or tripled easily (get the hint?… you'll want leftovers).

1. In a large stockpot, cook pasta according to package directions.
   Drain, transfer to a large bowl, and cover with foil to keep warm.
2. Meanwhile, heat oil in a large non-stick skillet over medium heat.
   Add onion and sauté 2 minutes. Add mushrooms and beef and cook
   until beef is browned on all sides and mushrooms are tender and
   releasing juice, about 5 minutes. Add salt and pepper and stir to coat.
   Add wine and simmer until liquid is absorbed. Add beef broth and
   bring mixture to a boil. Reduce heat and simmer 5 minutes.
3. Remove from heat and stir in sour cream. Spoon mixture over
   cooked pasta and serve.

Preparation and cooking time: 25 minutes   *Serves 2*

Needed items
large stockpot
large bowl
large non-stick skillet
aluminum foil

- 6 ounces uncooked bowtie (farfalle) pasta
- 2 teaspoons olive or vegetable oil
- 1 small onion, chopped (about ½ cup)
- 1 cup sliced Shiitake or cremini mushrooms
- ½ pound beef tenderloin, cut into 1-inch cubes
- ½ teaspoon salt
- ¼ teaspoon cracked black pepper
- ¼ cup dry red wine
- 1½ cups beef broth
- ½ cup sour cream (regular or nonfat)

Needed items
  small bowl
  large Dutch oven or oven-proof
    stockpot
  large bowl or food processor
  2-quart casserole dish
  rolling pin
  plastic wrap
  baking sheet

For the filling:
  2 tablespoons all-purpose flour
  2 teaspoons dried thyme
  ½ teaspoon salt
  ¼ teaspoon ground black pepper
  ¼ teaspoon paprika
  2 teaspoons olive or vegetable oil
  1 medium onion, chopped (about
       1 cup)
  1 pound boneless beef round or
       chuck, cut into 2-inch cubes
  2 carrots, peeled and chopped
  2 celery stalks, chopped
  4 medium red potatoes, cut into
       1-inch cubes
  1 14½-ounce can crushed
       tomatoes
  1 cup beef broth
  ¼ cup dry red wine
  1 tablespoon Dijon mustard
  ½ cup frozen corn

For the crust:
  ¾ cup all-purpose flour
  ½ teaspoon salt
  ¼ cup (½ stick) butter, chilled and
       cut up
  2 tablespoons cold water
  1 egg, lightly beaten

Beef Pot Pie

I love the crust on this pot pie, a tender, flaky pastry crust that crumbles into the stewed beef mixture as you cut into the top. If you're short on time, you can substitute prepared puff pastry (from the frozen foods section of the market) or a refrigerated pie crust. For a Shepherd's pie, top the beef mixture with mashed potatoes instead.

1. Preheat oven to 350° F.

2. To make the filling, in a small bowl, combine 2 tablespoons flour, thyme, salt, pepper, and paprika and set aside.

3. Heat oil in a large Dutch oven or oven-proof stockpot over medium heat. Add onion and sauté 2 minutes. Add beef and sauté 5-7 minutes, or until browned on all sides. Add flour mixture and stir to coat. Stir in carrots, celery, potatoes, tomatoes, beef broth, red wine, and Dijon mustard and mix well. Bring mixture to a boil. Remove from heat, cover, and transfer pot to the oven.

4. Bake 1 hour. Uncover and bake 30 more minutes.

5. Meanwhile, to make the crust, in a large bowl or food processor fitted with the metal blade, combine flour and salt. Work in butter with your fingers or process until mixture resembles coarse meal. Add cold water and mix or process until a manageable dough forms. Roll the dough into a round disc, press down slightly with the palm of your hand, wrap in plastic and refrigerate 20-30 minutes (chilling the dough makes it easier to work with).

6. Remove stew from oven and increase oven temperature to 425° F. Transfer stew to a clean 2-quart casserole dish and stir in corn.

7. Roll dough out into a circle that is ½-inch larger than the diameter of your casserole dish. Lay crust on top of casserole and pinch around the edges to seal the crust to the dish. Brush the top with beaten egg and prick the surface 1 or 2 times with a sharp knife to allow steam to escape during cooking.

8. Place dish on baking sheet and bake 20-25 minutes, or until crust is golden.

Preparation time: 25 minutes   *Serves 4*
Cooking time: 1 hour 50-55 minutes

Pot Roast with Root Vegetables

Any root vegetables will work in this recipe—celery root, sweet potatoes, parsnips—be adventurous and get to the root of it all.

1. Preheat oven to 300° F.

2. In a shallow baking dish, combine flour, salt, and pepper. Add roast and turn to coat all sides.

3. Heat 2 teaspoons of the oil in a large Dutch oven or oven-proof stockpot over medium heat. Add roast and sauté until browned on all sides, about 8-10 minutes. Remove roast from pan and set aside.

4. Heat remaining 2 teaspoons of oil in the same Dutch oven. Add onion and sauté 2 minutes. Add thyme, oregano, and basil and cook 1 minute. Return roast to pan.

5. Using a vegetable peeler, peel a ½-inch strip around the middle of each potato. Add potatoes to the roast with carrots, turnip, beef broth, and wine. Bring mixture to a boil. Remove from heat, cover, and transfer pot to the oven.

6. Bake 2 hours. Turn roast over and bake 1-1½ more hours, until meat pulls apart easily when tested with a fork.

7. To serve, transfer roast to a serving platter and surround with vegetables. Skim surface grease from simmering liquid and serve the sauce on the side.

Preparation time: 20-25 minutes
Cooking time: 3-3½ hours

Serves 8

Needed items
  shallow baking dish
  large Dutch oven or oven-proof
    stockpot
  vegetable peeler

¼ cup all-purpose flour
½ teaspoon salt
¼ teaspoon ground black pepper
4 teaspoons olive or vegetable oil, divided
1 4-pound bottom round or center cut rump roast, trimmed of fat
1 medium onion, chopped (about 1 cup)
2 teaspoons dried thyme
1½ teaspoons dried oregano
1 teaspoon dried basil
8 small red potatoes (about 1 pound)
4 carrots, peeled and cut into 1-inch chunks
1 yellow turnip or rutabaga (about 1 pound), peeled cut into 1-inch chunks
2½ cups beef broth
½ cup dry red wine

Needed items
   large bowl
   large non-stick skillet

For the meatballs:
   1   pound lean ground beef
   1   small onion, diced (about
         ½ cup)
   ¼   cup Italian-style dry bread
         crumbs
   1   egg
   2   tablespoons chopped fresh
         Italian parsley
   ½   teaspoon salt
   ¼   teaspoon ground black pepper
   2   teaspoons olive or vegetable oil

Sweet-n-Sour Sauce
   1   8¼-ounce can crushed
         pineapple in unsweetened
         pineapple juice
   2   tablespoons Hoisin sauce
   1   tablespoon light brown sugar

Wild Mushroom-Sherry Sauce
   1   cup sliced fresh Shiitake or
         other wild mushrooms
   1   teaspoon dried thyme
   1   cup beef broth
   1   tablespoon cornstarch
   ¼   cup sherry wine

Hearty Tomato Sauce
   1   14½-ounce can diced tomatoes
   2   tablespoons tomato paste
   1   teaspoon dried oregano
   1   teaspoon dried basil
   ¼   teaspoon crushed red pepper
         flakes

Meatballs with 5 Different Sauces

How could I stop at three sauces, or even four? These five delectable sauces, all very different, give you five choices depending on your mood.

Meatballs

1. In a large bowl, combine beef, onion, bread crumbs, egg, parsley, salt, and pepper. Mix well with your hands and form mixture into sixteen 2-inch meatballs.

2. Heat oil in a large non-stick skillet over medium heat. Add meatballs and sauté 5-7 minutes, or until browned on sides.

3. Add sauce ingredients as instructed below.

Sweet-n-Sour Sauce

1. Add all ingredients and simmer 5 minutes, or until meatballs are cooked through and sauce thickens and reduces.

Wild Mushroom-Sherry Sauce

1. Add mushrooms and sauté 5 minutes, until tender and releasing juice. Add thyme and stir to coat meatballs and mushrooms. Add beef broth and simmer 3 minutes.

2. Dissolve cornstarch in sherry and add to skillet. Simmer 1 minute, until sauce thickens.

Hearty Tomato Sauce

1. Add all ingredients and simmer 5 minutes, or until meatballs are cooked through and sauce thickens.

Red Wine Gravy

1. Add beef broth and simmer 5 minutes. Dissolve cornstarch in red wine and add to skillet. Simmer 1 minute, or until sauce thickens.

Cilantro-Soy Sauce

1. Add sesame oil and sauté 2 minutes. Add ½ cup of the beef broth and soy sauce and simmer 3 minutes.
2. Dissolve cornstarch in remaining ½ cup beef broth and add to skillet. Simmer 1 minute, or until sauce thickens. Remove from heat and stir in cilantro.

Preparation and cooking time: 20-25 minutes   Serves 4

Red Wine Gravy
- 1 cup beef broth
- 1 tablespoon cornstarch
- ¼ cup dry red wine

Cilantro-Soy Sauce
- 2 teaspoons dark sesame oil
- 1 cup beef broth, divided
- 1 tablespoon soy sauce
- 1 tablespoon cornstarch
- 2 tablespoons chopped fresh cilantro

Beef and Bean Burritos

This recipe makes six burritos, enough for six people if you serve rice and a salad on the side. Or, it serves two for dinner, leaving leftovers and a great lunch for the next day.

1. Preheat oven to 400° F.
2. Heat oil in a large non-stick skillet over medium heat. Add steak and sauté 4 minutes, or until cooked through. Remove from heat and set aside.
3. In a large bowl, combine beans, onion, cilantro, jalapeno pepper, chili powder, and cumin. Mash everything together with a potato masher or fork. Spoon mixture onto the center of each flour tortilla. Top with cooked steak. Roll up tortillas, fold in the ends and place side-by-side in shallow baking dish that has been coated with non-stick spray. Top with salsa and grated cheese.
4. Cover with foil and bake 20 minutes. Uncover and bake 10 more minutes, or until cheese is golden and bubbly.

Preparation time: 20 minutes
Cooking time: 30 minutes   Serves 2

Needed items
- large non-stick skillet
- large bowl
- shallow baking dish
- aluminum foil

- 2 teaspoons olive or vegetable oil
- ½ pound flank steak, sliced crosswise into thin strips
- 2 15-ounce cans pink beans, drained
- 1 small onion, chopped (about ½ cup)
- 2 tablespoons chopped fresh cilantro
- 2 teaspoons chili powder
- 1 small serrano or jalapeño pepper, seeded and minced
- 1 teaspoon ground cumin
- 6 8-inch flour tortillas
- ½ cup mild, medium or hot salsa
- ½ cup grated Monterey Jack cheese (regular or reduced-fat)
- non-stick cooking spray

Needed items
  large stockpot
  baking sheet
  large saucepan
  aluminum foil

2 butternut squash (about 1½
    pounds each), halved
    lengthwise and seeded
2 teaspoons olive or vegetable oil
½ pound baked ham, diced
1 small red onion, chopped
    (about ½ cup)
1 green bell pepper, seeded and
    diced
2 teaspoons dried sage
¼ teaspoon salt
¼ teaspoon ground black pepper
2 cups chicken broth
¾ cup uncooked pearl barley
2 tablespoons grated Parmesan
    cheese

Stuffed Butternut Squash with Barley and Ham

Note: To save time (and another dirty pan), skip the boiling of the butternut squash and increase baking time to 1 hour.

1. Preheat oven to 350° F.

2. Scoop the flesh from each butternut squash half, leaving about ½ inch of flesh with the skin. Chop the flesh into small dice and set aside.

3. In a large stockpot, boil squash shells in rapidly boiling water for 3 minutes. Drain and place upside down on a baking sheet. Set aside until ready to use.

4. Heat oil in a large saucepan over medium heat. Add ham, onion, green pepper, and diced squash and sauté 3 minutes. Add sage, salt, and pepper and stir to coat. Add chicken broth and bring to a boil. Gradually add barley and return to a boil. Reduce heat and simmer, uncovered, 25-30 minutes, or until barley is tender and liquid is absorbed.

5. Spoon barley mixture into each halved squash. Transfer stuffed squash to a foil-lined baking sheet and top with Parmesan cheese.

6. Bake 30 minutes, or until squash is tender and cheese is golden.

Preparation time: 40 minutes   *Serves 4*
Cooking time: 30 minutes

Honey-Mustard Glazed Ham

Baking a ham is very easy, and the finished product is incredibly versatile—served hot or cold, with vegetables, rolls and potatoes—it's a true crowd-pleasing feast. Just remember to tuck some of the ham away for ham sandwiches.

1. Preheat oven to 325° F.
2. If ham has skin, peel it away using a sharp knife and discard, leaving a thin (⅛-inch) layer of fat on the surface. Score remaining fat with a sharp knife by cutting diagonal lines (about ⅛-inch deep) from one side to the other, criss-crossing cuts to form diamond shapes on the surface. Transfer ham to a foil-lined roasting pan and set aside.
3. Whisk together honey, mustard, brown sugar, and cloves. Brush mixture all over ham.
4. Bake 14 minutes per pound (about 1 hour for a 4-pound ham), basting every 15 minutes with the pan juices. Cool slightly before slicing.

Preparation time: 15 minutes
Cooking time: 1 hour

Serves 8

Needed items
foil-lined roasting pan

1 4-pound fully cooked, boneless ham
½ cup honey
2 tablespoons Dijon mustard
1 tablespoon light brown sugar
¼ teaspoon ground cloves

Glazed Sesame Pork

Today's pork cuts are leaner and more tender than they used to be. In this dish, a few simple pantry staples come together to create a tasty, Asian-inspired glaze that also works well on chicken and turkey.

1. Season both sides of pork chops with salt and pepper.
2. Heat oil in a large non-stick skillet over medium heat. Add chops and sauté 2-3 minutes per side, until golden. Add ¼ cup of the chicken broth, sesame seeds, vinegar, brown sugar, and mustard. Simmer 6-8 minutes, or until chops are fork-tender.
3. Dissolve cornstarch in remaining ¼ cup of chicken broth and add to skillet. Simmer 1 minute, or until sauce thickens.

Preparation and cooking time: 20 minutes

Serves 4

* Toast sesame seeds by heating in a small skillet over medium heat until golden, shaking the pan frequently (it should take about 3-5 minutes).

Needed items
large non-stick skillet
small skillet

4 4-ounce boneless loin chops, trimmed of fat
½ teaspoon salt
¼ teaspoon ground black pepper
2 teaspoons dark sesame oil
½ cup chicken broth, divided
4 teaspoons raw sesame seeds, lightly toasted*
2 tablespoons white wine vinegar
1 tablespoon light brown sugar
1 tablespoon Dijon mustard
2 teaspoons cornstarch

Needed items
  shallow dish
  large Dutch oven or oven-proof
    stockpot

¼ cup packed light brown sugar
2 tablespoons chili powder
1 tablespoon paprika
2 teaspoons ground cumin
1 teaspoon salt
½ teaspoon ground black pepper
1 2-pound boneless pork butt or
   shoulder blade roast, trimmed
   of fat
1 tablespoon vegetable oil
½ cup chicken broth or water
1 tablespoon balsamic vinegar
6-8 Kaiser rolls, halved

Barbecued Pulled Pork Sandwiches

A great dish to start early so you can allow the ingredients to simmer and blend for hours. The shredded pork, smothered in tangy barbecue sauce, makes quite a sloppy and satisfying sandwich.

1. Preheat oven to 325° F.
2. In a shallow dish, combine brown sugar, chili powder, paprika, cumin, salt, and pepper. Add pork and turn to coat all sides.
3. Heat oil in a large Dutch oven or oven-proof stockpot over medium heat. Add pork (and any seasoning mixture that falls off) and sauté until browned on all sides. Add chicken broth, cover, and transfer pot to the oven.
4. Bake 2-2½ hours, or until meat shreds easily when pulled with a fork.
5. Remove pot from oven and, using 2 forks, shred entire pork roast (while it's still in the pot). Place pot over medium heat and simmer until liquid is absorbed. Stir in balsamic vinegar and mix well. Serve shredded pork over halved rolls.

Preparation time: 15 minutes   *Serves 6-8*
Cooking time: 2-2½ hours

Stuffed Pork Chops

Comfort food, for sure. Pork has a natural affinity for fruit (fresh or dried), and this sweet and savory stuffing unites the sweetness of apples and leeks with aromatic herbs, oregano and rosemary.

Note: The stuffing can be made in advance and refrigerated until ready to use. And, you can substitute pears for the apples, if desired.

1. Preheat oven to 350° F.
2. Heat 2 teaspoons of the oil in a large non-stick skillet over medium heat. Add leek and apple and sauté 4 minutes, or until tender and golden. Add oregano, rosemary, ½ teaspoon of the salt, and ¼ teaspoon of the pepper and stir to coat. Transfer mixture to a large bowl and add bread cubes and chicken broth. Mix well and set aside.
3. Using a sharp knife, slice pockets into chops by slicing horizontally into the side, and almost through to the other side. Season the outside with remaining ½ teaspoon salt and ¼ teaspoon pepper.
4. Heat remaining 2 teaspoons of the oil in the same non-stick skillet over medium heat. Add chops and sauté 2 minutes per side, or until golden. Remove from pan and stuff chops with apple mixture, allowing stuffing to overflow out of pockets.
5. Transfer chops to a shallow baking dish and pour vermouth over top.
6. Cover with foil and bake 30 minutes. Uncover and bake 15 more minutes, or until chops are cooked through and stuffing is golden brown.

Preparation time: 20-25 minutes
Cooking time: 45 minutes

Serves 4

Needed items
  large non-stick skillet
  large bowl
  shallow baking dish
  aluminum foil

4 teaspoons olive or vegetable oil, divided
1 leek, green portion discarded, white portion halved, rinsed and chopped
1 medium apple (preferably Mackintosh or Winesap), cored and diced
2 teaspoons dried oregano
½ teaspoon dried rosemary
1 teaspoon salt, divided
½ teaspoon ground black pepper, divided
1½ cups unseasoned bread cubes (or cut up day-old bread)
½ cup chicken broth
4 4-ounce boneless pork chops, about 1-inch thick, trimmed of fat
½ cup vermouth or dry white wine

Needed items
  large bowls
  large baking sheet
  aluminum foil
  large stockpot

For the chinese dumplings:
  2 cups finely chopped Napa
      (Chinese) cabbage
  1 teaspoon salt
  ½ pound ground pork
  2 garlic cloves, minced
  2 green onions, white and green
      parts divided and chopped
  1 tablespoon soy sauce
  2 teaspoons cornstarch, plus extra
      for dusting dumplings
  1 teaspoon dark sesame oil
  ¼ teaspoon ground black pepper
  40 3-inch square wonton skins
      (also called "wonton
      wrappers")

For the soy-ginger dipping sauce:
  ¼ cup soy sauce
  2 tablespoons water
  2 teaspoons grated fresh ginger
  1 teaspoon honey

Chinese Dumplings with Soy-Ginger Dipping Sauce

This recipe can easily be doubled or tripled so you can serve the dumplings as an appetizer or hors d'oeuvre at your next party.

Note: These dumpling freeze very well, so make them ahead and freeze before cooking. The dumplings can go straight from the freezer to the pot, just add 1-2 minutes to the cooking time. Remember this trick, when the dumplings float to the top, they're done.

1. In a large bowl, combine cabbage and salt. Let stand 30 minutes to draw out water.

2. Squeeze cabbage to remove excess water and place in a large bowl. Add pork, garlic, white portion of green onions, 1 tablespoon soy sauce, 2 teaspoons cornstarch, sesame oil, and pepper. Mix well with a fork (or your hands) until well blended.

3. Spread out 20 wonton skins on a clean, dry surface. Spoon 1 tablespoon of pork mixture onto each square. Brush the edges of the wonton with water and top with second wonton skin. Pinch around the edges to seal. Dab each corner with water and fold into the center, making an envelope. Transfer dumplings to a large baking sheet and dust the top with remaining cornstarch.

4. Bring a large pot of water to a boil. Add dumplings in batches (about 5-6 at a time) and boil 2 minutes (or until they float to the surface). Remove with a slotted spoon, transfer to a serving plate and cover with foil to keep warm while you boil remaining dumplings.

5. Meanwhile, to make the dipping sauce, combine green portion of green onions, ¼ cup soy sauce, water, ginger, and honey and mix well. Serve with dumplings.

Preparation and cooking time: 30 minutes

Makes 20 dumplings
(4 servings)

Barbecued Spareribs

Pull out the napkins for this one. This barbecue blend is a combination of sweet, sour and slightly hot, with a little "pungent" thrown in for good measure.

Note: You can prepare this dish up to twenty-four hours in advance and bake it just before serving. Keep the ribs refrigerated while marinating.

1. Preheat oven to 350° F.
2. In a large bowl, whisk together orange juice, brown sugar, soy sauce, mustard, ginger, chili powder, cumin, and pepper. Set aside until ready to use.
3. Parboil ribs in a large pot of rapidly boiling water 3-4 minutes (this helps boil off extra fat). Drain and add to prepared barbecue sauce. Turn to coat ribs with sauce and transfer ribs and sauce to a large roasting pan.
4. Bake uncovered 1 hour until tender, turning once and basting frequently with the pan juices.

Preparation time: 20 minutes
Cooking time: 1 hour

Serves 4

Needed items
large bowl
large stockpot
large roasting pan

½ cup orange juice
¼ cup packed light brown sugar
2 tablespoons soy sauce
1 tablespoon Dijon mustard
1 tablespoon grated fresh ginger
4 teaspoons chili powder
1½ teaspoons ground cumin
½ teaspoon ground black pepper
3 pounds trimmed, pork spareribs (about eight 2-inch pieces)

Olive-Crusted Veal Chops with Garlic and Rosemary

Roasting veal by high heat produces a crispy, brown crust and a pink, juicy middle. The crust in this recipe is an interesting blend of tangy-salty olives, fresh garlic, and floral rosemary.

1. Preheat oven to 425° F.
2. In a blender, combine olives, garlic, sherry vinegar, rosemary, salt, and pepper. Purée until mixture forms a thick paste. Pat veal chops dry and rub olive mixture all over both sides.
3. Heat oil in a large oven-proof skillet over medium heat. Add veal chops and sauté 2 minutes per side, or until golden brown. Transfer skillet to the oven and roast 10-15 minutes, or until veal is cooked through.

Preparation and cooking time: 30 minutes

Serves 4

Needed items
blender
large oven-proof skillet

¼ cup pitted Greek (Kalamata) olives
2 garlic cloves, peeled
2 tablespoons sherry vinegar
1 tablespoon fresh chopped rosemary
¼ teaspoon salt
¼ teaspoon ground black pepper
4 4-ounce boneless veal loin chops, about 1-inch thick
2 teaspoons olive oil

Needed items
    fine sieve
    meat mallet, the bottom of a heavy
        skillet, or a rolling pin
    shallow baking dish
    large non-stick skillet

½ ounce dried porcini or Shiitake
    mushrooms
½ cup warm water
4 4-ounce boneless veal chops,
    about 1-inch thick
¼ cup all-purpose flour
½ teaspoon salt
¼ teaspoon ground black pepper
1 tablespoon butter or margarine
½ cup sherry wine
½ cup milk (regular or nonfat)
1 tablespoon chopped fresh
    thyme, or 1 teaspoon dried

Veal Chops with Porcini-Sherry Sauce

Veal is the meat of young calves and is typically very pale in color, with a firm, dense flesh. Look for those characteristics when shopping for this dish. Reddish-colored meat will have a stronger flavor and tougher texture and is better suited for stews and long braising times. Serve this dish with pasta or rice, you don't want to waste any of the delicious sauce.

1. Combine dried mushrooms and warm water and let stand 15 minutes. Drain mushrooms through a paper towel-lined sieve, reserving liquid, and chop into small pieces. Set aside until ready to use.

2. Pound veal chops until ½-inch thick (use the flat side of a meat mallet, the bottom of a heavy skillet or a rolling pin). Set aside.

3. In a shallow baking dish, combine flour, salt, and pepper. Add veal chops and turn to coat both sides.

4. Melt butter in a large non-stick skillet over medium heat. Add veal chops and sauté 2 minutes per side, or until golden brown. Add chopped mushrooms, reserved soaking liquid, and sherry and simmer 2 minutes. Add milk and thyme and simmer 1-2 more minutes, or until sauce thickens.

Preparation and cooking time: 30 minutes   *Serves 4*

Chili-Crusted Venison

Venison is a versatile meat that's just as quick and easy to prepare as beef. It's lower in fat and cholesterol than beef, and pairs well with both savory and sweet (fruit-based) sauces.

1. Place venison on a foil-lined baking sheet and set aside.
2. In a small bowl, whisk together remaining ingredients. Rub mixture all over both sides of venison. Cover with plastic wrap and refrigerate 1 hour (and up to 24 hours).
3. Preheat grill or broiler.
4. Grill or broil venison 3-4 minutes per side, or until browned on the outside and pink in the center. Remove from heat, wrap with foil, and let stand 5 minutes (this keeps the venison moist). Slice crosswise into 1-inch thick slices and serve warm.

Preparation and cooking time: 1 hour 20 minutes   *Serves 4*

Needed items
foil-lined baking sheet
small bowl
plastic wrap

1 pound venison filet, trimmed of fat
1 tablespoon Dijon mustard
1 tablespoon sherry vinegar
1 tablespoon chili powder
1 teaspoon ground cumin
1 teaspoon dried thyme
1 teaspoon granulated sugar
1 teaspoon salt
½ teaspoon ground coriander

Curried Lamb and Lentil Stew

A robust stew with the distinct taste of lamb, perfect for wintry Sundays. Ladle the stew over couscous or rice to round out the meal. Pork tenderloin or chicken make great substitutes for the lamb, if desired.

1. Heat oil in a large saucepan over medium heat. Add onion, garlic, and carrots and sauté 2 minutes. Add lamb and sauté 5 minutes, or until browned. Add curry, cumin, bay leaf, salt, and cayenne and stir to coat. Add tomatoes, chicken broth, and lentils and bring mixture to a boil. Reduce heat, partially cover and simmer 45 minutes, or until lentils are tender, stirring occasionally.
2. Remove from heat, discard bay leaf, and stir in cilantro.

Preparation and cooking time: 1 hour   *Serves 4*

Needed items
large saucepan

2 teaspoons olive or vegetable oil
1 small onion, chopped (about ½ cup)
2 garlic cloves, minced
2 carrots, peeled and chopped
1 pound lamb shoulder or stew meat, trimmed of fat and cut into 1-inch cubes
1 tablespoon curry powder
1 teaspoon ground cumin
1 bay leaf
½ teaspoon salt
⅛ teaspoon cayenne pepper
1 28-ounce can crushed tomatoes
2 cups chicken broth
1 cup lentils, rinsed and picked over to remove any stones
2 tablespoons chopped fresh cilantro

Needed items
  medium bowl
  shallow dish
  plastic wrap

1 cup plain yogurt (regular or
     lowfat)
¼ cup fresh mint leaves, chopped
1 tablespoon ground coriander
½ teaspoon ground black pepper
4 4-ounce lamb chops, trimmed
     of fat

Grilled Lamb Chops with Yogurt-Mint Sauce

Many people have a love-hate relationship with lamb. The problem is, one experience with an overcooked piece of lamb, and you may never go back. When preparing this dish, keep an eye on those chops as they cook—just tender and cooked through is the ideal way to prepare this tender meat.

1. In a medium bowl, combine yogurt, mint, coriander, and pepper. Transfer half of the mixture to a shallow dish and add lamb chops. Turn to coat both sides, cover with plastic wrap, and refrigerate 1 hour (and up to 24 hours). Spoon remaining yogurt mixture into a serving bowl and set aside.

2. Preheat grill or broiler.

3. Remove chops from marinade (discard marinade). Grill or broil chops 5 minutes per side, or until no longer pink in the center. Serve chops with yogurt-mint sauce on the side.

Preparation and cooking time: 1 hour 15 minutes   *Serves 4*

Seafood and Shellfish

Herb-Grilled Salmon with Papaya-Chile Salsa

Fresh herbs pair exceptionally well with fish, and the distinct taste of thyme and rosemary seem to belong with salmon.

Note: The salmon and serrano chiles can be broiled instead of grilled.

1. To prepare the salmon, in a small bowl, combine mustard, lemon juice, thyme, rosemary, and pepper. Brush mixture all over both sides of salmon steaks and transfer salmon to a large, shallow baking dish. Cover with plastic wrap and refrigerate 30 minutes (and up to 4 hours).

2. Preheat grill or broiler.

3. To make the salsa, place serrano peppers on hot grill or under broiler and cook 4 minutes, turning frequently, until charred on all sides. Wrap peppers in plastic wrap and let stand 5 minutes. Remove skin from peppers, halve, seed, and cut into small dice-sized pieces. Transfer to a small bowl and add papaya and red onion. Set aside.

4. Place salmon steaks on grill or under broiler and cook 4 minutes per side, or until fork-tender and cooked through. When ready to serve, spoon salsa over salmon steaks.

Preparation and cooking time: 45 minutes

Serves 4

Needed items
   small bowls
   large shallow baking dish
   plastic wrap

For the herb grilled salmon:
   2 tablespoons Dijon mustard
   2 tablespoons fresh lemon juice
   1 tablespoon chopped fresh thyme
   1 tablespoon chopped fresh rosemary
   ½ teaspoon ground black pepper
   4 4-ounce salmon steaks, about 1-inch thick

For the papaya-chile salsa:
   2 serrano chile peppers
   1½ cups diced fresh papaya
   2 tablespoons minced red onion

Needed items
shallow baking dish
plastic wrap

1/4 cup orange juice
2 tablespoons fresh lemon juice
2 tablespoons light brown sugar
4 teaspoons chili powder
2 teaspoons finely grated
     lemon zest
1 teaspoon ground cumin
1/2 teaspoon salt
     pinch of cayenne pepper
4 6-ounce salmon fillets, about
     1-inch thick
     non-stick cooking spray

Barbecue-Roasted Salmon

It may seem odd to pair a strong, barbecue-type coating with fresh salmon. Don't fret, salmon can handle it. In fact, the spice coating caramelizes as it roasts (because of the brown sugar), and as the seasoning works its way into the flesh, the salmon takes on a new dimension while staying tender all the way through.

1. In a shallow baking dish, whisk together orange juice, lemon juice, brown sugar, chili powder, lemon zest, cumin, salt, and cayenne. Add salmon fillets and turn to coat both sides. Cover with plastic wrap and refrigerate 15-20 minutes.

2. Preheat oven to 400° F.

3. Remove salmon from marinade (discard marinade) and coat the bottom of the baking dish with non-stick spray.

4. Return salmon to baking dish and roast 15 minutes, or until fork-tender.

Preparation and cooking time: 25 minutes   *Serves 4*

Needed items
large oven-proof skillet

2 6-ounce salmon fillets, about
     1-inch thick
2 tablespoons chopped fresh
     tarragon
1/2 teaspoon salt
1/2 teaspoon cracked black pepper
4 teaspoons olive or vegetable
     oil, divided
1 shallot, minced
1/3 cup dry white wine or
     vermouth
1 tablespoon Dijon mustard
1 teaspoon cornstarch
1/2 cup chicken broth

Tarragon-Crusted Salmon with Mustard Sauce

The slight anise flavor of tarragon is the perfect accompaniment to salmon. A Dijon-white wine sauce pulls all the ingredients together to finish the dish.

1. Preheat oven to 350° F.

2. Coat both sides of salmon fillets with tarragon, salt, and pepper.

3. Heat 2 teaspoons of the oil in a large oven-proof skillet over medium heat. Add salmon fillets and cook 1 minute per side. Remove fish from pan and set aside.

4. Heat remaining 2 teaspoons of oil in the same skillet over medium heat. Add shallot and sauté 2 minutes. Add wine and Dijon mustard and simmer 1 minute. Dissolve cornstarch in chicken broth and add to skillet. Simmer 1 minute, or until mixture thickens.

5. Return salmon to the skillet, place the pan in the oven and bake 5 minutes, or until fish is fork-tender.

Preparation and cooking time: 20 minutes   *Serves 2*

Seared Tuna with Anchovy-Olive Crust and Roasted Fennel

It takes the strong taste of tuna to stand up to this Italian-inspired, intensely flavored crust (other strong-flavored fish that may be substituted include swordfish, bluefish, or king mackerel). The anise-scented fennel balances the flavors and completes the dish.

1. Preheat oven to 400° F.

2. In a blender, combine olives, lemon juice, garlic, anchovy paste, oregano, ¼ teaspoon of the salt, and pepper. Purée until smooth. Rub mixture all over both sides of tuna steaks. Set aside to marinate while you prepare the roasted fennel.

3. Arrange fennel slices in a large roasting pan that has been coated with non-stick spray. Sprinkle the top with remaining ¼ teaspoon salt. Roast 15 minutes, or until golden brown. Remove pan from oven and set aside.

4. Heat oil in a large non-stick skillet over medium heat. Add tuna steaks in batches (to prevent crowding) and sauté 1 minute per side. Remove from skillet and place steaks over fennel in roasting pan. Return pan to oven and roast 5-7 minutes, or until tuna is fork-tender (be careful not to over-cook the tuna). Serve tuna steaks with roasted fennel on the side.

Preparation and cooking time: 30 minutes

Serves 4

Needed items
blender
large roasting pan
large non-stick skillet

¼ cup pitted Greek (Kalamata) olives
3 tablespoons fresh lemon juice
2 garlic cloves, peeled and sliced
2 teaspoons anchovy paste
1 tablespoon chopped fresh oregano, or 1 teaspoon dried
½ teaspoon salt, divided
¼ teaspoon ground black pepper
4 6-ounce tuna steaks, about 1-inch thick
1 fennel bulb, sliced crosswise into ¼-inch thick slices
2 teaspoons olive oil
non-stick cooking spray

Needed items
blender
shallow dish
foil-lined baking sheet
plastic wrap

3   tablespoons sherry vinegar
2   heaping tablespoons drained
    capers
2   garlic cloves, peeled and sliced
¼   teaspoon salt
¼   teaspoon ground black pepper
2   6-ounce swordfish steaks
¼   cup pitted large black olives,
    sliced

Caper-Crusted Swordfish with Black Olives

Swordfish is a hearty, firm-fleshed fish that takes on the flavors of other ingredients quite well. This unique crust balances acidity from the capers with sweetness from the black olives.

1. In a blender, combine vinegar, capers, garlic, salt, and pepper. Purée until smooth. Place swordfish in a shallow dish, pour over caper mixture, and turn to coat. Cover with plastic wrap and refrigerate 20 minutes (and up to 4 hours).

2. Preheat broiler.

3. Transfer swordfish steaks to a foil-lined baking sheet (spoon over any remaining caper mixture if desired). Broil steaks 2 minutes. Flip, arrange black olive slices on top, and broil 3-4 more minutes, or until fish is fork-tender.

Preparation and cooking time: 35 minutes   *Serves 2*

Needed items
medium saucepan
large non-stick skillet

4   teaspoons olive or vegetable
    oil, divided
1   shallot, minced
2   garlic cloves, minced
1   14½-ounce can diced tomatoes
¼   cup dry white wine or
    vermouth
2   tablespoons drained capers
8   pitted Greek (or Gaeta) olives,
    minced
1   teaspoon dried thyme
¼   teaspoon crush red pepper
    flakes
2   4-ounce red snapper fillets
¼   teaspoon salt
¼   teaspoon ground black pepper
¼   teaspoon paprika

Red Snapper Livornese

Livornese, a traditional tomato-based sauce, is spruced up in this dish with the help of white wine, capers, and olives. A great sauce for snapper.

1. Heat 2 teaspoons of the oil in a medium saucepan over medium heat. Add shallot and garlic and sauté 2 minutes. Add tomatoes, vermouth, capers, olives, thyme, and red pepper flakes and bring mixture to a boil. Reduce heat and simmer 10 minutes.

2. Season both sides of snapper with salt, pepper, and paprika. Heat remaining 2 teaspoons of oil in a large non-stick skillet over medium heat. Add snapper fillets and sauté 1 minute per side. Add tomato sauce and simmer 2 minutes, or until fish is fork-tender.

Preparation and cooking time: 20-25 minutes   *Serves 2*

Braised Red Snapper in Cilantro Broth

A colorful, light dish that's ready to serve in minutes. The cilantro broth imparts an aromatic elegance to the fish, while keeping it moist.

1. Heat 2 teaspoons of the oil in a large non-stick skillet over medium heat. Add garlic and shallot and sauté 4 minutes, or until tender and golden. Transfer garlic and shallot to a blender and add chicken broth, cilantro, lemon juice, ¼ teaspoon of the salt, and ¼ teaspoon of the pepper. Purée until smooth and set aside.

2. Season both sides of snapper with remaining ¼ teaspoon salt and ¼ teaspoon pepper. Heat remaining 2 teaspoons of oil in the same non-stick skillet over medium heat. Add snapper fillets and sauté 1 minute per side, or until golden. Pour over cilantro mixture and simmer 2 minutes, or until fish is fork-tender.

3. To serve, transfer snapper fillets to individual plates and spoon remaining cilantro broth over top.

Preparation and cooking time: 20 minutes   *Serves 4*

Needed items
large non-stick skillet
blender

- 4 teaspoons olive oil, divided
- 2 garlic cloves, minced
- 1 shallot, minced
- 1¼ cups chicken broth
- ⅓ cup tightly packed fresh cilantro leaves
- ¼ cup fresh lemon juice
- ½ teaspoon salt, divided
- ½ teaspoon ground black pepper, divided
- 4 6-ounce skinless red snapper fillets

Parmesan-Crusted Flounder

This crust is so versatile, you can use it to coat any light fish, such as cod, tilapia, snapper, and bass.

1. In a shallow dish, combine bread crumbs, Parmesan, rosemary, and cayenne pepper. Mix well and set aside.

2. Season both sides of flounder fillets with salt and pepper. Dredge fillets in flour and turn to coat both sides. Dip fillets in egg and then into bread crumb mixture. Turn to coat both sides.

3. Heat oil in a large non-stick skillet over medium heat. Add flounder and sauté 3-4 minutes per side, or until golden brown. Add vermouth and sauté 1 minute, or until liquid is absorbed and flounder is fork-tender.

Preparation and cooking time: 20 minutes   *Serves 2*

Needed items
shallow dish
large non-stick skillet

- 3 tablespoons Italian-style dry bread crumbs
- 3 tablespoons grated Parmesan cheese
- ½ teaspoon dried rosemary
- ⅛ teaspoon cayenne pepper
- 2 4-ounce flounder fillets
- ¼ teaspoon salt
- ⅛ teaspoon ground black pepper
- 2 tablespoons all-purpose flour
- 1 egg, lightly beaten
- 2 teaspoons olive or vegetable oil
- ¼ cup vermouth or dry white wine

Needed items
large bowl
shallow roasting pan

2-3 parsnips (about 1 pound total),
    peeled and sliced crosswise
    into ¼-inch thick rounds
1 red onion, quartered
1 tablespoon olive oil
1 tablespoon granulated sugar
1 teaspoon salt, divided
½ teaspoon ground black pepper,
    divided
1 1 to 1½-pound Chilean sea bass
    fillet, about 1½-inches thick
2 tablespoons chopped fresh
    rosemary
¼ cup fresh lemon juice
    non-stick cooking spray

Roasted Chilean Sea Bass with Parsnips and Red Onion

The firm, wonderfully white flesh of Chilean sea bass is excellent with caramelized parsnips and onions. The parsnip-onion mixture is so awesome, any meat, fish, or poultry would make a great partner!

1. Preheat oven to 450° F.
2. In a large bowl, combine parsnips, onion, oil, sugar, ½ teaspoon of the salt, and ¼ teaspoon of the pepper. Toss to combine. Transfer mixture to a shallow roasting pan that has been coated with non-stick spray. Place pan in oven and roast 20 minutes, stirring halfway through cooking time.
3. Meanwhile, season both sides of bass with rosemary and remaining ½ teaspoon of salt and ¼ teaspoon of pepper.
4. Remove pan from oven and arrange bass over parsnips and onion. Spoon lemon juice over top. Return pan to oven and roast 15-20 minutes, or until fish is fork-tender.

Preparation and cooking time: 50 minutes   *Serves 4*

Spicy Paella

Paella is a popular dish in Spain, often made with shellfish, sausage, and beans. By using chorizo sausage and shrimp, my slight variation maintains the integrity of the original dish.

1. Heat oil in a large saucepan over medium heat. Add onion, garlic, and jalapeño and sauté 2 minutes. Add rice and sauté 2 minutes, or until translucent. Add rosemary, thyme, saffron, salt, and pepper and stir to coat.

2. Add tomatoes, chicken broth, and chorizo and bring mixture to a boil. Reduce heat, cover, and simmer 15 minutes.

3. Add shrimp, vermouth and peas and simmer uncovered, 3-5 minutes, or until shrimp are bright pink and cooked through and liquid is absorbed.

Preparation and cooking time: 25-30 minutes

Serves 4

Needed items
large saucepan

- 2 teaspoons olive oil
- 1 small onion, chopped (about ½ cup)
- 2 garlic cloves, minced
- 1 small jalapeño or habañero pepper, seeded and diced
- 1½ cups uncooked long grain white rice
- 1 teaspoon dried rosemary
- 1 teaspoon dried thyme
- ¼ teaspoon saffron threads
- ¼ teaspoon salt
- ¼ teaspoon ground black pepper
- 1 28-ounce can diced tomatoes
- 1½ cups chicken broth
- ½ pound chorizo sausage, sliced into ¼-inch thick rounds
- 1 pound large shrimp, peeled and deveined (leave tails on)
- ½ cup vermouth or dry white wine
- ½ cup frozen green peas

Needed items
  large bowl
  shallow dish
  large oven-proof skillet

  ¾ pound lump crabmeat (or two
       6-ounce cans, drained)
  ½ cup sour cream (regular or
       nonfat)
  ¼ cup Italian-style dry
       breadcrumbs
  2 teaspoons Dijon mustard
  1 teaspoon Old Bay seasoning
  ½ teaspoon dried oregano
  ¼ teaspoon ground black pepper
  ¼ cup all-purpose flour
  2 teaspoons olive or vegetable oil

Quick Crab Cakes

*Crab cakes hold together better when given a chance to chill. If you have the
time, after you form the mixture into cakes, wrap them in plastic and refrigerate
30 minutes (and up to 24 hours).*

1. Preheat oven to 400° F.
2. In a large bowl, combine crabmeat, sour cream, bread crumbs,
   mustard, Old Bay seasoning, oregano, and pepper. Gently mix
   ingredients together, being careful not to break up crabmeat too
   much.
3. Shape mixture into 2 cakes, each about 1-inch thick and 3-inches
   wide. Place flour in a shallow dish, add crab cakes, and turn to coat
   both sides.
4. Heat oil in a large oven-proof skillet. Add crab cakes and sauté
   2-3 minutes per side, or until golden brown. Transfer pan to oven
   and bake 20 minutes, or until crab cakes are cooked through.

Preparation and cooking time: 45 minutes   *Serves 2*

Crab-Stuffed Poblano Chiles with Mango Salsa

Poblano chiles are mildly hot and make a great "back-drop" for the subtly seasoned crab mixture.

1. Preheat oven to 350° F.

2. To make the stuffed poblanos, in a large bowl, whisk together ricotta, 2 tablespoons of the Romano cheese, mustard, oregano, salt, and pepper. Fold in crabmeat and artichokes.

3. Spoon mixture into center of each poblano chile. Place stuffed chiles in the bottom of a shallow roasting pan that has been coated with non-stick spray. Top with remaining Romano cheese.

4. Bake 30 minutes, or until golden.

5. To make the salsa, combine all ingredients in a medium bowl and mix well. Refrigerate until ready to serve.

Preparation time: 20 minutes
Cooking time: 30 minutes

Serves 4

Needed items
medium and large bowls
shallow roasting pan

For the crab-stuffed poblano chiles:
1 15-ounce container ricotta cheese (regular or nonfat)
3 tablespoons grated Romano or Parmesan cheese, divided
1 teaspoon Dijon mustard
1 teaspoon dried oregano
¼ teaspoon salt
¼ teaspoon ground black pepper
1 cup lump crabmeat (or two 6-ounce cans, drained)
1 14-ounce can artichoke hearts, drained and quartered
4 (5-inch) poblano chiles, halved and seeded
   non-stick cooking spray

For the mango salsa:
1½ cups chopped fresh mango
⅓ cup pitted black olives, sliced
2 tablespoons chopped fresh cilantro
1 tablespoon balsamic vinegar

Needed items
  large bowl
  shallow baking dish
  aluminum foil

  ¾ pound lump crabmeat (or two
       6-ounce cans, drained)
  ½ pound cooked medium shrimp,
       shelled and halved
  1 10-ounce package frozen
       chopped spinach, thawed
       and drained
  1 cup ricotta cheese (regular or
       reduced-fat)
  1 tablespoon Dijon mustard
  1 teaspoon dried oregano
  ½ teaspoon salt
  ¼ teaspoon ground black pepper
  ⅛ teaspoon cayenne pepper
  4 8-inch flour tortillas
  1 cup sour cream (regular or
       nonfat)
  ⅔ cup milk (regular or nonfat)
  2 tablespoons grated Parmesan
       cheese
     non-stick cooking spray

Crab and Shrimp Enchiladas

Any combination of seafood will work in this recipe, and leftover, cooked fish (monkfish, cod, tilapia, swordfish) work particularly well.

1. Preheat oven to 400° F.

2. In a large bowl, combine crabmeat, shrimp, spinach, ricotta, mustard, oregano, salt, pepper, and cayenne. Gently mix to combine.

3. Spoon mixture evenly onto the center of each tortilla. Roll up tortillas, fold in ends and place side-by-side in the bottom of a shallow baking dish that has been coated with non-stick spray. Set aside.

4. Whisk together sour cream and milk. Pour mixture over enchiladas and top with Parmesan cheese.

5. Cover with foil and bake 20 minutes. Uncover and bake 10 more minutes, or until top is golden.

Preparation time: 20 minutes
Cooking time: 30 minutes

Serves 4

Coriander Shrimp with Garlic Spinach

Note: You can broil the shrimp instead of grilling. Just place them under the broiler, 5 inches from the heat source, and broil 2-3 minutes per side. Also, when using wooden skewers, soak them in water first for at least 30 minutes to prevent them from scorching.

1. To make the shrimp, combine shrimp, lime juice, coriander, and pepper in a shallow dish and toss to coat shrimp with marinade. Cover with plastic wrap and refrigerate 15 minutes (and up to 1 hour).

2. Coat grill rack with non-stick spray and place rack over medium-hot coals.

3. Skewer shrimp, place on rack, and grill 2 minutes. Flip and grill 2 more minutes, or until bright pink and cooked through.

4. To prepare the spinach, heat oil in a large skillet over medium heat. Add shallot, garlic, and water chestnuts and sauté 3 minutes, or until golden. Add spinach, cover and steam 1 minute, or until spinach is wilted. Remove from heat and stir in balsamic vinegar and pepper.

5. To serve, arrange spinach mixture on 4 individual dinner plates and place shrimp skewers on top.

Preparation and cooking time: 25-30 minutes

Serves 4

Needed items
- shallow dish
- grill
- skewers
- large skillet
- plastic wrap

For the coriander shrimp:
- 1 pound large shrimp, peeled and deveined (leave tails on)
- ¼ cup fresh lime juice
- 1½ teaspoons ground coriander
- ¼ teaspoon ground black pepper
- non-stick cooking spray

For the garlic spinach:
- 2 teaspoons olive oil
- 1 shallot, minced
- 2 garlic cloves, minced
- 1 8-ounce can water chestnuts, drained and halved
- 1 10-ounce package fresh spinach, washed, drained and stems trimmed
- 2 teaspoons balsamic vinegar
- ¼ teaspoon ground black pepper

Needed items
large non-stick skillet

2 teaspoons olive oil
1 shallot, minced
2 garlic cloves, minced
1 small jalapeño or serrano
   seeded and minced
1 teaspoon dried oregano
½ teaspoon salt
⅛ teaspoon ground black pepper
1 pound medium shrimp, peeled
   and deveined (leave tails on)
½ cup dry white wine or
   vermouth
2 tablespoons chopped fresh
   Italian parsley

Needed items
large bowl
medium saucepan

1 3¾-ounce package uncooked
   cellophane or bean thread
   noodles
2 teaspoons olive or vegetable oil
2 garlic cloves, minced
2 teaspoons minced fresh ginger
3 cups chicken broth
¼ cup rice wine or vermouth
1 tablespoon soy sauce
¼ teaspoon ground black pepper
½ pound medium shrimp, peeled
   and deveined
2 tablespoons chopped fresh
   cilantro (optional)

Spicy Shrimp Scampi

Scampi is traditionally a rich seafood dish loaded with garlic and butter. This lightened-up version is packed with flavor, plus a little heat! Serve the shrimp mixture over pasta or rice for a complete meal.

1. Heat oil in a large non-stick skillet over medium heat. Add shallot, garlic, and jalapeño and sauté 2 minutes. Add oregano, salt, and pepper and stir to coat. Add shrimp and sauté 1 minute.

2. Add wine and simmer 2 minutes, or until shrimp are bright pink and cooked through. Remove from heat and stir in parsley.

Preparation and cooking time: 15 minutes   *Serves 4*

Shrimp Hot Pot

This was my favorite dish (the only one I would order) at my most-treasured, little Thai restaurant in Manhattan. After several dozen attempts to recreate the meal, this one seems to be just right!

Note: Cellophane, mung bean, and bean thread noodles are the same— translucent dried noodles made from the starch of the mung bean. The threadlike noodles have a slippery texture and work best when soaked in water for 10-15 minutes before using.

1. In a large bowl, soak noodles in enough hot water to cover for 10-15 minutes. Drain and set aside.

2. Heat oil in a medium saucepan over medium heat. Add garlic and ginger and sauté 2 minutes. Add chicken broth, wine, soy sauce, and pepper and bring mixture to a boil. Add shrimp and noodles and simmer 3 minutes, or until shrimp are bright pink and cooked through and noodles are just tender. Remove from heat and stir in cilantro if desired.

Preparation and cooking time: 20-25 minutes   *Serves 2*

Roasted Mussels in Garlic-Shallot Broth

This makes a great appetizer—just serve with a wedge of bread for the broth. For a complete meal, serve the mussels over angelhair pasta or white rice.

1. Preheat oven to 425° F.
2. In a large roasting pan, combine mussels, vermouth, water, garlic, shallots, parsley, salt, and pepper. Toss to combine.
3. Roast, uncovered, 15 minutes, stirring halfway through cooking, until shells have opened. Discard any shells that have not opened.
4. Transfer mussels to shallow serving bowls and spoon remaining broth over top.

Preparation and cooking time: 25 minutes   *Serves 2*

* To remove the "beards," use sharp scissors to cut away the dark, shaggy material protruding from one end of the shell.

Needed items
large roasting pan
sharp scissors

2½ pounds mussels, scrubbed and beards removed*
¾ cup vermouth or dry white wine
¼ cup water
4 garlic cloves, minced
2 shallots, minced
¼ cup tightly packed fresh Italian parsley leaves
¼ teaspoon salt
¼ teaspoon ground black pepper

Seafood Salad

Serve this salad over lettuce, stuff it into pita pockets, or spoon it onto hearty black bread. You can substitute lobster for the shrimp, if desired.

Note: The salad can be prepared in advance and refrigerated for up to two days.

1. Cook shrimp in a large pot of rapidly boiling water for 2 minutes, or until bright pink and cooked through. Drain and transfer to a large bowl. Add crabmeat, onion, and parsley and set aside.
2. In a small bowl, whisk together sour cream, vinegar, Old Bay, and pepper. Pour over shrimp mixture and gently toss to combine. Cover with plastic wrap and refrigerate until ready to serve.

Preparation and cooking time: 20 minutes   *Serves 4*

Needed items
large stockpot
small and large bowls
plastic wrap

1 pound medium shrimp, peeled and deveined
½ pound lump crabmeat (or two 6-ounce cans, drained)
¼ cup minced red onion
2 tablespoons chopped fresh Italian parsley
¾ cup sour cream (regular or nonfat)
2 tablespoons red wine vinegar
1 tablespoon Old Bay seasoning
¼ teaspoon ground black pepper

Needed items
  large stockpot
  large bowl
  large skillet
  sharp scissors
  aluminum foil

12 ounces uncooked spaghetti
2 teaspoons olive oil
1 shallot, minced
2 garlic cloves, minced
2 bay leaves
1 teaspoon dried oregano
1 teaspoon dried basil
½ teaspoon dried rosemary
½ teaspoon salt
¼ teaspoon crushed red pepper
    flakes
1 28-ounce can crushed tomatoes
¼ cup dry red wine
½ pound large shrimp, peeled and
    deveined (leave tails on)
½ pound fresh mussels, scrubbed
    and beards removed*
½ pound fresh clams, scrubbed

Shellfish Marinara

Feel free to use your favorite seafood in this versatile, classic Italian dish.

1. In a large stockpot, cook pasta according to package directions. Drain, transfer to a large bowl, and cover with foil to keep warm.

2. Meanwhile, heat oil in a large skillet over medium heat. Add shallot and garlic and sauté 2 minutes. Add bay leaves, oregano, basil, rosemary, salt, and red pepper flakes and stir to coat. Add tomatoes and red wine and bring mixture to a boil. Reduce heat, cover, and simmer 10 minutes.

3. Add shrimp, mussels, and clams, cover and simmer 3-5 minutes, or until shells have opened and shrimp are bright pink and cooked through. Discard any shells that have not opened. Discard bay leaves.

4. Pour sauce and seafood over pasta and toss to combine.

Preparation and cooking time: 25-30 minutes   *Serves 4*

* To remove the "beards," use sharp scissors to cut away the dark, shaggy material protruding from one end of the shell.

Side Dishes, Salads, and Salsas

Sourdough Salad with Tomatoes and Mozzarella

In Sicily, it's common to brush hearty bread with olive oil, rub it with garlic, and toast it until golden. This variation on that theme makes the perfect first-course salad by combining all the stand-out ingredients of the region.

1. Preheat oven to 400° F.
2. Arrange bread slices and garlic cloves on a baking sheet. Toast in oven 10 minutes, or until bread is golden. Remove from oven, cut bread into 2-inch pieces and chop garlic.
3. Place bread slices in a large bowl, pour over enough water to cover, and let stand 5 minutes. Drain and squeeze bread to remove excess water.
4. In a large bowl, combine bread, garlic, tomatoes, basil, onion, and mozzarella. Set aside.
5. Whisk together vinegar, oil, and pepper and pour over bread mixture. Toss gently to combine. Cover with plastic wrap and refrigerate 30 minutes (and up to 2 days).
6. To serve, spoon bread salad onto lettuce leaves.

Preparation and cooking time: 45 minutes　　　　　　　　*Serves 4*

* It's important that the bread be stale, so it absorbs the moisture and flavor of the other ingredients.

Needed items
baking sheet
large bowls
plastic wrap

1　stale* sourdough baguette (about ½ pound), cut crosswise into 1-inch thick slices
3　garlic cloves, peeled
4　ripe tomatoes, halved, seeded and cut into 1-inch pieces
½　cup chopped fresh basil
¼　cup diced red onion
4　ounces mozzarella cheese (regular or part-skim), cut into ½-inch cubes
⅓　cup balsamic vinegar
1　tablespoon olive oil
½　teaspoon ground black pepper
4　curly lettuce leaves, rinsed

Needed items
blender

1   large ripe tomato, peeled,
     halved, seeded, and chopped
¼   cup chopped sundried
     tomatoes (packed without oil)
1   tablespoon minced fresh ginger
1   garlic clove, peeled
2   tablespoons balsamic vinegar
½   cup water
2   tablespoons olive oil
¼   teaspoon salt
¼   teaspoon ground black pepper
4   cups mixed greens (any
     combination of Romaine,
     Red leaf, Bibb, and Boston
     lettuces; mustard greens and
     spinach taste great too!)

Needed items
large saucepan
large bowl

½   pound lentils, rinsed and
     picked over to remove stones
2   bay leaves
2   garlic cloves, peeled
1   yellow bell pepper, seeded and
     diced
1   red bell pepper, seeded and
     diced
8   Greek (Kalamata) olives
¼   cup diced red onion
¼   cup chopped fresh Italian
     parsley
¼   cup red wine vinegar
1   tablespoon olive oil
½   teaspoon salt
¼   teaspoon ground black pepper
4   Romaine lettuce leaves
⅓   cup crumbled feta cheese

Mixed Greens with Tomato-Ginger Dressing

This recipe serves four. If you're just cooking for the two of you, reduce the amount of greens and store the leftover dressing in an airtight container in the refrigerator.

Time saver: Make the dressing ahead and refrigerate until ready to serve.

Another time saver: Make the dressing ahead, refrigerate it, and go out to dinner. Have the dressing tomorrow.

1. In a blender, combine tomato, sundried tomatoes, ginger, garlic, and vinegar. Process until smooth. Add water, oil, salt, and pepper and purée until smooth.
2. Divide greens evenly among 4 salad plates and spoon dressing over top.

Preparation time: 10-15 minutes   *Serves 4*

Lentil Salad with Feta and Bell Peppers

There's probably not a kitchen in Greece without olives and feta cheese (it's like a refrigerator in this country without ketchup and mustard). Add tender lentils, bell peppers, and few seasonings and you've got one incredible salad. Serve the mixture over mixed greens or cooked rice for a filling, satisfying meal.

1. Combine lentils, bay leaves, and garlic in a large saucepan and pour over enough water to cover. Place pot over medium-high heat and bring to a boil. Reduce heat, cover, and simmer 25 minutes, or until lentils are tender. Drain, discard bay leaves, and mince garlic.
2. In a large bowl, combine lentils, garlic, bell peppers, olives, onion, and parsley. Toss to combine.
3. Whisk together vinegar, oil, salt, and pepper, pour over lentil mixture and toss to combine.
4. Spoon lentil mixture onto lettuce leaves and sprinkle feta cheese on top.

Preparation and cooking time: 35-40 minutes   *Serves 4*

Roasted Corn and Garlic Couscous

Roasting corn brings out its inherent sweetness while adding a smoky, toasted flavor.

1. Preheat oven to 425° F.
2. Wrap garlic cloves tightly in foil and place on a baking sheet that has been coated with non-stick spray. Arrange corn on baking sheet next to garlic and sprinkle with ¼ teaspoon of the salt.
3. Roast 15 minutes, or until garlic is soft and corn is golden, stirring every 5 minutes to prevent corn from burning. Unwrap garlic and mince.
4. Combine garlic, corn, and chicken broth in a medium saucepan. Set over medium-high heat and bring mixture to a boil. Stir in couscous, remove from heat, cover, and let stand 5 minutes.
5. Stir in green onions, pimento, pepper, and remaining ½ teaspoon salt and toss to combine.

Preparation and cooking time: 25 minutes　　　　　　*Serves 4*

Needed items
 baking sheet
 medium saucepan
 aluminum foil

 3 garlic cloves, peeled
 2 cups fresh cob corn (about
　 4 ears)
 ¾ teaspoon salt, divided
 1½ cups chicken broth
 1 cup uncooked couscous
 ¼ cup chopped green onions
 2 tablespoons chopped pimento
 ¼ teaspoon ground black pepper
　 non-stick cooking spray

Rice and Peas with Lemon-Chipotle Dressing

Chipotle chiles are dried and smoked jalapeños, and they are mild to very hot. When combined with tomato sauce and other seasonings the mixture is called "adobo."

1. In a blender, combine chicken broth, chipotle pepper, lemon juice, sugar, oregano, and salt. Purée until smooth.
2. Transfer mixture to a medium saucepan and set over medium-high heat. Add rice and bring to a boil. Reduce heat, cover, and simmer 15-20 minutes, or until rice is tender and liquid is absorbed. Stir in peas and heat through.

Preparation and cooking time: 30 minutes　　　　　　*Serves 4*

Needed items
 blender
 medium saucepan

 2¼ cups chicken broth
 1 chipotle pepper in adobo sauce
　 (from 7-ounce can)
 ¼ cup fresh lemon juice
 1 tablespoon granulated sugar
 1 teaspoon dried oregano
 ½ teaspoon salt
 1 cup uncooked Basmati or long
　 grain white rice
 1 cup frozen green peas

Needed items
large stockpot

6 cups chicken broth or water
1 smoked ham hock (about
  ½ pound)
2 bay leaves
1½ cups uncooked long grain
  white rice
2 19-ounce cans black beans
2 teaspoons minced chipotle in
  adobo (from 7-ounce can)
½ teaspoon salt
¼ teaspoon ground black pepper

Black Beans and Rice

Give yourself plenty of time to make this dish because the longer the cooking time, the more intense the flavor. I like to make big batches of rice and beans to serve as a main course (with a small amount of leftovers!). Feel free to cut the recipe in half if you need less.

1. Combine chicken broth, ham hock, and bay leaves in a large stockpot over medium-high heat. Bring to a boil, reduce heat, cover, and simmer 1 hour.

2. Add rice, black beans (with canned liquid), chipotle in adobo, salt, and pepper. Cover and simmer 20 minutes, or until rice is tender and liquid is absorbed.

3. Discard bay leaves. Remove ham hock, pull away any edible pieces of meat, and return the meat to the pan. Toss to combine.

Preparation and cooking time: 1½ hours   *Serves 4*

Needed items
large non-stick skillet

2 teaspoons olive oil
2 tablespoons pine nuts
2 garlic cloves, minced
1 10-ounce package fresh
  spinach, rinsed well and
  stems trimmed
2 teaspoons balsamic vinegar
¼ teaspoon ground black pepper

Sautéed Spinach with Garlic and Pine Nuts

Balsamic vinegar? Yes, believe it or not, it brings out the wonderful blend of garlic, spinach, and pine nut flavors without losing its inherent, mildly sweet taste.

1. Heat oil in a large non-stick skillet over medium heat. Add pine nuts and sauté 1 minute. Add garlic and sauté 2 more minutes, or until pine nuts and garlic are both golden brown.

2. Add spinach, cover, and steam 1 minute, or until wilted. Remove from heat and stir in vinegar and pepper.

Preparation and cooking time: 10 minutes   *Serves 4*

Italian-Style Stuffed Artichokes

To eat a stuffed artichoke, work your way from the outside in—pull leaves from the sides and scrape off the bread filling and tender flesh with your top teeth (whatever doesn't come off easily is discarded). When you get to the "heart," simply slice and enjoy!

1. Slice 1 inch off the top of each artichoke to remove the tough, thorn-like tips. Slice the stem end so it's even with the base and pull away any dry or tough outer leaves from the bottom (the leaves are tough by nature, so don't peel away too many!). Stand artichokes upright in a large stockpot. Pour over enough water to reach 3 inches up the sides of the pot. Slice one of the lemons and add it to the water. Set pot over medium-high heat and bring to a boil. Reduce heat to medium, cover, and boil 20 minutes, or until an outer leaf pulls off easily. Drain artichokes upside down.

2. Preheat oven to 350° F.

3. Using a spoon, remove inner core of artichoke (pale inner leaves) and scrape away the fuzzy middle.

4. In a medium bowl, combine bread crumbs, Parmesan, and salt. Spoon mixture into the center of artichokes, and then inside outer leaves. Transfer stuffed artichokes to a shallow baking dish and squeeze the juice from the second lemon over top.

5. Cover with foil and bake 30 minutes. Serve in shallow bowls, with an extra bowl on the side for discarded leaves.

Preparation time: 30 minutes
Cooking time: 30 minutes

Serves 4

Needed items
large stockpot
medium bowl
shallow baking dish
aluminum foil

4 large or jumbo artichokes, about 12 ounces each
2 whole lemons
1 cup Italian-style dry bread crumbs
¼ cup grated Parmesan cheese
½ teaspoon salt

Needed items
large skillet

2 tablespoons diced, oil-packed
   sundried tomatoes, plus 2
   teaspoons oil from jar
2 garlic cloves, minced
2 medium zucchini, sliced
   crosswise into ¼-inch thick
   rounds
¼ cup vermouth or dry white
   wine
¼ teaspoon salt
¼ teaspoon ground black pepper

Braised Zucchini with Sundried Tomatoes

Sundried tomatoes have a rich tomato flavor and they add tremendous depth to this simple side dish.

1. Heat sundried tomato oil in a large skillet over medium heat. Add garlic and diced sundried tomatoes and sauté 2 minutes. Add zucchini and sauté 2 minutes, or until golden brown.

2. Add vermouth, salt, and pepper, cover and simmer 2-3 minutes, or until zucchini is just tender.

Preparation and cooking time: 15 minutes   *Serves 4*

Needed items
large stockpot
large bowl
plastic wrap

2 pounds small red potatoes
   (about 8-10)
2 cups fresh string beans (about
   ½ pound), ends trimmed and
   halved
1 6-ounce jar marinated
   artichoke hearts
8 Greek (Kalamata) olives
2 tablespoons balsamic vinegar
2 tablespoons chopped fresh
   Italian parsley
½ teaspoon salt
¼ teaspoon ground black pepper

New Potato Salad with String Beans and Artichokes

A twist on a classic. Bring this salad to your next tailgate party or picnic and redefine the meaning of potato salad. It's not that white glob next to the cheeseburger anymore.

1. Place potatoes in a large stockpot, pour over enough water to cover, and set over medium-high heat. Bring to a boil and cook 20 minutes. Add string beans and simmer 2 more minutes, or until potatoes are fork-tender and string beans are tender-crisp. Drain, and when cool enough to handle, quarter potatoes. Combine potatoes and string beans in a large bowl and set aside.

2. Drain artichokes, reserving 1 tablespoon of the oil. Add artichokes to potatoes and string beans. Add reserved oil and remaining ingredients and toss to combine. Cover with plastic wrap and refrigerate until ready to serve.

Preparation and cooking time: 30 minutes   *Serves 6*

Sweet Potato Bay Fries

Now is a good time to pull out the Mandoline or French fry attachment that came with your new food processor. You can also make Bay fries with Idaho or Yukon Gold potatoes.

1. Preheat oven to 400° F.
2. Spread potatoes out on a large baking sheet that has been coated with olive oil spray. Coat potatoes with an even layer of olive oil spray. Sprinkle with Old Bay.
3. Bake 30-35 minutes, or until golden.

Preparation time: 5 minutes
Cooking time: 30-35 minutes

Serves 2

Needed items
large baking sheet

2 large sweet potatoes, cut lengthwise into ¼-inch thick fries
olive oil cooking spray
1 tablespoon Old Bay seasoning

Scalloped Potatoes with Gorgonzola

Scalloped potatoes are typically sliced potatoes, smothered in milk and other ingredients and baked until tender. The addition of Gorgonzola takes this classic dish to a new level.

1. Preheat oven to 375° F.
2. In a medium bowl, whisk together milk, Gorgonzola, sour cream, and pepper. Set aside.
3. Arrange half of the potato and onion slices in the bottom of a cast iron or large oven-proof skillet that has been coated with non-stick spray. Pour over half of the milk mixture. Top with remaining potatoes and onions, and pour over remaining milk mixture. Top with chopped green onions. Cover with foil and bake 30 minutes. Uncover and bake 30 more minutes, or until potatoes are tender and top is golden brown.

Preparation time: 15 minutes
Cooking time: 1 hour

Serves 6

Needed items
medium bowl
cast iron or large oven-proof skillet
aluminum foil

1 cup milk (regular or nonfat)
½ cup (about 2 ounces) finely crumbled Gorgonzola cheese
3 tablespoons sour cream (regular or reduced-fat)
¼ teaspoon ground black pepper
4 large Idaho potatoes (about 2½ pounds), peeled and sliced crosswise into ¼-inch thick slices
1 large Spanish onion, halved and sliced crosswise into ¼-inch thick slices
¼ cup chopped green onions
non-stick cooking spray

Needed items
small bowl
2-quart casserole dish
aluminum foil

1 cup milk (regular or nonfat)
1 tablespoon Dijon mustard
½ teaspoon ground black pepper
4 large Yukon Gold potatoes
  (about 2½ pounds), peeled,
  halved lengthwise and sliced
  crosswise into ¼-inch thick
  slices
¼ pound lean ham, diced and
  divided
¾ cup grated Monterey Jack
  cheese (regular or reduced-
  fat), divided
¾ cup grated cheddar cheese
  (regular or reduced-fat),
  divided
2 tablespoons chopped fresh
  Italian parsley (optional)
  non-stick cooking spray

Needed items
large non-stick skillet

1 teaspoon olive oil
1 pound baby carrots
¼ cup chicken broth
1 tablespoon fresh lemon juice
1 teaspoon finely grated lemon
  zest
½ teaspoon celery salt
¼ teaspoon ground black pepper
1 tablespoon minced fresh dill

Oven-Roasted Scalloped Potatoes with Ham and Two Cheeses

The buttery flavor and creamy texture of Yukon Gold potatoes pair beautifully with the saltiness of the ham and sharpness of the cheddar cheese.

1. Preheat oven to 375° F.
2. In a small bowl, whisk together milk, mustard, and pepper. Set aside.
3. Arrange half of the potato slices in the bottom of a 2-quart casserole dish that has been coated with non-stick spray. Pour over half of milk mixture. Top with half of the diced ham and ½ cup each of the Monterey Jack and cheddar cheeses. Top with remaining potato slices and pour over remaining milk mixture. Top with remaining diced ham and ¼ cup each of the Monterey Jack and cheddar cheeses.
4. Cover with foil and bake 45 minutes. Uncover and bake 15 more minutes, or until potatoes are tender and cheese is golden and bubbly. Garnish with fresh chopped parsley if desired.

Preparation time: 15 minutes
Cooking time: 1 hour

Serves 4

Sautéed Baby Carrots with Dill

Talk about a convenience product—ready-to-eat baby carrots. Just pop open the bag and whip up this colorful, refreshing side dish in minutes.

1. Heat oil in a large non-stick skillet over medium heat. Add carrots and sauté 2 minutes. Add chicken broth, lemon juice, lemon zest, celery salt, and pepper and toss to coat.
2. Reduce heat, cover, and simmer 7-8 minutes, or until carrots are tender-crisp.
3. Stir in fresh dill and toss to combine.

Preparation and cooking time: 15 minutes

Serves 6

Garlic Mashed Potatoes with Celery Root and Fresh Chives

Celery root adds a distinct, concentrated celery flavor to these already incredible, garlic-infused, creamy mashed potatoes.

1. Combine potatoes, celery root, and garlic cloves in a large stockpot. Pour over enough water to cover and set pot over medium-high heat. Bring to a boil, reduce heat, and simmer 10 minutes, or until potatoes are fork-tender.

2. Drain and transfer to a large bowl or food processor fitted with the metal blade. Add buttermilk and mash or process until smooth (do not overmix or potatoes will become "gummy").

3. Fold in parsley, chives, salt, and pepper.

Preparation and cooking time: 30 minutes   *Serves 4*

Needed items
  large stockpot
  large mixing bowl or food
    processor

  4 large Idaho potatoes (about
      2½ pounds), peeled and cut
      into 2-inch pieces
  1 celery root (about ½ pound),
      peeled and cut into 2-inch
      pieces
  4 garlic cloves, peeled
  ¾ cup buttermilk
  ¼ cup chopped fresh Italian
      parsley
  2 tablespoons minced fresh
      chives
  ¾ teaspoon salt
  ¼ teaspoon ground black pepper

Whipped Candied Sweet Potatoes

Serve this beautifully orange purée along-side roasted chicken, pork, or turkey. For a different presentation, skip the purée step and serve the sweet potatoes in tender, 1-inch chunks.

1. Melt butter in a large saucepan over medium heat. Add sweet potatoes and onion and sauté 5 minutes.

2. Add remaining ingredients, bring to a boil, reduce heat, cover, and simmer 20 minutes, or until potatoes are fork-tender.

3. Remove from heat, transfer potato mixture to a food mill or food processor fitted with the metal blade, and process until smooth.

Preparation and cooking time: 35 minutes   *Serves 4*

Needed items
  large saucepan
  food mill or food processor

  1 tablespoon butter or margarine
  4 large sweet potatoes (about
      3 pounds), peeled and cut
      into 2-inch pieces
  ½ cup sliced yellow onion
  2 cups chicken broth
  1 tablespoon Dijon mustard
  1 tablespoon honey
  ¼ teaspoon salt

Needed items
large stockpot
baking dish

2 whole leeks, green and root
    ends trimmed and discarded
1 teaspoon olive oil
1 teaspoon granulated sugar
2 teaspoons Italian-style dry
    bread crumbs
2 teaspoons grated Parmesan
    cheese
   non-stick cooking spray

Broiled Leeks with Parmesan Bread Crumbs

Leeks are ancient members of the onion family, with a milder, sweeter taste than their onion cousins. The inside layers of leeks often contain dirt because the white portion is buried in the soil to keep it pale in color (I prefer sunscreen). To remove the dirt, just halve the leeks lengthwise and rinse out the layers.

1. Preheat broiler.
2. In a large stockpot, blanch leeks in rapidly boiling water for 3 minutes. Drain and when cool enough to handle, slice in half lengthwise.
3. Brush each half with olive oil and top the cut side with sugar, bread crumbs, and Parmesan cheese. Transfer leeks to a baking dish that has been coated with non-stick spray.
4. Broil 5 minutes, or until golden.

Preparation and cooking time: 15 minutes   *Serves 2*

Needed items
foil-lined baking sheet
large stockpot
large skillet
plastic bag

4 large red bell peppers, halved
    and seeded
1 pound fresh string beans,
    ends trimmed
¾ cup balsamic vinegar
2 garlic cloves, minced
¼ teaspoon ground black pepper

Roasted Red Peppers and String Beans

Any seasonal green vegetable, such as sugar snap peas and fresh, thin asparagus, will work in this recipe.

1. Preheat broiler.
2. Place pepper halves, skin-side up, on a foil-lined baking sheet and press down to flatten. Place under broiler, 4 inches from heat source, and broil until blackened all over. Place peppers in a plastic bag and let steam 5 minutes. Remove from bag and peel away blackened skin. Slice peppers into thin strips and set aside.
3. Blanch string beans in a large pot of rapidly boiling water for 4 minutes, or until tender-crisp. Drain and set aside.
4. Meanwhile, combine balsamic vinegar and garlic in a large skillet over medium heat. Simmer until liquid reduces and forms a thick syrup, about 5 minutes, stirring frequently. Stir in roasted peppers and string beans and stir to coat vegetables with syrup. Stir in pepper.

Preparation and cooking time: 25 minutes   *Serves 6*

Baked Polenta with Spicy Vegetable Ragout

Ragout is a French term for stew that literally means "restores the appetite." This hearty ragout is the ideal partner for polenta (cornmeal cooked in a liquid—preferably chicken or beef broth—until smooth and creamy). In this recipe, the polenta is baked until firm so you can slice and serve it over the highly seasoned vegetables.

1. Preheat oven to 400° F.
2. To make the polenta, bring chicken broth to a boil in a large saucepan over medium-high heat. Reduce heat, and gradually add cornmeal in a steady stream, whisking constantly. Cook 5 minutes, or until smooth and thick, stirring frequently.
3. Remove from heat, stir in cheese, salt, and pepper. Pour mixture into a 9-inch round cake pan that has been coated with non-stick spray and place pan on a baking sheet.
4. Bake 25 minutes, or until top is golden. Cool on a wire rack before slicing.
5. To prepare vegetable ragout, heat oil in a large non-stick skillet over medium heat. Add onion and sauté 2 minutes. Add eggplant, squash, carrots, and jalapeño and sauté 4 minutes. Add chili powder and stir to coat. Add tomatoes, bring to a boil, reduce heat, and simmer 15 minutes. Remove from heat and stir in cilantro and salt.
6. To serve, spoon vegetable ragout onto 4 dinner plates or into shallow bowls. Slice polenta into wedges and place on top of ragout.

Preparation and cooking time: 35-40 minutes   *Serves 4*

Needed items
   large saucepan
   9-inch round cake pan
   wire rack
   large non-stick skillet
   baking sheet

For the baked polenta:
   3 cups chicken broth or water
   1 cup yellow cornmeal
   ⅓ cup grated Romano or
      Parmesan cheese
   ½ teaspoon salt
   ½ teaspoon ground black pepper
      non-stick cooking spray

For the vegetable ragout:
   2 teaspoons olive oil
   1 small onion, chopped (about
      ½ cup)
   1 medium eggplant, diced (about
      2 cups)
   1 yellow squash, diced
   2 carrots, peeled and diced
   1 jalapeño pepper, seeded
      and diced
   1 tablespoon chili powder
   1 14½-ounce can crushed
      tomatoes
   2 tablespoons chopped fresh
      cilantro
   ½ teaspoon salt

Needed items
small bowl
medium saucepan
wire whisk

1 cup cold water
1 cup yellow cornmeal
3 cups chicken broth or water
¼ teaspoon salt
¼ teaspoon ground black pepper
½ cup grated smoked Gouda
    cheese

Creamy Polenta with Smoked Gouda

There's nothing worse than lumpy polenta. Mix dry cornmeal with cold water first, and then gradually add the mixture to boiling liquid. Viola, no lumps!

1. In a small bowl, combine cold water and cornmeal. Let stand 5 minutes.

2. Meanwhile, in a medium saucepan over medium-high heat, combine chicken broth, salt, and pepper. Bring mixture to a boil. Gradually whisk in cornmeal mixture and reduce heat to low. Cook 20 minutes, stirring frequently with a wire whisk, until mixture is thick and creamy.

3. Stir in smoked Gouda and simmer until cheese melts, stirring constantly.

Preparation and cooking time: 30 minutes   *Serves 4*

Needed items
small bowl
large skillet
fine sieve

½ ounce dried porcini mushrooms
½ cup warm water
1 tablespoon olive oil
2 shallots, diced
2 garlic cloves, minced
3 large portobello mushrooms
    (about 1 pound), stems
    discarded, caps halved and
    sliced into ½-inch thick slices
½ pound Shiitake mushrooms,
    stems discarded, caps sliced
    into ½-inch thick slices
¼ cup sherry wine
1 teaspoon dried thyme
½ teaspoon salt
¼ teaspoon ground black pepper
2 tablespoons chopped fresh
    Italian parsley

Wild Mushroom Sauté

This tender, earthy side dish is great spooned over beef, pork, chicken, turkey, and creamy mashed potatoes.

Note: My mother nearly fainted when she read "mushroom stems discarded"! She uses the stems to make an incredible mushroom stock or to add depth to her mixed vegetable stocks. So, if you want, toss the stems into a zip-top bag and freeze until stock-making day.

1. In a small bowl, combine dried mushrooms and warm water and let stand 15 minutes.

2. Heat oil in a large skillet over medium heat. Add shallots and garlic and sauté 2 minutes. Add portobello and Shiitake mushrooms and sauté 5 minutes, or until mushrooms are tender and releasing juice.

3. Meanwhile, drain porcini mushrooms through a paper towel-lined sieve, reserving liquid, and chop mushrooms into small pieces. Add chopped porcinis and reserved soaking liquid to skillet. Stir in sherry, thyme, salt, and pepper. Bring to a boil, reduce heat and simmer 5 minutes, or until liquid is absorbed. Stir in parsley and toss to combine.

Preparation and cooking time: 35 minutes   *Serves 6*

Parmesan-Almond-Crusted Broccoli

You may think, "Why bother, when I can just microwave the broccoli?" It's actually not a bother, and the golden Parmesan-almond crust adds a nice crunch and toasted flavor to this gorgeous green vegetable.

1. Preheat oven to 450° F.
2. Blanch broccoli in a large pot of rapidly boiling water for 2 minutes. Drain, rinse under cold water to prevent further cooking, and transfer to a shallow baking dish.
3. In a medium bowl, combine bread crumbs, Parmesan, almonds, basil, oregano, salt, and pepper and mix well with a fork. Pour bread crumb mixture over broccoli.
4. Bake, uncovered, 15 minutes, or until topping is golden brown.

Preparation and cooking time: 30 minutes　　　　　　　*Serves 6*

Needed items
large stockpot
shallow baking dish
medium bowl

6　cups broccoli florets
⅓　cup plain dry bread crumbs
2　tablespoons grated Parmesan cheese
2　tablespoons finely chopped almonds
1　teaspoon dried basil
1　teaspoon dried oregano
½　teaspoon salt
¼　teaspoon ground black pepper

Two Bean Mango Salsa

The sweetness of mango coupled with the salty-tender beans makes this salsa the perfect topping for fish, chicken, and pork.

1. Combine all ingredients in a large bowl and mix well. Cover with plastic wrap and refrigerate until ready to serve.

Preparation and cooking time: 15 minutes　　　　　　*Makes 4 cups*

Needed items
large bowl
plastic wrap

1　15-ounce can black beans, rinsed and drained
1　15-ounce can cannellini (white kidney) beans, rinsed and drained
2　ripe mangoes, seeded and diced
½　cup diced red onion
1　jalapeño pepper, seeded and minced
¼　cup chopped fresh cilantro
1　tablespoon balsamic vinegar
1　teaspoon ground coriander
1　teaspoon ground cumin

Needed items
  baking sheet
  large bowl
  plastic wrap

  2 cups fresh cob corn (about
       4 ears)*
  2 cups diced fresh tomatoes
  ¼ cup chopped fresh cilantro
  ¼ cup diced red onion
  2 tablespoons red wine vinegar
  ½ teaspoon minced chipotle in
       adobo (from 7-ounce can)
  ¼ teaspoon salt
  ¼ teaspoon ground black pepper
       non-stick cooking spray

Tomato and Roasted Corn Salsa

Salsa pairs well with practically everything—grilled and roasted meat, fish, and poultry—and, of course, tortilla chips.

1. Preheat oven to 425° F.
2. Spread corn out on a baking sheet that has been coated with non-stick spray. Roast 15 minutes, or until golden, stirring halfway through cooking to prevent burning.
3. Transfer corn to a large bowl and add remaining ingredients. Mix well. Cover with plastic wrap and refrigerate until ready to serve.

Preparation and cooking time: 25 minutes   *Makes 3 cups*

  * Cut kernels from cob using a sharp knife, pushing down along ear.

Desserts and Other Sweet Treats

Banana-Nut Scones

Scones may sound difficult to make, but they're actually pretty easy. In fact, after you've had these, make a batch using different fruit—applesauce, mashed ripe peaches, or mangoes. Keep experimenting and you can have a different scone every time!

1. Preheat oven to 400° F.

2. In a large bowl or food processor fitted with the metal blade, combine flour, ⅓ cup of the sugar, baking powder, baking soda, and salt. Add butter and process or mix together with your fingers until mixture resembles coarse meal.

3. In a medium bowl, whisk together egg whites, buttermilk, and vanilla. Stir in bananas. Fold mixture into dry ingredients and mix until just blended.

4. Transfer dough to a lightly floured surface and knead 5 times. Place dough on baking sheet that has been coated with non-stick spray and shape into a 9-inch circle. Using a sharp knife, make 12 (¼-inch deep) cuts in a spoke pattern across top of dough. Sprinkle the top with walnuts and remaining tablespoon of sugar. Press walnuts slightly into dough.

5. Bake 15-20 minutes, or until golden and a knife inserted near the center comes out clean. Cool on a wire rack before slicing into 12 wedges.

Preparation time: 15 minutes
Cooking time: 15-20 minutes

Makes 12 scones

Needed items
large bowl or food processor
medium bowl
baking sheet
wire rack

2¾ cups all-purpose flour
⅓ cup plus 1 tablespoon granulated sugar, divided
2 teaspoons baking powder
½ teaspoon baking soda
¼ teaspoon salt
3 tablespoons butter or margarine, chilled and cut up
2 egg whites
¼ cup buttermilk
1 teaspoon vanilla extract
2 medium ripe bananas, mashed (about 1 cup)
⅓ cup chopped walnuts
non-stick cooking spray

Needed items
  medium and large bowls
  muffin cups
  wire rack

1   6-ounce bag mixed dried fruit
    bits (or mixed dried fruit, cut
    in pieces)
2   cups warm water
2   cups all-purpose flour
1½ cups rolled oats (regular or
    quick cooking)
3   teaspoons baking powder
1   teaspoon ground cinnamon
½   teaspoon baking soda
½   teaspoon salt
1   cup milk (regular or nonfat)
1   cup chunky applesauce
½   cup packed light brown sugar
1   egg
1   tablespoon butter or margarine,
    melted
½   teaspoon vanilla extract
1   Mackintosh or Winesap apple,
    peeled, cored, and diced
    non-stick cooking spray

Apple-Oat Muffins with Mixed Fruit

I like to make large, bakery-sized muffins. Little, tennis ball-sized muffins just won't do. If you prefer smaller muffins, fill the muffin cups two-thirds full and make eighteen.

1. Preheat oven to 400° F.

2. Combine dried fruit and water and let stand 10 minutes.

3. In a large bowl, combine flour, oats, baking powder, cinnamon, baking soda, and salt. Mix well with a fork, make a well in the center, and set aside.

4. In a medium bowl, whisk together milk, applesauce, brown sugar, egg, melted butter, and vanilla. Drain dried fruit and add to mixture. Stir in diced apple. Fold mixture into dry ingredients until just blended.

5. Spoon batter into 12 muffin cups that have been coated with non-stick spray.

6. Bake 20-25 minutes, or until a wooden pick inserted in the center of one muffin comes out almost clean. Cool in pan, on a wire rack, 10 minutes. Remove muffins from pan and cool completely.

Preparation time: 15 minutes   *Makes 12 muffins*
Cooking time: 20-25

Blueberry Muffins

The hint of almond (from almond extract) brings out the sweetness of the blueberries, while adding a unique, nutty flavor.

1. Preheat oven to 400° F.
2. In a large bowl, combine flour, oats, sugar, baking powder, baking soda, and salt. Mix well with a fork, make a well in the center, and set aside.
3. In a small bowl, whisk together yogurt, milk, egg, melted butter, and almond extract. Fold mixture into dry ingredients until just blended. Fold in blueberries.
4. Spoon batter into 12 muffin cups that have been coated with non-stick spray.
5. Bake 25-30 minutes, or until a wooden pick inserted in the center of one muffin comes out almost clean. Cool in pan, on a wire rack, 10 minutes. Remove muffins from pan and cool completely.

Preparation time: 15 minutes
Cooking time: 25-30 minutes

Makes 12 muffins

Needed items
small and large bowls
muffin cups
wire rack

2½ cups all-purpose flour
1 cup rolled oats (regular or quick cooking)
¾ cup granulated sugar
2 teaspoons baking powder
1 teaspoon baking soda
½ teaspoon salt
2 cups vanilla yogurt (regular or nonfat)
¼ cup milk (regular or nonfat)
1 egg
2 tablespoons butter or margarine, melted
1 teaspoon almond extract
2 cups blueberries, fresh or frozen (keep frozen until ready to use)
non-stick cooking spray

Needed items
 large mixing bowl
 mixer
 8-inch square cake pan
 wire rack

10 tablespoons butter or
  margarine, softened
¼ cup confectioners' sugar
3 tablespoons granulated sugar,
  divided
¼ teaspoon salt
1 teaspoon vanilla extract
1½ cups all-purpose flour
¾ cup dried cherries (about
  3 ounces)

Cherry Shortbread

Any dried fruit—cranberries, blueberries, apricots, raisins—will work in this versatile shortbread dough. You can also skip the fruit and simply add a little cinnamon and nutmeg. You'd have to change the name of the recipe, of course.

1. Preheat oven to 325° F.

2. In a large mixing bowl, beat together butter, confectioners' sugar, 2 tablespoons of the granulated sugar, and salt until smooth and creamy. Beat in vanilla. Gradually beat in flour. Fold in cherries. Transfer dough to a flat surface and lightly knead until well-blended and smooth.

3. Press mixture into the bottom of an 8-inch square cake pan and deeply prick the surface all over with a fork.

4. Bake 45-50 minutes, or until pale gold and slightly darker at the edges.

5. Remove from oven and sprinkle the top with remaining tablespoon of granulated sugar. Cool on a wire rack before cutting into 24 squares (it's easier to cut into bars while shortbread is still slightly warm).

Preparation time: 15 minutes
Cooking time: 45-50 minutes

Makes 24 shortbread cookies

Creamy Vanilla Cheesecake

This velvety smooth dessert is light enough to follow even the heaviest main course. It makes a great breakfast with fresh fruit, too. There are no rules in my kitchen.

1. Preheat oven to 300° F.

2. To make the crust, combine graham cracker crumbs, sugar, and melted butter in a medium bowl. Mix well with a fork to combine. Press the mixture into the bottom of a 9-inch springform pan that has been coated with non-stick spray. Set aside.

3. To make the filling, whisk together ricotta, sour cream, cream cheese, egg, and vanilla in a large bowl. Fold in sugar and flour. Pour filling into prepared pan.

4. Bake 1 hour, or until center is set. Turn off oven, prop open the oven door (not all the way, just slightly), and allow the cake to cool for 15 minutes (slow cooling prevents cracking).

5. Transfer pan to a wire rack and cool completely. Cover with plastic wrap and chill until ready to serve.

Preparation time: 20 minutes
Cooking and cooling time: 1 hour 15 minutes

Makes one 9-inch cheesecake
(12 servings)

Needed items
  medium and large bowls
  9-inch springform pan
  wire rack
  plastic wrap

For the crust:
  ½ cup plus 2 tablespoons graham cracker crumbs
  2 tablespoons granulated sugar
  2 tablespoons butter or margarine, melted
  non-stick cooking spray

For the filling:
  1 cup ricotta cheese (regular or nonfat)
  1 cup sour cream (regular or nonfat)
  8 ounces cream cheese (regular or nonfat), softened
  1 egg
  2 teaspoons vanilla extract
  ¾ cup granulated sugar
  6 tablespoons all-purpose flour

Needed items
  double boiler or small bowl and
      medium saucepan
  large mixing bowl
  mixer
  8-inch square cake pan
  wire rack

  ¼ cup (½ stick) butter
  4 1-ounce squares unsweetened
      chocolate
  2 eggs
  ¼ teaspoon salt
  1½ cups granulated sugar
  ¼ cup buttermilk
  1 teaspoon vanilla extract
  ¾ cup all-purpose flour
  2 cups whipped cream or
      non-dairy whipped topping
  2 cups fresh raspberries
      non-stick cooking spray

Gooey Chocolate Squares with Whipped Cream and Fresh Raspberries

While I was deciding on a name for this dessert, "gooey" was the one word that kept creeping into my mind! Whip up a batch and you'll see why. I suggest serving this dish with napkins.

1. Preheat oven to 350° F.

2. Melt butter and chocolate together in a double boiler or small bowl over simmering water. Remove from heat and set aside to cool slightly.

3. In a large mixing bowl, beat together eggs and salt until mixture doubles in size, about 2 minutes. Gradually beat in sugar. Beat in buttermilk and vanilla. Gradually add chocolate mixture and mix until blended. Fold in flour until just blended.

4. Transfer batter to an 8-inch square cake pan that has been coated with non-stick spray.

5. Bake 35-40 minutes, or until edges begin to pull away from the sides of the pan and a wooden pick inserted near the center comes out almost (not totally) clean. Cool in pan, on a wire rack, before cutting.

6. To serve, slice cake into 8 equal squares and top each portion with ¼ cup each whipped cream and fresh raspberries.

Preparation time: 15-20 minutes
Cooking time: 35-40 minutes

Serves 8

Apple Pie

A simple pie recipe that encourages dozens of variations. Once you've mastered this version, try adding grated lemon or orange zest, raisins or cranberries, allspice and cloves, and even sliced almonds.

1. Preheat oven to 375° F.
2. Press one of the pie crusts into the bottom and up the sides of a 9-inch pie plate, allowing dough to hang over the sides. Sprinkle the bottom with cornstarch and set aside.
3. In a large bowl, combine apples, sugar, and cinnamon and toss to coat apples. Transfer apples to prepared pie shell and arrange slices to form an even mound (don't worry that the apples form a mound higher than the pie plate—they shrink as they cook). Place second crust on top of apples and pinch the two crusts together to seal. Roll the edge under and, using two fingers, pinch around the edge of the plate to form a decorative rim.
4. Brush the surface with beaten egg (if you plan to cut leftover dough into decorations, such as leaves, hearts, or stars, brush the surface with egg, add decorations, and brush the decorations with egg). Pierce the surface all over with a fork to allow steam to escape during cooking and place pie on a baking sheet.
5. Bake 1 hour, or until golden brown. Cool on rack at least 10 minutes before slicing.

For the pie crusts:

1. In a large bowl or food processor fitted with the metal blade, combine flour, sugar, salt, and butter. Process or mix together with your fingers until mixture resembles coarse meal.
2. Add cold water, one tablespoon at a time, and process or mix just until you can form dough into a ball. Transfer dough to a lightly floured surface and roll into a round disk. Wrap in plastic and refrigerate 15 minutes (and up to 3 days).
3. Remove plastic wrap and transfer dough to a lightly floured surface. Divide dough into two equal portions and roll each portion into a 12-inch circle. Use as directed.

Preparation time: 30 minutes
Cooking time: 1 hour

Makes one, double-crust, 9-inch pie
(8-12 servings)

Needed items
  9-inch pie plate
  large bowl
  large bowl or food processor
  rolling pin
  plastic wrap

  2 uncooked 9-inch pie crusts
       (recipe follows)
1½ teaspoons cornstarch
  6 Mackintosh or Granny Smith
       apples (about 2½ pounds),
       cored and sliced (and peeled
       if desired)
⅓ cup granulated sugar
  1 teaspoon ground cinnamon
  1 egg, lightly beaten

For the pie crusts:
  3 cups all-purpose flour
  3 tablespoons granulated sugar
½ teaspoon salt
  1 cup (2 sticks) butter or
       margarine (butter makes a
       flakier crust), chilled and cut
       up
6-8 tablespoons cold water

Needed items
rolling pin
medium and large bowls
baking sheet
wire rack

1 puff pastry sheet (½ package),
  thawed according to package
  directions
4 Granny Smith apples (about
  2 pounds), peeled, cored and
  thinly sliced
½ cup granulated sugar
1 teaspoon ground cinnamon
1 teaspoon vanilla extract
1 egg
1 tablespoon water
  non-stick cooking spray

Apple Strudel

The idea of making "strudel" may seem intimidating, but it's actually quite easy. Puff pastry sheets can be bought pre-made, and they're located in the frozen foods section of the supermarket. Your job is just to assemble and bake.

1. Preheat oven to 375° F.

2. Unfold pastry on a lightly floured surface. Roll into a 12x15-inch rectangle.

3. In a large bowl, combine apples, sugar, cinnamon, and vanilla and toss to coat apples. Arrange apple mixture on top of pastry, to within ½-inch of edges. Starting from the shorter end, roll up pastry like a jellyroll. Place seam-side down on a baking sheet that has been coated with non-stick spray.

4. In a medium bowl, whisk together egg and water. Brush egg wash all over surface of pastry. Using a sharp knife, cut several 2-inch long slits (about ⅛-inch deep), 2 inches apart, on top of pastry.

5. Bake 35 minutes, or until golden. Cool on baking sheet on a wire rack 15 minutes before slicing.

Preparation time: 20 minutes
Cooking time: 35 minutes

Serves 8

Fruit Tart with Chocolate Ganache

A secret chocolate ganache layer lies between fresh fruit and a tender, flaky crust. You can add an additional layer of vanilla pudding or custard on top of the chocolate if desired (just chill the tart until pudding is firm before placing fruit on top).

1. Preheat oven to 400° F.

2. To make the crust, in a large bowl or food processor fitted with the metal blade, combine flour, sugar, salt, and butter. Process or mix together with your fingers until mixture resembles coarse meal.

3. Add cold water, one tablespoon at a time, and process or mix just until you can form dough into a ball. Transfer dough to a lightly floured surface and roll into a 12-inch circle. Drape dough over a 9-inch, removable-bottom tart pan and press dough into bottom and up the sides. Prick the bottom and sides with a fork and cover the crust with foil or wax paper. Top the foil with beans or rice (to weigh down the crust and prevent it from puffing up during cooking—this is called "blind baking").

4. Bake 10 minutes. Remove beans and foil and bake 15-20 more minutes, or until crust is golden brown. Remove from oven and cool completely, in pan, on a wire rack.

5. Meanwhile, to make the ganache layer, melt chocolate in a double boiler or medium bowl over simmering water. Set aside to cool slightly. Scald heavy cream in a small saucepan just until bubbles appear around the edges. Whisk scalded cream into chocolate. Whisk in vanilla. Pour ganache into prepared crust and tilt pan slightly to make an even layer. Set aside or chill until firm.

6. When ganache is firm, top with fresh fruit, alternating each to form decorative circles. Brush the top with apricot preserves (if your preserves are thick and unspreadable, warm them slightly in the microwave) until fruit is glazed and shiny. Serve chilled or room temperature.

Preparation time: 30-40 minutes
Cooking time: 25-30 minutes

Serves 10-12

Needed items
large bowl or food processor
rolling pin
9-inch removable-bottom tart pan
wire rack
double boiler or medium bowl
    and medium saucepan
small saucepan
aluminum foil or wax paper
beans or rice

For the crust:
1½ cups all-purpose flour
  2 tablespoons granulated sugar
  ½ teaspoon salt
  ½ cup (1 stick) butter or
       margarine, chilled and cut up
3-4 tablespoons cold water

For the ganache layer:
  4 1-ounce squares semi-sweet
       chocolate
  ½ cup heavy cream
  ½ teaspoon vanilla extract

For the fruit layer:
  2 ripe peaches or nectarines,
       pitted and sliced
  2 ripe kiwis, peeled and sliced
  ½ cup strawberries, hulled
       and sliced
  ½ cup blueberries
  ¼ cup apricot preserves

Needed items
large mixing bowl
mixer
9-inch loaf pan
wire rack

1   cup (2 sticks) unsalted butter,
     softened
2   cups granulated sugar
5   eggs
2   cups all-purpose flour
1   teaspoon vanilla extract
½   teaspoon ground nutmeg
1   12-ounce package semi-sweet
     chocolate morsels
     non-stick cooking spray

Chocolate Chip Pound Cake

Talk about decadence. Sweet chocolate chips nestled in a dense, buttery cake. Pass me a treadmill.

Note: Pound cake freezes very well, so feel free to make this cake ahead of time. Once the cake has cooled completely, wrap it tightly in plastic wrap and freeze for up to 2 months. Thaw at room temperature before slicing.

1. Preheat oven to 325° F.
2. In a large mixing bowl, beat together butter and sugar until creamy. Add eggs, one at a time, mixing well after each addition. Gradually add flour and mix well. Blend in vanilla and nutmeg. Fold in chocolate morsels.
3. Pour mixture into a 9-inch loaf pan that has been coated with non-stick spray.
4. Bake 90 minutes, or until a knife inserted near the center comes out clean. Cool in pan, on a wire rack, before slicing.

Preparation time: 15 minutes
Cooking time: 90 minutes

Makes 1 loaf (8-10 servings)

Best-Ever Chocolate Cake with Chocolate Cream Icing

Perfect for birthday parties! Although boxed cake mixes are tempting, making a cake from scratch is not only easy, it's much more satisfying in the end.

1. Preheat oven to 350° F.
2. Melt chocolate in a double boiler or small bowl over simmering water. Set aside to cool slightly.
3. In a medium bowl, sift together flour, baking soda, and salt and set aside.
4. In a large mixing bowl, beat together butter and brown sugar until blended. Add eggs, one at a time, mixing well after each addition. Beat in vanilla. Gradually beat in chocolate. Gradually add flour mixture and buttermilk, alternating each and ending with flour mixture. Gradually add boiling water and mix until just blended.
5. Transfer mixture to two 9-inch round cake pans that have been coated with non-stick spray.
6. Bake 30-35 minutes, or until a wooden pick inserted near the center comes out almost clean (little bits clinging to the pick mean the cake's still moist).
7. Cool cakes, in pans, on wire racks 10 minutes. Loosen the edges with a sharp knife, invert pans, and cool completely on wire racks.

To make the icing:

1. Melt chocolate morsels in a double boiler or medium bowl over simmering water. Set aside to cool slightly.
2. Whisk together sour cream and vanilla extract. Gradually whisk in melted chocolate. Mix until smooth and spreadable.

To assemble cake:

1. Spread ½ cup of icing on one cake layer. Top with second cake layer. Spread remaining icing over top and sides of cake.

Preparation time: 25 minutes
Cooking time: 30-35 minutes

Makes one double layer, 9-inch cake
(12 servings)

Needed items
 double boiler or small and
  medium bowls and medium
  saucepan
 mixer
 medium and large bowls
 2 9-inch round cake pans
 wire rack

 4 1-ounce squares unsweetened
  chocolate
 2½ cups all-purpose flour
 2 teaspoons baking soda
 ½ teaspoon salt
 ½ cup (1 stick) butter or
  margarine, softened
 2 cups packed light brown sugar
 3 eggs
 2 teaspoons vanilla extract
 1½ cups buttermilk
 1 cup boiling water
  non-stick cooking spray

For the chocolate cream icing:
 1 12-ounce package semi-sweet
  chocolate morsels
 1⅔ cups sour cream
 1 teaspoon vanilla extract

Needed items
  baking sheet
  large bowl
  8-inch square cake pan
  plastic wrap or wax paper

  2   cups rolled oats (regular or
        quick cooking)
1½   cups puffed rice cereal
  ½   cup sunflower seeds
  ¾   cup honey
  ¼   cup crunchy peanut butter
  ¼   cup raisins
      non-stick cooking spray

Peanut Bars

Excellent, high-energy snack for those days on the go!

1. Preheat oven to 350° F.
2. Spread oats out on a baking sheet and bake 10 minutes, or until lightly toasted, shaking the pan occasionally to promote even browning. Transfer to a large bowl and add remaining ingredients. Mix well.
3. Press mixture into an 8-inch square cake pan that has been coated with non-stick spray (use plastic wrap or a piece of wax paper to prevent mixture from sticking to your fingers!).
4. Cover with plastic wrap and refrigerate 1 hour (and up to 2 days). Cut into 12 squares and serve chilled or room temperature.

Preparation and cooking time: 20 minutes   *Makes 12 bars*

Needed items
  baking sheet
  large bowl
  8-inch square cake pan
  plastic wrap or wax paper

2½   cups rolled oats (regular or
        quick cooking)
  ½   cup sliced almonds
  1   6-ounce bag dried apricots,
        chopped
  2   tablespoons nonfat dry
        milk powder
  1   teaspoon ground cinnamon
  1   teaspoon almond extract
  1   cup honey
  ¼   cup apple juice
      non-stick cooking spray

Apricot-Almond Bars

These chewy, granola-type bars are perfect anytime—for breakfast, a mid-afternoon snack, a source of fuel during a long walk, or a great dessert when served with a scoop of frozen yogurt or ice cream.

1. Preheat oven to 350° F.
2. Spread oats and almonds out on a baking sheet and bake 10 minutes, or until lightly toasted, shaking the pan occasionally to promote even browning. Transfer to a large bowl and add apricots, dry milk, cinnamon, and almond extract. Stir in honey and apple juice and mix well.
3. Press mixture into an 8-inch square cake pan that has been coated with non-stick spray (use plastic wrap or a piece of wax paper to prevent mixture from sticking to your fingers!).
4. Cover with plastic wrap and refrigerate 1 hour (and up to 2 days). Cut into 12 squares and serve chilled or room temperature.

Preparation and cooking time: 20 minutes   *Makes 12 bars*

Chocolate Oat Squares

This is my version of puffed rice treats. The oats add a distinct texture, and the combination of raisins, cocoa, and peanut butter creates a candy-bar-like experience.

1. Preheat oven to 350° F.

2. Spread oats out on a baking sheet and bake 10 minutes, or until lightly toasted, shaking the pan occasionally to promote even browning. Transfer to a large bowl and add toasted rice cereal and raisins. Set aside.

3. In a small saucepan over low heat, combine milk and cocoa. Simmer until cocoa is dissolved, stirring constantly with a wire whisk. Whisk in honey, peanut butter, and vanilla. Add mixture to oat mixture and mix well.

4. Press mixture into an 8-inch square cake pan that has been coated with non-stick spray (use plastic wrap or a piece of wax paper to prevent mixture from sticking to your fingers!).

5. Cover with plastic wrap and refrigerate 1 hour (and up to 2 days). Cut into 12 squares and serve chilled or room temperature.

Preparation and cooking time: 20 minutes

Makes 12 squares

Needed items
- baking sheet
- large bowl
- small saucepan
- 8-inch square cake pan
- wire whisk
- plastic wrap or wax paper

- 2½ cups rolled oats (regular or quick cooking)
- 1 cup toasted rice cereal
- 1 cup raisins
- 1 cup milk (regular or nonfat)
- ¼ cup cocoa powder
- ⅓ cup honey
- ¼ cup crunchy or creamy peanut butter
- 1 teaspoon vanilla extract
- non-stick cooking spray

Needed items
large bowls
mixer
8-inch square cake pan
wire rack

1½ cups all-purpose flour
½   cup yellow cornmeal
1   teaspoon baking powder
½   teaspoon baking soda
¼   teaspoon salt
2   tablespoons butter or
     margarine, softened
½   cup packed light brown sugar
2   egg whites
½   cup milk (regular or nonfat)
2   tablespoons fresh lemon juice
2   teaspoons finely grated
     lemon zest
¼   cup sliced almonds
     non-stick cooking spray

Lemon Cornmeal Bars

*Blending lemon, cornmeal, and almonds is a marriage made in heaven's kitchen.
The result is a wonderfully dense bar with a nutty, fresh lemon taste.*

1. Preheat oven to 325° F.

2. In a large bowl, combine flour, cornmeal, baking powder, baking
   soda, and salt. Set aside.

3. In a large mixing bowl, beat together butter and sugar until light and
   fluffy. Add egg whites and mix well. Add milk, lemon juice, and
   lemon zest and mix well. Gradually add flour mixture and mix until
   just blended (do not overmix).

4. Pour mixture into an 8-inch square cake pan that has been coated
   with non-stick spray. Top with sliced almonds, pressing almonds
   slightly into surface.

5. Bake 20 minutes, or until a knife inserted near the center comes out
   clean. Cool on a wire rack before cutting into 12 bars.

Preparation time: 15 minutes
Cooking time: 20 minutes

Makes 12 bars

Carrot Cake Bars

This also makes a great carrot cake, just skip the "cut into bars" part and add sweet cream cheese icing*!

1. Preheat oven to 350° F.

2. In a large bowl, combine oats, flour, baking powder, cinnamon, baking soda, and salt. Set aside.

3. In a large mixing bowl, beat together butter and sugar until light and fluffy. Add egg whites, buttermilk, and vanilla and mix well. Gradually add flour mixture and mix until just blended. Fold in carrots and raisins.

4. Pour batter into an 8-inch square cake pan that has been coated with non-stick spray.

5. Bake 20 minutes, or until a knife inserted near the center comes out almost clean. Cool on a wire rack before cutting into 12 squares.

* Cream Cheese Icing:

1. In a large mixing bowl, combine cream cheese and vanilla. Sift in confectioners' sugar and beat until smooth.

2. Spread on top and sides of cooled carrot cake.

Preparation time: 15 minutes
Cooking time: 20 minutes

Makes 12 bars

Needed items
  large bowls
  mixer
  8-inch square cake pan
  wire rack

For carrot cake bars:
  1½ cups rolled oats (regular or quick cooking)
  1 cup all-purpose flour
  2 teaspoons baking powder
  1 teaspoon ground cinnamon
  ½ teaspoon baking soda
  ¼ teaspoon salt
  2 tablespoons butter or margarine, softened
  ½ cup packed light brown sugar
  2 egg whites
  ¾ cup buttermilk
  1 teaspoon vanilla
  1 cup grated fresh carrots
  ½ cup raisins
     non-stick cooking spray

For icing:
  8 ounces cream cheese (regular or light)
  1 teaspoon vanilla
  3½ cups confectioners' sugar

Needed items
    small and large bowls
    baking sheet

2   cups all-purpose flour
⅔   cup granulated sugar
¾   teaspoon baking soda
¼   teaspoon salt
2   eggs
2   egg whites
⅓   cup crunchy peanut butter
1   teaspoon vanilla extract
    non-stick cooking spray

Peanut Biscotti

In Italy, it's common to see biscotti-lovers rest the cookies over steaming cups of coffee, cappuccino, or espresso. While the coffee flavor is infused into the dough, the steam softens the cookie's crisp center. In my house, it's common to see me eating these before the coffee's finished brewing.

1. Preheat oven to 325° F.
2. In a large bowl, combine flour, sugar, baking soda, and salt. Set aside.
3. In a small bowl, whisk together eggs and egg whites. Whisk in peanut butter and vanilla. Add egg mixture to dry ingredients and mix until a manageable dough forms.
4. Transfer the dough to a lightly floured surface and shape into a 10-inch log. Place log on a baking sheet that has been coated with non-stick spray.
5. Bake 30-35 minutes, or until a knife inserted near the center comes out clean.
6. Reduce oven temperature to 300° F.
7. Cut log crosswise into 18 slices and arrange slices on baking sheet.
8. Bake 20 more minutes, turning once, until golden. Cool until crisp.

Preparation time: 30 minutes
Cooking time: 50-55 minutes

Makes 18 biscotti cookies

Super-Rocky, Rocky Road Brownies

You may need a 4-wheel drive to truly enjoy this bumpy ride.

1. Preheat oven to 350° F.

2. Melt chocolate in a double boiler or small bowl over simmering water. Set aside to cool slightly.

3. In a medium bowl, combine flour, baking powder, and salt. Set aside.

4. In a large mixing bowl, beat together butter and sugar until blended. Add eggs, one at a time, mixing well after each addition. Gradually add melted chocolate and mix well. Beat in vanilla. Gradually add flour mixture and mix well. Fold in chocolate morsels, peanut butter chips, and marshmallows. Pour batter into an 8-inch square cake pan that has been coated with non-stick spray.

5. Bake 40 minutes, or until a wooden pick inserted near the center comes out almost clean. Cool in pan, on a wire rack, before cutting into 12 squares.

Preparation time: 20 minutes
Cooking time: 40 minutes

Makes 12 brownies

Needed items
double boiler or small bowl and
    medium saucepan
medium and large bowls
mixer
8-inch square cake pan
wire rack

2 1-ounce squares unsweetened
    chocolate
⅔ cup all-purpose flour
½ teaspoon baking powder
¼ teaspoon salt
¼ cup (½ stick) butter or
    margarine, softened
1 cup granulated sugar
2 eggs
1 teaspoon vanilla extract
1 6-ounce package semi-sweet
    chocolate morsels
1 cup peanut butter chips
1 cup mini marshmallows
    non-stick cooking spray

Needed items
  medium and large bowls
  mixer
  baking sheets
  wire rack

  ⅔ cup all-purpose flour
  1 teaspoon ground cinnamon
  ½ teaspoon baking powder
  ½ teaspoon baking soda
  ½ teaspoon salt
  ¼ teaspoon ground nutmeg
  12 tablespoons (1½ sticks) butter
      or margarine, softened
  1 cup packed light brown sugar
  ½ cup granulated sugar
  1 egg
  2 tablespoons water
  1 teaspoon vanilla extract
  3 cups rolled oats (regular or
      quick cooking)
  1 cup raisins
    non-stick cooking spray

Oatmeal Raisin Cookies

These cinnamony, chewy cookies are a welcome addition to any cookie jar.

1. Preheat oven to 350° F.

2. In a medium bowl, combine flour, cinnamon, baking powder, baking soda, salt, and nutmeg. Set aside until ready to use.

3. In a large mixing bowl, beat together butter and both sugars until light and fluffy. Beat in egg. Beat in water and vanilla. Gradually add flour mixture and mix until blended. Fold in oats and raisins.

4. Drop batter by slightly heaping tablespoons onto baking sheets that have been coated with non-stick spray, at least 1 inch apart.

5. Bake 10-12 minutes, or until golden brown in the middle and slightly darker around the edges.

6. Cool on baking sheets 5 minutes. Transfer to wire racks to cool completely.

Preparation time: 15 minutes
Cooking time: 10-12 minutes

Makes 36 cookies

Butter Cookies

Great for Christmas or any other festive occasion that calls for decorated cookies.

1. In a large mixing bowl or food processor fitted with the metal blade, beat together butter and sugar until light and fluffy. Add egg, vanilla, and salt and mix well. Gradually add flour and mix until a manageable dough forms. Form dough into a disc, wrap in plastic wrap, and refrigerate 1 hour (and up to 1 week).

2. Preheat oven to 375° F.

3. Transfer dough to a lightly floured surface and roll out to ¼-inch thickness. Cut into desired shapes using a variety of cookie cutters. Transfer cookies to baking sheets and bake 10-12 minutes, or until golden around the edges.

4. Transfer to wire racks to cool completely.

Note: For chocolate-filled sandwich cookies, spread melted semi-sweet chocolate between 2 cookies (let cool before serving). For decorated cookies, top with colored icing. To top with sprinkles, dissolve 1 tablespoon powdered egg whites in 2 tablespoons water, brush the mixture over cooled cookies, and sprinkle decorations on top.

Preparation time: 20 minutes
Chilling time: 1 hour
Cooking time: 10-12 minutes

Makes 36 cookies

Needed items
large mixing bowl or food processor
rolling pin
cookie cutters
baking sheets
wire rack
plastic wrap

½ cup (1 stick) unsalted butter, softened
½ cup granulated sugar
1 egg
1 teaspoon vanilla extract
⅛ teaspoon salt
1¼ cups all-purpose flour

Needed items
    large and medium bowls
    mixer
    rolling pin
    2- or 3-inch round cookie cutters
    baking sheets
    wire rack
    plastic wrap

2¾ cups all-purpose flour
 1   tablespoon ground ginger
 1   teaspoon ground cinnamon
 1   teaspoon baking soda
 ¼   teaspoon salt
 ½   cup packed light brown sugar
 ¼   cup plus 2 tablespoons
         granulated sugar, divided
 3   tablespoons butter or
         margarine, softened
 ½   cup plus 2 tablespoons
         molasses
 ¼   cup water
 1   teaspoon vanilla extract
     non-stick cooking spray

Ginger Snaps

A heaping plate of fresh-baked ginger snaps screams "Autumn is here!" These crisp, spicy wafers are great for dunking into apple cider or hot spiced cider drinks.

1. Preheat oven to 350° F.

2. In a medium bowl, combine flour, ginger, cinnamon, baking soda, and salt. Mix well with a fork and set aside.

3. In a large mixing bowl, beat together brown sugar, ¼ cup of the granulated sugar, and butter until light and fluffy. Beat in molasses, water, and vanilla. Gradually add flour mixture and mix on low speed until blended. Roll dough into a ball, wrap in plastic wrap, and press down gently to form a disc. Refrigerate 30 minutes (and up to 4 days).

4. Transfer dough to a lightly floured surface and roll out to ¼-inch thickness. Using 2- or 3-inch round cookie cutters, cut dough into cookies. Transfer cookies to baking sheets that have been coated with non-stick spray.

5. Bake 12 minutes, or until puffed up and slightly golden around the edges. Remove from oven and sprinkle the tops with remaining 2 tablespoons granulated sugar. Transfer to wire racks to cool completely.

Preparation time: 15 minutes   *Makes 36 cookies*
Cooling time: 30 minutes
Cooking time: 12 minutes

Peanut Butter Cookies

The addition of dry-roasted peanuts add a distinct crunch and extra burst of peanut flavor.

1. Preheat oven to 375° F.
2. In a medium bowl, combine flour, baking soda, and salt. Set aside.
3. In a large mixing bowl, beat together butter, peanut butter, and both sugars until light and fluffy. Add eggs, one at a time, mixing well after each addition. Beat in milk and vanilla. Gradually add flour mixture and mix until blended. Fold in oats and chopped peanuts.
4. Drop batter by rounded tablespoons onto baking sheets that have been coated with non-stick spray, at least 1 inch apart (the cookies spread out as they cook).
5. Bake 12-14 minutes, or until cookies are puffed up and golden brown. Transfer to wire racks to cool completely.

Preparation time: 15 minutes
Cooking time: 12-14 minutes

Makes 48 cookies

Needed items
  large and medium bowls
  mixer
  baking sheets
  wire rack

  2 cups all-purpose flour
  1 teaspoon baking soda
  ¼ teaspoon salt
  ¾ cup (1½ sticks) butter or margarine, softened
  ¾ cup creamy peanut butter
  1 cup granulated sugar
  1 cup packed light brown sugar
  2 eggs
  ¼ cup milk
  1½ teaspoons vanilla extract
  2 cups rolled oats (regular or quick cooking)
  1 cup dry-roasted peanuts, coarsely chopped
     non-stick cooking spray

Chocolate Chip Meringue Kisses

This little "clouds" are sweet, light, and wonderful.

1. Preheat oven to 200° F.
2. Spray a large baking sheet with non-stick spray and coat with a light dusting of flour. Shake off excess flour and set aside.
3. In a large mixing bowl, beat egg whites until they hold soft peaks. Gradually add sugar and beat until stiff, glossy peaks form. Gently fold in chocolate morsels and vanilla.
4. Drop mixture by heaping tablespoons (in the shape of kisses) onto prepared baking sheet.
5. Bake 1 hour, or until pale gold and no longer sticky on the surface. Turn oven off and let meringue kisses sit in the oven for 1 hour. Transfer kisses to wire racks to cool completely.

Preparation time: 15 minutes
Cooking and cooling time: 2 hours

Makes 24 kisses

Needed items
  large baking sheet
  large bowl
  mixer
  wire rack

     all-purpose flour
  4 large egg whites
  1 cup granulated sugar
  ½ cup mini semi-sweet chocolate morsels
  ½ teaspoon vanilla extract
     non-stick cooking spray

Needed items
  large bowl
  mixer
  baking sheets
  wire rack

  1   cup (2 sticks) unsalted butter or
        margarine, softened
  ¾   cup granulated sugar
  ¾   cup packed light brown sugar
  2   eggs
  1½ teaspoons vanilla extract
  1½ cups all-purpose flour
  1   teaspoon salt
  ⅛   teaspoon ground white pepper
  1   teaspoon baking soda
  2   teaspoons hot water
  ¾   cup rolled oats (regular or
        quick cooking)
  1   12-ounce bag semi-sweet
        chocolate chunks or
        mega-size morsels
  1   12-ounce bag white chocolate
        chunks or morsels
      non-stick cooking spray

Chocolate Chunk Cookies

This is my mother's signature recipe, one that soothes the soul (if ever a cookie **could** *soothe the soul, this one's it).*

1. Preheat oven to 375° F.

2. In a large mixing bowl, beat together butter and both sugars until smooth and creamy. Add eggs, one at a time, mixing well after each addition. Beat in vanilla. Gradually add flour, salt, and pepper and beat on low speed until blended. Dissolve baking soda in hot water and add to mixing bowl. Fold in oats and both chocolates.

3. Drop batter by heaping teaspoons onto baking sheets that have been coated with non-stick spray, at least 1 inch apart.

4. Bake 12 minutes, or until golden brown in the middle and slightly darker around the edges.

5. Cool on baking sheets 5 minutes. Transfer to wire racks to cool completely (or should I say: cool what's left after samples are taken!).

Preparation time: 15 minutes   *Makes 48 cookies*
Cooking time: 12 minutes

Special Occasions

I always find a reason to celebrate. I figure it must be a holiday somewhere! Whether it's the first day of summer, Flag Day, the President's birthday, or the Ides of March, there's always some reason to throw a party. I know, it's a stretch, but it works.

Special occasions are a great opportunity to bring together friends and family. Whether the focus is an anniversary, Thanksgiving, or an annual football game, the theme is the same—spending time with the people you love, having fun, and eating well. This year, surprise everyone by having a gathering at your place. The fool-proof recipes in this chapter were designed to coax you into entertaining. All the menus and recipes are simple-to-prepare crowd-pleasers. Once you get over your initial fear of cooking for a crowd, the rest is easy, and you'll be throwing regular parties with ease. Plus, your wedding guests will get to see what you did with those candlesticks, or what picture you chose for their frame, or better yet, how you learned to use the food processor.

New Year's Eve

I met my husband on New Year's Eve, just before midnight. While everyone was "kissing-in" the New Year, we were introducing ourselves.

This special meal incorporates all the wonderful ingredients associated with New Year's Eve—bubbly champagne, exotic mushrooms, a rich cream sauce, and confetti (for eating, not throwing). The meal concludes with a decadent pecan pie, the perfect blend of nuts and sugar, nestled in a buttery, flaky crust. Serve dinner with a chilled bottle of champagne on ice.

Menu

Chicken and Wild
Mushrooms in
Champagne Cream

Orzo Confetti

Sugar Snap Peas with
Roasted Shallots

Orange-Pecan Pie

Needed items
large skillet
aluminum foil

2 whole skinless chicken breasts
   (with bone), halved
2 teaspoons dried tarragon
1 teaspoon salt
½ teaspoon ground black pepper
2 teaspoons olive or vegetable oil
12 fresh Shiitake mushrooms,
   stems discarded, caps thinly
   sliced
2 cups dry champagne
1 tablespoon all-purpose flour
1 cup heavy cream

Needed items
large stockpot
large bowl

1 pound uncooked orzo pasta
   (rice-shaped pasta)
¼ cup balsamic vinegar
1 tablespoon olive oil
2 tablespoons crumbled
   feta cheese
1 carrot, peeled and diced
1 roasted red pepper (bottled in
   water), diced
1 small yellow bell pepper,
   seeded and diced
½ cup frozen green peas, thawed
¼ cup minced red onion
¼ cup chopped fresh basil
¼ cup chopped fresh cilantro
½ teaspoon salt
¼ teaspoon ground black pepper

Chicken and Wild Mushrooms in Champagne Cream

1. Rinse chicken and pat dry. Coat both sides with tarragon, salt, and pepper and set aside.

2. Heat oil in a large skillet over medium heat. Add mushrooms and sauté 5 minutes, or until tender and releasing juice. Add chicken and sauté until golden brown on both sides. Add champagne and bring mixture to a boil. Reduce heat, partially cover, and simmer 10 minutes, or until chicken is cooked through.

3. Remove chicken and mushrooms with a slotted spoon, transfer to a serving plate, and cover with foil to keep warm.

4. Dissolve flour in cream and whisk until blended. Add mixture to pan and simmer 5 minutes, or until mixture thickens to the consistency of gravy. Spoon cream sauce over chicken and mushrooms and serve hot.

Preparation and cooking time: 30 minutes   *Serves 4*

Orzo Confetti

1. In a large stockpot, cook pasta according to package directions, drain, and transfer to a large bowl. Add balsamic vinegar and olive oil and mix well. Stir in remaining ingredients and toss to combine.

2. Serve warm or chilled.

Preparation and cooking time: 25 minutes   *Serves 4*

Sugar Snap Peas with Roasted Shallots

Although this sounds like a time-consuming side dish, it's not. Plus, you can trim the ends of the snap peas while the shallots roast!

1. Preheat oven to 400° F.
2. Place shallot quarters on a baking sheet that has been coated with non-stick spray. Roast 30 minutes, or until tender and golden brown. Remove from oven and chop into small pieces.
3. Meanwhile, blanch peas in a large pot of rapidly boiling water for 2 minutes. Drain and set aside.
4. Heat oil in a large skillet over medium heat. Add garlic and sauté 2 minutes. Add roasted shallots, snap peas, salt, and pepper and sauté 2 minutes to heat through.

Preparation and cooking time: 40 minutes   *Serves 4*

Needed items
 baking sheet
 large stockpot
 large skillet

 2 shallots, peeled and quartered
 ¾ pound sugar snap peas, ends trimmed
 2 teaspoons olive oil
 1 garlic clove, minced
 ½ teaspoon salt
 ¼ teaspoon ground black pepper
   non-stick cooking spray

Needed items
   large bowl or food processor
   rolling pin
   9-inch pie plate
   large bowl
   wire rack

For the crust:
   1½ cups all-purpose flour
   3 tablespoons granulated sugar
   ½ teaspoon salt
   ½ cup (1 stick) butter or
         margarine, chilled and cut up
   3-4 tablespoons cold water

For the filling:
   1 cup light corn syrup
   ½ cup granulated sugar
   ½ cup packed light brown sugar
   3 tablespoons butter or
         margarine, melted
   3 egg whites
   2 teaspoons grated orange zest
   1 teaspoon vanilla extract
   2¼ cups pecan pieces
   12 whole pecan halves

Orange-Pecan Pie

The addition of orange zest adds a refreshing taste to this sweet treat.

Note: You can substitute a ready-made pie crust for home-made. If you make the crust from scratch, you can make it up to three days ahead of time (wrap it in plastic wrap and refrigerate until ready to use).

1. Preheat oven to 400° F.

2. To make the crust, in a large bowl or food processor fitted with the metal blade, combine flour, sugar, salt, and butter. Process or mix together with your fingers until mixture resembles coarse meal. Add cold water, one tablespoon at a time, and process or mix just until you can form dough into a ball. Transfer dough to a lightly floured surface and roll into a 12-inch circle. Press dough into the bottom of a 9-inch pie plate, allowing dough to hang over the sides. Roll the overlapping dough under and, using two fingers, pinch around the edge of the plate to form a decorative rim. Set aside until ready to use.

3. To make the filling, in a large bowl, whisk together corn syrup, both sugars, butter, egg whites, orange zest, and vanilla. Fold in pecan pieces. Pour mixture into prepared pie shell. Arrange pecan halves on top of filling, near the inside edge.

4. Bake 10 minutes. Reduce oven temperature to 350° F and bake 40 more minutes, or until center and top are firm to the touch (the filling will harden as it cools). Cool on a wire rack completely before cutting.

Preparation time: 20 minutes
Cooking time: 50 minutes

Makes one 9-inch pie (12 servings)

Valentine's Day

Stay home this year and avoid sharing the most romantic night of the year with dozens of strangers. This meal is light and easy—you won't be stuffed or too tired for a little romance! Nothing says "it's a special occasion" quite like lobster. And as you tie those asparagus spears together into tight bundles, remember the bond you have with the one you love. Serve the meal with a bottle of wine, a few candles, some special music and the night is off and running.

Menu

Broiled Lobster Tails

Steamed Asparagus Bundles
with Tomato Vinaigrette

Basmati Pilaf with Toasted
Almonds and Cumin Seeds

Mixed Berry Sweetheart
Shortcake

Needed items
  sharp scissors
  skewers
  foil-lined baking sheet
  medium bowl

2 lobster tails (about 6-8 ounces
     each)
⅓ cup fresh lemon juice
1 tablespoon olive oil
1 tablespoon chopped fresh
     oregano, or 1 teaspoon dried
1 teaspoon paprika
½ teaspoon salt
¼ teaspoon ground black pepper

Broiled Lobster Tails

1. Using sharp scissors, cut away the thin under-tissue of lobster tails, exposing the meat. Place a skewer through the back, just below the shell, to prevent tails from curling up during cooking. Place tails on a foil-lined baking sheet and set aside.

2. In a medium bowl, whisk together lemon juice, olive oil, oregano, paprika, salt, and pepper. Brush mixture over prepared lobster tails.

3. Preheat broiler.

4. Broil tails, 5 inches from heat source, 5 minutes per side, or until bright red and cooked through.

Preparation time: 15 minutes
Cooking time: 10 minutes
                                                          Serves 2

Needed items
  blender or food processor
  steamer basket or colander
  large stockpot
2 6-inch pieces colored string

1 beefsteak tomato, halved,
     seeded, and chopped
1 tablespoon Dijon mustard
1 tablespoon water
½ teaspoon grated lemon zest
¼ teaspoon ground black pepper
12 thin asparagus spears, stem
     ends trimmed

Steamed Asparagus Bundles with Tomato Vinaigrette

1. In a blender or food processor fitted with the metal blade, combine tomato, mustard, water, lemon zest, and pepper. Process until smooth. Set aside.

2. Using string, tie 6 asparagus spears together into a tight bundle. Repeat with remaining 6 asparagus spears.

3. Place a steamer basket or colander in a large stockpot. Add enough water to reach 1 inch. Bring water to a boil. Add asparagus bundles to steamer basket and cover pot. Steam 5 minutes, or until asparagus is tender-crisp. Remove bundles from pot and transfer to individual plates. Drizzle tomato vinaigrette over top.

Preparation time: 10 minutes
Cooking time: 5 minutes
                                                          Serves 2

Basmati Pilaf with Toasted Almonds and Cumin Seeds

1. Heat oil in a medium saucepan over medium heat. Add almonds and cumin seeds and sauté until golden, about 2-3 minutes, stirring constantly. Add rice and sauté until translucent, about 3 minutes.

2. Add chicken broth, salt, and pepper and bring mixture to a boil. Reduce heat, cover, and simmer 20 minutes, or until rice is tender and liquid is absorbed. Remove from heat and stir in green onions.

Preparation and cooking time: 30 minutes   *Serves 2*

Needed items
  medium saucepan

  2   teaspoons olive oil
  2   tablespoons sliced almonds
  ½   teaspoon whole cumin seeds
  ½   cup uncooked Basmati rice
  1   cup chicken broth or water
  ½   teaspoon salt
  ¼   teaspoon ground black pepper
  ¼   cup chopped green onions

Mixed Berry Sweetheart Shortcake

You can make the shortcake and mixed berry filling in advance. Assemble shortcake just before serving.

1. In a medium bowl, combine berries, orange juice, and 1 teaspoon of the sugar. Mix well and set aside until ready to use.

2. Preheat oven to 400° F.

3. In a large bowl or food processor fitted with the metal blade, combine 3 tablespoons of the sugar, flour, baking powder, salt, and butter. Mix together with your hands or process until mixture resembles coarse meal. Gradually add milk and mix or process until mixture forms a manageable dough.

4. Transfer dough to a lightly floured surface and roll out to 2-inch thickness. Using a sharp knife or heart-shaped cookie cutter, cut dough into two hearts (about 4 inches in diameter). Place hearts on a baking sheet that has been coated with non-stick spray. Brush the surface with egg white and sprinkle the top with remaining teaspoon of sugar.

5. Bake 15-20 minutes, or until golden. Remove from oven, and while still warm, split cakes in half crosswise (like an English muffin).

6. To serve, spoon berry mixture on the bottom half of each heart. Top with sugar-coated second half. Garnish with whipped cream and any remaining berries.

Preparation time: 20 minutes   *Serves 2*
Cooking time: 15-20 minutes

Needed items
  medium bowl
  large bowl or food processor
  rolling pin
  sharp knife or heart-shaped
    cookie cutter
  baking sheet
  wire rack

  1   cup mixed berries (blueberries,
        raspberries, strawberries)
  1   tablespoon orange juice
  3   tablespoons plus 2 teaspoons
        granulated sugar, divided
  1   cup all-purpose flour
  2   teaspoons baking powder
  ¼   teaspoon salt
  2   tablespoons butter or margarine,
        chilled and cut up
  ⅓   cup milk
  1   egg white
      non-stick cooking spray
      whipped cream for garnish

Thanksgiving

When you say the word "Thanksgiving," all kinds of wonderful images and childhood memories come to mind. And those images are almost exclusively about food. Thanksgiving is probably one of the most comforting nights of the year, and a great time to bring the family together. This year, start a tradition of your own. Hosting a Thanksgiving feast may sound like a daunting task, but it doesn't have to be. These recipes are simple to prepare, yet boast the flavors of a labor-intensive meal. And, don't worry, people love to "pitch in" and help on Thanksgiving day.

Feel free to add a mixed green salad or a steamed green vegetable (broccoli, spinach, or green beans) to add color to the plate.

Roast Turkey with Fresh Herbs

When selecting a turkey, plan on about 1-1½ pounds per person. That ensures enough meat and the possibility of leftovers.

1. Preheat oven to 450° F.
2. Rinse turkey inside and out and pat dry.
3. Remove leaves from thyme, rosemary, and tarragon stems. Reserve stems and coarsely chop leaves. Coat the outside of turkey with the chopped leaves, salt, and pepper. Place turkey in a shallow roasting pan and loosely stuff the cavity with the reserved herb stems, leeks, and apples. Insert a meat thermometer deep into the thickest part of the thigh next to the body, not touching the bone. Pour chicken broth into bottom of roasting pan.
4. Place turkey in oven and immediately reduce oven temperature to 325° F. Roast 20 minutes per pound, or until thermometer reads 180°-185° F. Let stand 10 minutes before carving.
5. Remove leeks and apples (serve on the side if desired), and carve turkey.

Preparation time: 10 minutes
Cooking time: 2 hours 45 minutes-3½ hours

Serves 6-8

Needed items
  shallow roasting pan
  meat thermometer

  1 8- to 10-pound turkey, giblets removed and discarded
 10 sprigs fresh thyme
  5 sprigs fresh rosemary
  5 sprigs fresh tarragon
  1 teaspoon salt
  ½ teaspoon ground black pepper
  2 leeks, green portion discarded, white portion halved, rinsed and chopped
  2 apples, cored and sliced
  1 cup chicken broth

Caramelized Bell Peppers and Pearl Onions

1. Melt butter and sugar together in a large skillet over medium heat. Add onions and sauté 10 minutes, or until tender and golden brown.
2. Add bell peppers, rosemary, salt, and pepper and sauté 3-5 minutes, or until peppers are tender-crisp.

Preparation and cooking time: 20 minutes

Serves 6

Needed items
  large skillet

  1 tablespoon butter or margarine
  1 tablespoon granulated sugar
  1 16-ounce package frozen small onions, thawed
  1 green bell pepper, seeded and chopped
  1 red bell pepper, seeded and chopped
  1 tablespoon chopped fresh rosemary
  ½ teaspoon salt
  ¼ teaspoon ground black pepper

Needed items
  large skillet
  large bowl
  4-quart casserole dish
  aluminum foil

  1   teaspoon olive oil
  3   links (about ⅓ pound) sweet
        Italian turkey sausage, casing
        removed, crumbled
  1   large onion, chopped (about
        1½ cups)
  3   celery stalks, chopped
  2   tablespoons chopped fresh
        Italian parsley
  3½ teaspoons dried sage
  1½ teaspoons dried thyme
  1   teaspoon dried marjoram
  ¾   teaspoon salt
  ¼   teaspoon ground black pepper
  2   stale sourdough baguettes
        (½ pound each), cut into
        ½-inch cubes
  2   cups chicken broth
      non-stick cooking spray

Sourdough Stuffing with Sweet Italian Sausage

1. Preheat oven to 350° F.

2. Heat oil in a large skillet over medium heat. Add sausage and sauté until browned and cooked through, breaking up the meat as it cooks. Add onion and celery and sauté 2 minutes. Add parsley, sage, thyme, marjoram, salt, and pepper and stir to coat everything with herbs and spices.

3. Transfer mixture to a large bowl and add cubed bread and chicken broth. Toss to combine. Spoon mixture into a 4-quart casserole dish that has been coated with non-stick spray.

4. Cover with foil and bake 20 minutes. Uncover and bake 15 more minutes, or until top is golden brown.

Preparation time: 20 minutes
Cooking time: 35 minutes

Serves 6

Needed items
  shallow baking dish
  medium bowl
  aluminum foil

  4   large sweet potatoes (about 2½
        pounds), peeled, halved
        lengthwise and cut into ½-inch
        thick slices
  ¼   cup orange juice
  ¼   cup maple syrup
  2   tablespoons light brown sugar
  1   tablespoon butter or margarine,
        melted
  ½   teaspoon salt
  ¼   teaspoon ground cloves

Maple-Orange Sweet Potatoes

1. Preheat oven to 350° F.

2. Arrange sweet potatoes in the bottom of a shallow baking dish and set aside.

3. In a medium bowl, whisk together orange juice, maple syrup, brown sugar, butter, salt, and cloves. Pour mixture over sweet potatoes and stir to coat potatoes with mixture.

4. Cover with foil and bake 45 minutes. Uncover, stir to coat potatoes with sauce, and bake 15 more minutes, or until potatoes are tender and sauce is thick and bubbly.

Preparation time: 10 minutes
Cooking time: 1 hour

Serves 6

Wild Mushroom Gravy

1. In a small bowl, combine dried mushrooms and ½ cup warm water and let stand
15 minutes.

2. Heat oil in a large skillet over medium heat. Add shallots and garlic and sauté 2 minutes. Add portobello and Shiitake mushrooms and sauté 5 minutes, or until mushrooms are tender and releasing juice.

3. Meanwhile, drain porcini mushrooms through a paper towel-lined sieve, reserving liquid, and chop mushrooms into small pieces. Add chopped mushrooms and reserved soaking liquid to skillet. Stir in chicken broth, sherry, thyme, salt, and pepper. Bring to a boil, reduce heat, and simmer 15 minutes.

4. Dissolve cornstarch in ¼ cup water and add to mushroom mixture. Simmer 2 minutes, or until sauce thickens.

Preparation and cooking time: 35-40 minutes   *Serves 6*

Needed items
small bowl
large skillet
fine sieve

½ ounce dried porcini mushrooms
¾ cup warm water, divided
1 tablespoon olive oil
2 shallots, diced
2 garlic cloves, minced
3 large portobello mushrooms
   (about 1 pound), stems
   discarded, caps sliced
½ pound Shiitake mushrooms,
   stems discarded, caps sliced
2 cups chicken broth
¼ cup sherry wine
1 teaspoon dried thyme
½ teaspoon salt
¼ teaspoon ground black pepper
1 tablespoon cornstarch

Cranberry-Corn Relish

This dish can be made a day or two in advance and refrigerated until ready to serve.

1. Combine all ingredients in a medium bowl. Cover with plastic wrap and refrigerate until ready to serve.

Preparation time: 10 minutes   *Serves 6*

Needed items
medium bowl
plastic wrap

1 16-ounce can whole berry
   cranberry sauce
1 15-ounce can whole kernel
   sweet corn, drained
1 4-ounce can chopped
   green chiles
¼ cup diced red onion
2 tablespoons chopped
   fresh cilantro

Needed items
  baking sheet
  food processor
  rolling pin
  9-inch pie plate
  large bowl
  wire rack
  plastic wrap

For the crust:
  4   ounces whole hazelnuts
  1   cup all-purpose flour
  3   tablespoons granulated sugar
  ½   teaspoon salt
  6   tablespoons butter, chilled and
      cut up
2-3   tablespoons cold water

For the filling:
  1   15-ounce can pumpkin (not
      pie filling)
  3   egg whites
  ½   cup granulated sugar
  ¼   cup packed light brown sugar
1¼   teaspoons ground cinnamon
  ¼   teaspoon ground ginger
  ¼   teaspoon ground cloves
1½   cups evaporated skim milk

Pumpkin Pie with Hazelnut Crust

1. Preheat oven to 350° F.

2. To make the crust, spread hazelnuts out on a baking sheet and toast in oven for 5 minutes, or until outer brown skin begins to crack. Remove from oven, place nuts in a dish towel and rub together to remove brown skin (don't worry, not all skin needs to be removed).

3. Place peeled hazelnuts in a food processor fitted with the metal blade. Add flour, sugar, and salt and process until hazelnuts are finely minced. Add butter and process until mixture resembles coarse meal. Add water and process just until a manageable dough forms. Roll dough into a round disc, wrap in plastic wrap, and refrigerate 30 minutes (and up to 4 days).

4. Preheat oven to 400° F.

5. Transfer dough to a lightly floured surface and roll into a 12-inch circle. Press dough into the bottom of a 9-inch pie plate, allowing dough to hang over the sides. Roll the overlapping dough under and, using two fingers, pinch around the edge of the plate to form a decorative rim. Prick the bottom and sides with a fork and set aside.

6. To make the filling, whisk together all ingredients in a large bowl. Pour mixture into prepared pie crust.

7. Bake 10 minutes, reduce oven temperature to 350° F, and bake 50 more minutes, or until a knife inserted near the center comes out clean.* Cool on a wire rack before slicing.

Preparation time: 45 minutes
Cooking time: 1 hour

Makes one 9-inch pie (12 servings)

* If edges of crust begin to brown before cooking time is complete, cover with foil, leaving the center of the pie exposed.

Christmas Dinner

My mother prepared Christmas dinner every year while I was growing up. She would labor for weeks in advance and get up at the crack of dawn on Christmas day to make sure everyone's favorite dish was made to perfection. One year (many years ago), she decided to play in a racquetball tournament on Christmas eve. That decision forever changed Christmas as we knew it. During one of the games, she sprained her ankle and was unable to walk. What about Christmas dinner? My dad stepped in (a man who couldn't even make scrambled eggs), he followed Chef Tell's recipes for a holiday dinner, and the rest is history. Now, every year, my father prepares the same sensational meal (he still can't scramble an egg) and my mom gets the night off.

Note: My dad usually prepares the entire meal the day before Christmas. On Christmas day it's reheat and serve! Why? So he can enjoy the festivities (and the bubbly) along with everyone else!

If desired, serve a side salad of mixed greens, sliced fennel, and grated carrots in a light vinaigrette dressing.

Menu

Christmas Goose

Cranberry Cornbread Dressing

Spaetzle

Red Cabbage

Walnut-Fudge Torte

Oven-Roasted Chestnuts

Needed items
    large roasting pan
    instant-read thermometer
    sharp knife
    carving board

1 8- to 10-pound goose, giblets
        removed and discarded
2 teaspoons dried thyme
1 teaspoon salt
½ teaspoon ground black pepper
1 apple, cored and sliced
1 medium onion, sliced
    water

Christmas Goose

1. Preheat oven to 425° F.
2. Rinse goose inside and out and pat dry. Season bird, inside and out, with thyme, salt, and pepper. Place breast-side down in a large roasting pan. Arrange apple and onion slices around bird and pour over enough water to equal 1 inch.
3. Place goose in oven and immediately reduce oven temperature to 350° F. Roast 2 hours, basting frequently and removing excess water periodically.
4. Remove goose from oven and pour off all but 1 cup of liquid. Return goose to pan, breast side up, and roast 30-60 more minutes, or until golden brown (an instant-read thermometer inserted in the thickest part of the thigh, not touching the bone, should read 165°-170° F). Remove goose from pan and transfer to a carving board to cool (let stand 15-30 minutes before carving).
5. To deglaze the roasting pan (to make gravy*), set it over medium heat. Add 1 cup of water and simmer, stirring constantly and scraping up the brown bits from the bottom of the pan. Simmer until liquid has reduced to a gravy-like consistency. Strain off any surface grease and serve along side carved goose.
6. Once goose has cooled, debone,** slice, and serve.

Cooking time: 2½-3 hours   *Serves 6*

*   Dad doesn't make his own gravy, he buys packaged sauce mix and prepares it the day before. It's not cheating, it's smart!

** To debone goose:
      Place breast-side down on a carving board. Using a sharp, strong knife, cut down along either side of the backbone and remove it. Reach into the cavity and remove breast bone. Cut off wings and legs and split breast in half. Slice each breast half crosswise into ½-inch thick slices. Slice meat from wings, thighs, and legs (as much as possible, discard any fatty meat). Serve or cover with foil and refrigerate. To reheat, place covered roasting pan in a preheated 350° F oven and bake 1 hour, or until goose is warm.

Cranberry Cornbread Dressing

Dressing and stuffing are practically the same thing, the difference being that dressing is not stuffed into the turkey. This version gets a spicy kick from the green chiles and sweetness from the cranberries.

Note: For an excellent cornbread, just skip the "cut into cubes" part.

1. Preheat oven to 400° F.
2. Combine cornmeal, flour, baking powder, salt, baking soda, and cayenne pepper in a large bowl. Mix well with a fork, make a well in the center, and set aside.
3. In a medium bowl, whisk together milk, egg whites, and oil. Stir in corn, cheese, chiles, and cranberries. Fold milk mixture into dry ingredients and mix until just blended.
4. Pour batter into an 8-inch square cake pan that has been coated with non-stick spray.
5. Bake 20 minutes, or until a wooden pick inserted near the center comes out clean. Cool in pan, on a wire rack, 10 minutes. Remove cornbread from pan and cut into 1-inch cubes. Transfer to a serving dish and serve warm.

Preparation time: 15 minutes
Cooking time: 20 minutes

Serves 6

Needed items
  medium and large bowls
  8-inch square cake pan
  wire rack

  1 cup yellow cornmeal
  1 cup all-purpose flour
  2 teaspoons baking powder
  1 teaspoon salt
  ½ teaspoon baking soda
  ¼ teaspoon cayenne pepper
  1 cup milk (regular or nonfat)
  2 egg whites
  2 tablespoons corn oil
  1 14-ounce can whole kernel corn, drained
  ⅓ cup grated Monterey Jack cheese (regular or reduced-fat)
  1 4-ounce can chopped green chiles
  1 cup sweetened dried cranberries
     non-stick cooking spray

Spaetzle

If you make this ahead, transfer to a shallow roasting pan, cover with foil, and refrigerate. To reheat, place covered roasting pan in a preheated 350° F oven and bake 1 hour (with the goose) until warm.

1. In a large stockpot, cook spaetzle according to package directions, drain, and set aside.
2. Melt butter in a large skillet over medium heat. Add garlic and sauté 2 minutes, or until golden. Add spaetzle and stir to coat. Add salt, pepper, and nutmeg and heat through.

Preparation and cooking time: 20 minutes

Serves 6

Needed items
  large stockpot
  large skillet

  1 pound uncooked spaetzle*
  1 tablespoon butter or margarine
  2 garlic cloves, minced
  ½ teaspoon salt
  ¼ teaspoon ground black pepper
  ¼ teaspoon ground nutmeg

  * Spaetzle is a Swiss, egg pasta that can be found in supermarkets and gourmet food stores.

Needed items
    grater or the shredder attachment
        on a food processor
    large saucepan

    1   head red cabbage, outer leaves
            removed, cored
    2   tablespoons olive oil
    1   medium onion, chopped
    2   apples, cored and thinly sliced
    ½   cup red wine vinegar
    1   cup dry red wine
    1   cup water
    ½   cup granulated sugar
    1   teaspoon ground cinnamon
    ½   teaspoon salt
    ¼   teaspoon ground black pepper
    1   small potato, peeled and grated

Needed items
    food processor
    small, medium, and large bowls
    mixer
    2 9-inch round cake pans
    wire rack
    double boiler or medium bowl
        and medium saucepan
    small saucepan
    fine sieve

For the walnut torte:
    1   cup chopped walnuts
    1   cup all-purpose flour
    1   teaspoon baking powder
    ¼   teaspoon salt
    4   eggs, separated
    1   cup granulated sugar, divided
    ¼   cup butter or margarine
            (½ stick), melted
    2   teaspoons vanilla extract
        non-stick cooking spray

Red Cabbage

If you make this ahead, keep it refrigerated, and then reheat in a large saucepan over medium-low heat until hot.

1. Using a grater or the shredder attachment on a food processor, shred the cabbage. Set aside.

2. Heat oil in a large saucepan over medium heat. Add onion and apples and sauté 3-4 minutes, or until tender. Add shredded cabbage, vinegar, wine, water, sugar, cinnamon, salt, and pepper. Bring mixture to a boil, reduce heat, partially cover and simmer 1 hour, stirring occasionally.

3. Add grated potato and simmer, uncovered, 30 minutes, or until mixture thickens and potato is tender, stirring frequently.

Preparation and cooking time: 1 hour 45 minutes   *Serves 6*

Walnut-Fudge Torte

To make the torte:

1. Preheat oven to 325° F.

2. Place walnuts in a food processor fitted with the metal blade. Process until finely crushed. Add flour, baking powder, and salt and process until blended. Set aside.

3. In a large mixing bowl, beat 4 egg whites until soft peaks form. Gradually beat in ½ cup of the granulated sugar and beat until stiff, shiny peaks form.

4. In a separate bowl, beat together egg yolks and remaining ½ cup sugar until thick and pale. Beat in melted butter and vanilla extract. Fold one spoonful of egg whites into egg yolk mixture. Mix well and then fold in remaining egg whites. Fold in flour mixture.

5. Pour batter into two 9-inch round cake pans that have been coated with non-stick spray.

6. Bake 25 minutes, or until top is golden and cakes begin to pull away from the sides of pans. Cool cakes in pans 10 minutes on a wire rack. Invert and cool completely.

To make the filling:

1. Melt chocolate in a double boiler or medium bowl over simmering water. Set aside to cool slightly.
2. Scald ½ cup of the heavy cream (keep the remaining ½ cup chilled) by heating in a small saucepan over medium heat just until bubbles appear around the edges. Stir scalded cream into chocolate and whisk until blended. Refrigerate until firm, about 1 hour.
3. Transfer mixture to a medium mixing bowl and beat until light and fluffy, about 30 seconds (although the ganache is firm, it still beats up light and fluffy).
4. In a small mixing bowl, beat remaining ½ cup of chilled heavy cream until stiff peaks form. Fold into chocolate mixture with vanilla.

To assemble the torte:

1. Spread chocolate filling on one cake layer. Place second cake layer on top and press down slightly. In a small bowl, combine confectioners' sugar and cocoa. Transfer mixture to a fine sieve and sift over top of torte (for a pretty presentation, sift a little confectioners' sugar-cocoa mixture around the edges of the plate, too).

Preparation time: 30 minutes
Chilling time (filling): 1 hour
Cooking time: 25 minutes

Makes one 9-inch torte (12 servings)

For the fudge filling:
  4   1-ounce semi-sweet chocolate squares
  1   cup heavy cream, divided
  1   teaspoon vanilla extract

For the topping:
  1   tablespoon confectioners' sugar
  ½   teaspoon unsweetened cocoa

Needed items
  large bowl
  sharp knife
  shallow roasting pan

1 pound whole chestnuts
   water

Oven-Roasted Chestnuts

For best results, soak the chestnuts in clear water for 2-3 hours before roasting.

1. Place chestnuts in a large bowl and pour over enough cold water to cover. Let stand 2-3 hours.

2. Preheat oven to 400° F.

3. Drain chestnuts and discard water. Using a sharp knife, cut a small X on the top of each chestnut, deep enough to break through the skin to get to the inside flesh.

4. Spread chestnuts out in a shallow roasting pan and roast 30 minutes. Remove from oven and cool slightly before serving.

Preparation time: 2-3 hours
Cooking time: 30 minutes

Serves 6

One-Year Anniversary

Although you may be tempted to eat out on your anniversary, making dinner together can be much more romantic. Start off with a tangy Caesar salad, and then enjoy a light dinner of scallops and black beans. Toss cooked egg noodles with a little olive oil and serve them on the side to round out the meal. And although you may be pulling your wedding cake out of the freezer for dessert, I've given you a passionate recipe just in case! Serve this menu with your favorite bottle of white or rosé wine.

Menu

Caesar Salad with
Sourdough Croutons

Crispy Broiled Scallops
with Spicy Black Beans

Passion Fruit Sherbet

Needed items
baking sheet
blender or food processor
large bowl

½   sourdough baguette, cut into
        1-inch cubes
¼   cup fresh lemon juice
2   tablespoons olive oil
2   tablespoons grated Parmesan
        cheese
2   garlic cloves, sliced
1   tablespoon red wine vinegar
1½ teaspoons anchovy paste
1   teaspoon Dijon mustard
½   teaspoon Worcestershire sauce
¼   teaspoon ground black pepper
4   Romaine lettuce leaves, rinsed,
        dried, and chopped

Needed items
shallow dish
foil-lined baking sheet
small saucepan

For the crispy broiled scallops:
1   tablespoon all-purpose flour
1   teaspoon ground cumin
1   teaspoon ground fennel
½   teaspoon salt
¼   teaspoon ground black pepper
1   pound sea scallops
2   egg whites

For the spicy black beans:
1   15-ounce can black beans,
        undrained
2   teaspoons minced chipotle in
        adobo (from 7-ounce can)
1   teaspoon chili powder
¼   cup chopped green onions

Caesar Salad with Sourdough Croutons

1. Preheat oven to 400° F.

2. Spread bread cubes out on a baking sheet and toast in oven 5-10 minutes, or until golden. Remove from oven and set aside.

3. In a blender or food processor fitted with the metal blade, combine lemon juice, oil, Parmesan, garlic, vinegar, anchovy paste, mustard, Worcestershire sauce, and pepper. Purée until smooth.

4. Place lettuce leaves and sourdough croutons in a large bowl (make sure lettuce is dry so the dressing sticks to it). Pour over dressing and toss to coat.

Preparation and cooking time: 20 minutes   *Serves 2*

Crispy Broiled Scallops with Spicy Black Beans
You can substitute shrimp for the scallops, if desired. Just remember to call the dish "crispy broiled shrimp" so you don't look silly.

1. To make the scallops, preheat broiler.

2. In a shallow dish, combine flour, cumin, fennel, salt, and pepper. Dip scallops into egg whites and then into flour mixture, turning to coat both sides.

3. Place scallops on a foil-lined baking sheet and broil, 5 inches from heat source, 5 minutes per side, or until golden brown and cooked through.

4. Meanwhile, to make the black beans, in a small saucepan over medium heat, combine beans, chipotle in adobo, and chili powder. Simmer uncovered for 10 minutes. Remove from heat and stir in green onions.

5. To serve, spoon black beans onto dinner plates and arrange scallops over top.

Preparation and cooking time: 20 minutes   *Serves 2*

Passion Fruit Sherbet

For easy clean-up, freeze the sherbet in large zip-top bags.

1. In a blender or food processor fitted with the metal blade, combine fruit salad (with the liquid) and remaining ingredients. Process until smooth.
2. Transfer mixture to a shallow baking dish, cover with plastic wrap, and freeze until firm (about 2-4 hours).
3. Remove from freezer, spoon sherbet into a blender or food processor, and process until smooth. Spoon sherbet into dessert bowls or return to freezer until ready to serve.

Preparation time: 10 minutes
Freezing time: 2-4 hours

Serves 2

Needed items
blender or food processor
shallow baking dish
plastic wrap

1 15¼-ounce can tropical fruit salad in light syrup and passion-fruit juice
1 cup milk (regular or nonfat)
½ cup buttermilk
1 teaspoon vanilla extract

Sunday Brunch

Menu

Spinach and Cheese Quiche
with Caramelized Shallots

Onion Tart with Parmesan

Swirled Pumpkin Cake

Pecan-Raisin Sticky Buns

Apple-Cinnamon
Coffee Cake

Chocolate Chip Pancakes

Crunchy Roasted Granola

I love Sundays—those casual days when everyone just kicks back and relaxes. I also love serving Sunday brunch to friends and family. There's no "Saturday Night" stress, and nobody's in a rush to go anywhere. Invite a few friends over for brunch and serve some or all of the recipes below. If you want, serve a fresh fruit salad on the side to round out the menu. Make a big batch of Bloody Mary's or Mimosas (champagne and freshly squeezed orange juice) to serve with the meal. A brunch party is an excellent way to wind down the weekend, or kick off the work-week with a revived spirit.

Spinach and Cheese Quiche with Caramelized Shallots

1. Preheat oven to 375° F.

2. To make the crust, in a large bowl or food processor fitted with the metal blade, combine flour, salt, and butter. Process or mix together with your hands until mixture resembles coarse meal. Add cold water, one tablespoon at a time, and process or mix until a manageable dough forms. Transfer dough to a lightly floured surface and roll into a 12-inch circle. Press dough into the bottom and up the sides of a 9-inch, removable-bottom tart pan (or 9-inch pie pan). Refrigerate until ready to use.

3. To make the filling, heat oil in a large skillet over medium heat. Add shallots and sugar and sauté 10 minutes, or until shallots are caramelized and golden brown. Transfer shallots to a large bowl and add spinach, ricotta, Swiss cheese, milk, eggs, mustard, oregano, salt, and pepper. Mix well. Spoon mixture into prepared crust and top with Parmesan cheese.

4. Bake 35-40 minutes, or until a knife inserted near the center comes out clean and crust is golden brown. Let stand 10 minutes before slicing.

Preparation time: 25 minutes
Cooking time: 35-40 minutes

Makes one 9-inch quiche (6-8 servings)

Needed items
   large bowl or food processor
   rolling pin
   9-inch removable-bottom tart pan
      or 9-inch pie pan
   large skillet
   large mixing bowl

For the crust:
   1½ cups all-purpose flour
   ½   teaspoon salt
   ½   cup (1 stick) butter or
         margarine, chilled and cut up
   3-4 tablespoons cold water

For the filling:
   2   teaspoons olive or vegetable oil
   4   shallots, halved and thinly
         sliced
   2   tablespoons granulated sugar
   1   10-ounce package frozen
         chopped spinach, thawed
         and drained
   1   cup ricotta cheese (regular or
         part-skim)
   ¾   cup grated Swiss cheese
         (regular or reduced-fat)
   ¼   cup milk (regular or nonfat)
   2   eggs, lightly beaten
   1   tablespoon Dijon mustard
   1   teaspoon dried oregano
   ½   teaspoon salt
   ¼   teaspoon ground black pepper
   1   tablespoon grated Parmesan
         cheese

Needed items
  rolling pin
  9-inch removable-bottom tart pan
  large non-stick skillet
  baking sheet
  small bowl

1 11-ounce can refrigerated
     breadstick dough
2 teaspoons olive oil
1 medium Spanish onion,
     chopped (about 1½ cups)
1 leek, green portion discarded,
     white portion halved, rinsed
     and chopped
2 garlic cloves, minced
1 medium Idaho or Yukon Gold
     potato, diced
1 tablespoon chopped fresh
     rosemary, or 1 teaspoon dried
2 teaspoons dried oregano
½ teaspoon salt
½ teaspoon ground black pepper
¾ cup milk (regular or nonfat)
4 tablespoons grated Parmesan
     cheese, divided
1 tablespoon Dijon mustard
1 egg
   non-stick cooking spray

Onion Tart with Parmesan

I love to find alternative uses for convenience products—after all, they're supposed to be "convenient." Refrigerated breadstick dough makes the perfect crust for this tart, while eliminating the time-consuming process of making dough from scratch.

1. Unroll dough and knead together on a lightly floured surface for 1 minute. Shape into a ball, cover with a dish towel, and let stand 20 minutes.

2. Roll dough into a 12-inch circle and set over a 9-inch, removable-bottom tart pan that has been coated with non-stick spray, allowing the dough to hang over sides by ¼ inch. Set aside.

3. Preheat oven to 375° F.

4. Heat oil in a large non-stick skillet over medium heat. Add onion, leek, and garlic and sauté 2 minutes. Add potato and sauté 4 minutes, or until onion and potato are golden. Add rosemary, oregano, salt, and pepper and stir to coat. Transfer mixture to tart pan and, using the back of a spoon, press mixture into dough. Place tart pan on a baking sheet and set aside.

5. In a small bowl, whisk together milk, 2 tablespoons of the Parmesan, mustard, and egg. Pour mixture over onion mixture. Top with remaining 2 tablespoons of Parmesan cheese.

6. Bake tart (on baking sheet) 45 minutes, or until a knife inserted near the center comes out clean. Let stand 10 minutes before slicing.

Preparation time: 45 minutes   *Makes one 9-inch tart (6-8 servings)*
Cooking time: 45 minutes

Swirled Pumpkin Cake

I must be honest, the swirl was not intended at first. The first time I tested this recipe, just before I popped the pumpkin mixture into the oven, I realized I forgot to add the cream cheese. I quickly added some orange juice to thin the cream cheese, added a little vanilla for flavor, and swirled the concoction into the pumpkin mixture. The cake was fantastic and the swirl stays!

1. Preheat oven to 350° F.

2. To make cream cheese swirl, whisk together all ingredients until smooth and creamy. Set aside until ready to use.

3. To make the cake, sift together flour, sugar, baking powder, cinnamon, baking soda, nutmeg, cloves, and salt in a large bowl. In a medium bowl, whisk together pumpkin, milk, egg whites, butter, and orange zest. Fold pumpkin mixture into dry ingredients and mix until just blended. Spoon about ⅔ of batter into the bottom of a 9-inch tube pan that has been coated with non-stick spray. Spoon cream cheese mixture over top of pumpkin batter. Top with remaining batter.

4. Using a skewer or knitting needle, swirl cream cheese mixture into batter by making figure eights.

5. Bake 40-45 minutes, or until edges start to pull away from the sides of the pan, and a knife inserted near the center comes out clean. Cool on a wire rack before inverting onto a serving plate.

Preparation time: 25 minutes
Cooking time: 40-45 minutes

Serves 10-12

Needed items
  medium and large bowls
  sifter
  9-inch tube pan
  skewer or knitting needle
  wire rack

For the swirl:
  8 ounces cream cheese (regular or reduced-fat)
  2 tablespoons orange juice
  1 teaspoon vanilla extract

For the cake:
  3 cups all-purpose flour
  1 cup granulated sugar
  3 teaspoons baking powder
  1½ teaspoons ground cinnamon
  1 teaspoon baking soda
  ½ teaspoon ground nutmeg
  ½ teaspoon ground cloves
  ¼ teaspoon salt
  1 15-ounce can pumpkin (not pie filling)
  1 cup milk (regular or nonfat)
  2 egg whites
  2 tablespoons butter or margarine, melted
  1 tablespoon finely grated orange zest
  non-stick cooking spray

Needed items

mixer with dough hook
  attachment (optional)
small, medium and large bowls
2 9-inch round cake pans
rolling pin
plastic wrap

1   cup warm milk (about 110° F)
1   packet active dry yeast
2   eggs, lightly beaten
¼   cup granulated sugar
½   teaspoon salt
3½ cups all-purpose flour
1   cup packed light brown sugar,
      divided
¾   cup maple syrup, divided
2   tablespoons butter or
      margarine, melted
1½ cups raisins, divided
1½ cups pecans or walnuts,
      broken up, divided
2   teaspoons ground cinnamon
    non-stick cooking spray

Pecan-Raisin Sticky Buns

You can substitute frozen bread dough if desired—just thaw according to package directions and pick up at step 3.

Make ahead tip: After you arrange slices in the cake pans (step 5), cover the pans with plastic wrap (or wax paper that has been coated with non-stick spray). Cover the plastic with foil and refrigerate overnight or freeze for up to 1 month. Let refrigerated dough stand at room temperature 2 hours before baking and let frozen sticky buns thaw completely (about 4 hours) before baking.

1. In a large mixing bowl (fitted with a dough hook if possible), dissolve yeast in warm milk. Let stand 5 minutes. Add eggs, granulated sugar, and salt and whisk until blended. Add flour and mix until a manageable dough forms. Knead with the dough hook for 2 minutes (or transfer to a lightly floured surface and knead 10 minutes by hand).

2. Transfer dough to a large bowl that has been coated with non-stick spray and turn to coat all sides. Cover bowl with a dish towel and let rise in a warm place free from draft until doubled in bulk, about 1 hour.

3. Meanwhile, in a small bowl, whisk together ¼ cup of the brown sugar, ¼ cup plus 2 tablespoons of the maple syrup, and melted butter. Divide mixture in half and pour into the bottom of two 9-inch round cake pans. Tilt the pans to coat the surface. Top mixture with ½ cup each raisins and pecans (¼ cup each per pan). Set aside.

4. To make the filling, combine remaining ¾ cup brown sugar, remaining ¼ cup plus 2 tablespoons maple syrup, and cinnamon in a medium bowl. Mix until blended.

5. Punch dough down, transfer to a lightly floured surface and roll out to an 11x15-inch rectangle. Top dough with filling mixture, spreading mixture to within ½-inch of the edges. Top with remaining raisins and pecans. Starting at the shorter end, roll up dough into a tight pinwheel (jellyroll fashion). Slice roll crosswise into 1-inch thick slices and place slices, side-by-side, in prepared cake pans (place one slice in the middle of the pan and remaining slices around the outside). Cover pans loosely with plastic wrap and let rise in a warm place free from draft for 45 minutes.

6. Preheat oven to 375° F.

7. Remove plastic wrap and bake sticky buns 18 minutes, or until golden. Remove from oven and let stand 1 minute. Invert pans onto serving plates and serve warm.

Preparation and rising time: 2 hours
Cooking time: 18 minutes

Serves 6-8

Apple-Cinnamon Coffee Cake

Add toasted almonds or walnuts to the topping for added flavor and crunch.

1. Preheat oven to 350° F.
2. In a large bowl, combine flour, sugar, baking powder, cinnamon, and salt. Mix well with a fork, make a well in the center, and set aside.
3. In a medium bowl, whisk together applesauce, milk, melted butter, egg, and vanilla. Fold mixture into dry ingredients until just blended.
4. Pour batter into an 8-inch square cake pan that has been coated with non-stick spray.
5. Bake 45 minutes, or until a wooden pick inserted near the center comes out almost clean (little bits clinging to the pick mean the cake's still moist).
6. Remove cake from the oven and while still warm, sprinkle the top with a mixture of the cinnamon and sugar. Cool cake in pan on a wire rack 10 minutes before slicing.

Preparation time: 20 minutes
Cooking time: 45 minutes

Makes one 8-inch cake (6-8 servings)

Needed items
  medium and large bowls
  8-inch square cake pan
  wire rack

1½ cups all-purpose flour
1   cup granulated sugar
1½ teaspoons baking powder
1   teaspoon ground cinnamon
½   teaspoon salt
1   cup chunky applesauce
½   cup milk (regular or nonfat)
2   tablespoons butter or
       margarine, melted
1   egg
1   teaspoon vanilla extract
     non-stick cooking spray

For the topping:
½   teaspoon ground cinnamon
2   tablespoons granulated sugar

Needed items
    griddle or a large non-stick skillet
    medium and large bowls

1½ cups all-purpose flour
 3 tablespoons granulated sugar
1¾ teaspoons baking powder
 ½ teaspoon salt
 1 cup milk (regular or nonfat)
 2 egg whites
 1 teaspoon vanilla extract
 4 tablespoons mini semi-sweet
      chocolate chips
    non-stick cooking spray

Chocolate Chip Pancakes

A little indulgence in the wee hours? Why not? If chocolate chips aren't your passion, substitute fresh fruit (blueberries, raspberries, diced apples, or sliced bananas) and start the day off with a smile.

1. Preheat griddle or a large non-stick skillet that has been coated with non-stick spray.
2. In a medium bowl, combine flour, sugar, baking powder, and salt. Mix well with a fork and set aside.
3. In a large bowl, whisk together milk, egg whites, and vanilla. Add milk mixture to dry ingredients and whisk until almost smooth (ignore any small lumps).
4. Ladle 3 tablespoons of batter onto hot griddle for each pancake. Spoon 1 teaspoon of the chocolate chips onto each pancake. When bubbles appear around the edges, flip pancake and cook 1 minute. Transfer to a warm plate and keep warm (in a 250° F oven) while you cook remaining pancakes.

Preparation and cooking time: *Makes twelve 4-inch pancakes*
30 minutes

Needed items
    medium bowls
    large baking sheet

 1 6-ounce package mixed dried
      fruit bits (or mixed dried fruit
      cut in pieces)
 ½ cup dried cranberries
 2 tablespoons light brown sugar
 1 cup hot water
 3 cups rolled oats (regular or
      quick cooking)
 ½ cup sliced almonds
 ½ cup raw sunflower seeds
 ¼ cup shredded coconut
 2 tablespoons nonfat dry milk
      powder
 1 teaspoon ground cinnamon

Crunchy Roasted Granola

A great snack to have on hand. Eat this wonderfully crunchy mixture by itself, with milk, or sprinkled over yogurt, ice cream, or fresh fruit. In between snack-attacks, store the granola in an airtight container or zip-top bag.

1. Preheat oven to 250° F.
2. In a medium bowl, combine dried fruit, cranberries, and brown sugar. Pour over hot water and let stand 15 minutes.
3. Meanwhile, combine oats, almonds, sunflower seeds, coconut, dry milk, and cinnamon. Add raisin mixture (with soaking liquid) to dry ingredients, mix well, and transfer to a large baking sheet.
4. Bake 1 hour, stirring every 15 minutes, or until golden and crisp.

Preparation and cooking time: 1½ hours   *Makes 7 cups*

Super Bowl Sunday

I start thinking about the Superbowl in December. Not because I love football, but because I love cooking for a crowd of friends. And, they love my chili. Serve this hearty chili with Parmesan-Sesame Bread Sticks (they look really cool laying across the bowl) and a tossed green salad topped with slices of tart green apples (the apples are the perfect accompaniment for spicy chili). Don't forget to keep lots of cold beer on hand!

Menu

Super Chili

Four Bean Vegetarian Chili

Goat Cheese Quesadillas
with Green Chile Salsa

Parmesan-Sesame
Bread Sticks

Almond-Raisin
Oatmeal Bars

Needed items
large stockpot
colander

4   teaspoons olive oil, divided
2   pounds lean ground beef or
      turkey
1   Spanish onion, chopped (about
      2 cups)
4   celery stalks, chopped
2   garlic cloves, minced
1   jalapeño pepper, seeded and
      minced
4   tablespoons chili powder
2   tablespoons ground cumin
2   teaspoons dried Mexican
      oregano or regular oregano
2   bay leaves
½   teaspoon salt
½   teaspoon crushed red pepper
      flakes, or more to taste
2   28-ounce cans diced tomatoes
3   cups beef or chicken broth
2   8-ounce cans tomato sauce
4   19-ounce cans red kidney
      beans, rinsed and drained
      grated cheddar cheese or sour
      cream
      chopped green onions
      (optional)

Super Chili

Feel free to make the chili a day or two in advance. Keep refrigerated and on game day, just reheat and serve. If any fat rises to the surface when the chili is "chilled," skim it off with a spoon before reheating.

1. Heat 2 teaspoons of the oil in a large stockpot over medium heat. Add ground beef and sauté until browned and cooked through, breaking up the meat as it cooks. Transfer to a colander to drain fat.

2. Heat remaining 2 teaspoons of oil in the same stockpot over medium heat. Add onion, celery, garlic, and jalapeño and sauté 4 minutes, or until tender and golden. Return beef to pot. Add chili powder, cumin, oregano, bay leaves, salt, and red pepper flakes and stir to coat vegetables and meat with spices. Add tomatoes, broth, tomato sauce, and beans and bring mixture to a boil. Reduce heat, partially cover, and simmer 1 hour.

3. To serve, discard bay leaves, ladle chili into bowls and top with grated cheddar or sour cream and chopped green onions.

Preparation and cooking time: 1½ hours   *Serves 6-8*

Four Bean Vegetarian Chili

A great vegetarian version. Couscous is added at the end to thicken the broth and round out the dish (you can add up to ½ cup couscous for a super-thick chili). You can also substitute any small pasta or rice, if desired.

1. Heat oil in a large stockpot over medium heat. Add onion, leek, green pepper, garlic, and jalapeño and sauté 4 minutes, or until tender.

2. Add chili powder, oregano, cumin, coriander, bay leaf, and salt and stir to coat vegetables with herbs and spices. Add tomatoes and simmer 2 minutes.

3. Add vegetable broth and canned beans and bring mixture to a boil. Reduce heat, partially cover, and simmer 20 minutes.

4. Add couscous, lima beans, and habañero sauce and simmer 5 minutes, or until mixture thickens.

Preparation and cooking time: 40 minutes   *Serves 6*

Needed items
large stockpot

- 2 teaspoons olive or vegetable oil
- 1 Spanish onion, chopped (about 2 cups)
- 1 leek, green portion discarded, white portion halved, rinsed and chopped
- 1 green bell pepper, seeded and chopped
- 2 garlic cloves, minced
- 1 jalapeño pepper, seeded and minced
- 2 tablespoons chili powder
- 1 tablespoon dried Mexican oregano or regular oregano
- 2 teaspoons ground cumin
- 1 teaspoon ground coriander
- 1 bay leaf
- ½ teaspoon salt
- 1 28-ounce can diced tomatoes
- 4 cups vegetable broth or water
- 1 19-ounce can black beans, rinsed and drained
- 1 19-ounce can white kidney (cannellini) beans, rinsed and drained
- 1 19-ounce can red kidney beans, rinsed and drained
- ⅓ cup uncooked couscous
- 1 cup frozen baby or regular lima beans
- 1-2 teaspoons habañero or other hot sauce

Needed items
baking sheets
medium bowls
aluminum foil

For the goat cheese quesadillas:
8 8-inch flour tortillas
4 ounces mild goat cheese
4 ounces grated Monterey Jack
   cheese (regular or reduced-fat)
1 19-ounce can black beans,
   rinsed and drained
¼ cup chopped fresh cilantro
1 tablespoon chili powder
   non-stick cooking spray

For the green chile salsa:
1 ripe beefsteak tomato, halved
   crosswise
1 4-ounce can chopped green
   chiles
1 tablespoon fresh lime juice
¼ teaspoon ground black pepper

Needed items
large saucepan
baking sheet
wire whisk

1 cup water
2 tablespoons butter or margarine
½ teaspoon salt
¼ teaspoon ground black pepper
1 cup all-purpose flour
½ teaspoon baking powder
⅓ cup buttermilk
1 egg
½ cup grated Parmesan cheese
¼ cup raw sesame seeds
   non-stick cooking spray

Goat Cheese Quesadillas with Green Chile Salsa

1. Preheat oven to 350° F.

2. To make the quesadillas, place four tortillas on baking sheets (2 tortillas per sheet) that have been coated with non-stick spray. Set aside.

3. In a medium bowl, combine goat cheese, Monterey Jack, beans, cilantro, and chili powder. Mix well and spoon mixture evenly onto the center of each tortilla, leaving a ½-inch border around the edges. Top with second tortilla and press down gently.

4. Cover with foil and bake 25 minutes.

5. Meanwhile, to make the salsa, squeeze tomato halves to remove seeds. Chop tomato into small dice and transfer to a medium bowl. Add remaining ingredients and toss to combine.

6. Slice each tortilla into wedges and serve with salsa.

Preparation time: 20 minutes
Cooking time: 25 minutes

Serves 4-6

Parmesan-Sesame Bread Sticks

1. Preheat oven to 425° F.

2. Combine water, butter, salt, and pepper in a large saucepan over medium-high heat. Bring mixture to a boil. When butter is melted, gradually add flour and baking powder, stirring constantly with a wire whisk (a whisk works better than a wooden spoon in this recipe). Cook just until mixture pulls away from the sides of the pan. Remove from heat and stir in buttermilk, egg, and Parmesan cheese.

3. Transfer dough to a smooth surface and form into twelve 6-inch logs, about 1 inch wide. Roll logs in sesame seeds to coat all sides.

4. Place logs on a baking sheet that has been coated with non-stick spray and bake 30-35 minutes, until golden.

Preparation time: 20 minutes
Cooking time: 30-35 minutes

Makes 12 breadsticks

Almond-Raisin Oatmeal Bars

1. Preheat oven to 350° F.

2. In a medium bowl, combine flour, cinnamon, baking powder, baking soda, and salt. Mix well with a fork and set aside.

3. In a large mixing bowl, beat together butter and both sugars until blended. Add egg and vanilla and beat until light and fluffy. Beat in milk. Gradually add flour mixture and mix until blended. Fold in oats, raisins, and almonds.

4. Press mixture into a 11x7-inch baking pan that has been coated with non-stick spray.

5. Bake 35-40 minutes, or until a wooden pick inserted near the center comes out almost clean (little bits clinging to the pick are fine). Cool in pan, on a wire rack, before slicing into 24 bars.

Preparation time: 20 minutes
Cooking time: 35-40 minutes

Makes 24 bars

Needed items
  medium and large bowls
  mixer
  11 x 7-inch baking pan
  wire rack

⅔ cup all-purpose flour
1 ½ teaspoons ground cinnamon
½ teaspoon baking powder
½ teaspoon baking soda
¼ teaspoon salt
½ cup (1 stick) butter or margarine, softened
1 cup packed light brown sugar
¼ cup granulated sugar
1 egg
2 teaspoons vanilla extract
⅓ cup milk (regular or nonfat)
3 cups rolled oats (regular or quick cooking)
1 cup raisins
½ cup sliced almonds
  non-stick cooking spray

Picnic for Two

Menu

Pasta Salad with Almonds
and Grapes

Sundried Tomato Pesto
with Sourdough Bread

Chocolate-Hazelnut
Cookies with White
Chocolate Chips

Imagine yourself sitting on a blanket under a huge tree, sipping wine and eating wonderful food with the one you love. Add a couple of friendly ants, and you've got a picnic. This menu was designed for a few reasons: first, the salad is made with pasta, so you don't have to worry about the food safety issues associated with chicken. Second, the pesto can be made in advance. And third, the cookies are really good. As for beverages, bring along a chilled bottle of white wine (don't forget the bottle opener!) or a thermos of home-made lemonade.

Pasta Salad with Almonds and Grapes

This recipe makes enough for four people, meaning there can be great leftovers for the return home.

1. In a large stockpot, cook pasta according to package directions, drain, and transfer to a large bowl. Add sour cream, sherry vinegar, and salt and mix well. Fold in grapes, almonds, and diced cucumber.

2. Cover with plastic wrap and refrigerate until ready to serve.

Preparation and cooking time: 25 minutes   *Serves 4*

* Toast almonds by heating in a small skillet over medium heat until golden, shaking the pan frequently (it should take about 3-5 minutes).

Needed items
  large stockpot
  large bowl
  small skillet
  plastic wrap

  8 ounces uncooked bowtie (farfalle) pasta
  1 cup sour cream (regular or nonfat)
  2 tablespoons sherry vinegar
  ½ teaspoon salt
  1 cup green seedless grapes, halved
  1 cup red seedless grapes, halved
  ½ cup sliced almonds, lightly toasted*
  1 cucumber, peeled and diced

Sundried Tomato Pesto with Sourdough Bread

1. In a blender or food processor fitted with the metal blade, combine tomatoes, water, garlic, basil, balsamic vinegar, sugar, and salt. Process until smooth. Transfer mixture to a sealable container and refrigerate until ready to serve.

2. Slice sourdough crosswise into thick slices and top with pesto.

Preparation time: 10 minutes   *Serves 2*

Needed items
  blender or food processor
  sealable container

  1 cup sundried tomatoes (packed without oil)
  1 cup warm water
  1 garlic clove
  ¼ cup packed fresh basil leaves
  1 tablespoon balsamic vinegar
  1 tablespoon granulated sugar
  ½ teaspoon salt
  1 sourdough baguette (about ½ pound)

Needed items
double boiler or medium bowl
and medium saucepan
large mixing bowl
mixer
baking sheets
wire rack

½ cup (1 stick) unsalted butter
or margarine
8 1-ounce squares semi-sweet
chocolate
4 1-ounce squares unsweetened
chocolate
4 eggs
2 cups granulated sugar
2 teaspoons vanilla extract
1 ¼ cups all-purpose flour
½ teaspoon baking powder
2 cups chopped hazelnuts
12 ounces white chocolate morsels
non-stick cooking spray

Chocolate-Hazelnut Cookies with White Chocolate Chips

These decadent cookies stay puffed up when they cook, yielding a chocolatey, chunky dream-come-true. You can substitute macadamia nuts for the hazelnuts and white chocolate chunks for the morsels, if desired.

1. Preheat oven to 350° F.
2. Melt butter and both chocolates (semi-sweet and unsweetened) together in the top of a double boiler or medium bowl over simmering water. Set aside to cool slightly.
3. In a large mixing bowl, beat together eggs and sugar until pale and foamy. Gradually add chocolate mixture and vanilla. Stir in flour and baking powder. Fold in nuts and white chocolate morsels.
4. Drop dough by heaping tablespoons onto baking sheets that have been coated with non-stick spray, at least 1 inch apart.
5. Bake 15 minutes, or until firm. Cool on baking sheets 5 minutes. Transfer to wire racks to cool completely.

Preparation time: 20 minutes
Cooking time: 15 minutes

Makes 48 cookies

Breakfast in Bed

There's no better way to start a morning than with breakfast in bed. The sneaky cook enjoys preparing this special, loving meal (quickly, before his or her spouse wakes up), while the recipient gets to stay snuggled in bed (pretending to be asleep, but smelling wonderful smells and waiting with great anticipation).

Menu

Breakfast Quesadillas

Strawberry Smoothie

Corn and Red Potato Hash

Needed items
  medium bowl
  large non-stick skillet
  baking sheet
  oven-proof plates

  5 eggs
  ¼ cup mild, medium or hot salsa
  2 tablespoons milk (regular or
       nonfat)
  ½ teaspoon salt
  ¼ teaspoon ground black pepper
  2 teaspoons olive or vegetable oil
  4 6-inch flour tortillas
  ⅔ cup grated Monterey Jack
       cheese (regular or reduced-fat)
     non-stick cooking spray

Breakfast Quesadillas

1. Preheat oven to 400° F.

2. In a medium bowl, whisk together eggs, salsa, milk, salt, and pepper.

3. Heat oil in a large non-stick skillet over medium heat. Add egg mixture and cook until just cooked through (not dry), about 3-4 minutes, stirring constantly.

4. Place two tortillas on a baking sheet that has been coated with non-stick spray. Spoon an equal amount of egg mixture onto each tortilla and top with an equal amount of cheese. Place second flour tortilla on top. Weigh down both quesadillas with oven-proof plates.

5. Bake 10 minutes, or until cheese melts. Slide quesadillas onto plates and slice into quarters.

Preparation time: 20 minutes
Cooking time: 10 minutes

Serves 2

Needed items
  blender

  1 cup fresh strawberries, hulled
  1 banana
  1 cup vanilla yogurt (regular
       or nonfat)
  1 cup ice
  1 teaspoon vanilla extract

Strawberry Smoothie

1. In a blender, combine all ingredients and process until smooth. Pour mixture into tall glasses and serve.

Preparation time: 10 minutes

Serves 2

Corn and Red Potato Hash

A favorite since colonial times, hash is traditionally a combination of corned beef, roast beef, bell peppers, and potatoes. This variation eliminates meat altogether and substitutes sweet corn. The distinct taste of red wine vinegar livens up the dish and intensifies the potato flavor.

1. Blanch potatoes in a large pot of rapidly boiling water for 8 minutes. Drain and set aside.

2. Heat oil in a large non-stick skillet over medium heat. Add onion and sauté 2 minutes, or until tender. Add potatoes, corn, paprika, salt, and pepper and stir to coat. Add chicken broth and vinegar and simmer 2 minutes, or until liquid is absorbed.

Preparation and cooking time: 25 minutes   *Serves 2*

Needed items
  large stockpot
  large non-stick skillet

  4 small red potatoes, diced
  2 teaspoons olive or vegetable oil
  1 small onion, diced (about
       ½ cup)
  ½ cup fresh or frozen corn
       (thawed)
  ½ teaspoon paprika
  ½ teaspoon salt
  ¼ teaspoon ground black pepper
  ¼ cup chicken broth
  2 tablespoons red wine vinegar

When In-Laws Come for Dinner

Menu

Sure-Fire Shish Kebabs

Rice, Corn, and Green
Chile Timbales

Chocolate-Swirled
Cheesecake

Preparing that first meal for in-laws can be pretty frightening. You want the meal to be perfect, and you want parents to rest assured you're both "eating well." Don't be nervous. In fact, with these recipes, be proud. Serve tangy beef kabobs with impressive rice timbales—little towers of flavor. Whip up a salad by tossing together mixed baby greens, arugula, and halved cherry tomatoes. Top the salad with shaved Parmesan (use a vegetable peeler) and your favorite vinaigrette dressing. For the grand finale, impress everyone with a silky-smooth, chocolate-swirled cheesecake. Serve dinner with a deep red wine, such as a Merlot or Cabernet Sauvignon.

Have all the ingredients cut up and ready to go before your guests arrive. That way you'll have time to socialize before dinner, and you won't be stuck in the kitchen.

Sure-Fire Shish-Kebabs

1. In a shallow dish, combine soy sauce, mustard, brown sugar, garlic powder, and pepper. Add steak, onion, bell peppers, and mushrooms and toss to coat. Cover with plastic wrap and refrigerate 15 minutes (and up to 24 hours).

2. Preheat grill or broiler.

3. Remove meat and vegetables from marinade (discard marinade) and skewer alternating pieces onto metal or wooden skewers (when using wooden skewers, soak them in water first to prevent burning).

4. Grill skewers 8 minutes, turning frequently, or until meat is cooked through and vegetables are tender-crisp.

Preparation and cooking time: 35 minutes   *Serves 4*

Needed items
  shallow dish
  skewers
  plastic wrap

¼ cup soy sauce
1 tablespoon Dijon mustard
1 tablespoon light brown sugar
¼ teaspoon garlic powder
¼ teaspoon ground black pepper
1 pound sirloin steak, cut into
    2-inch cubes
1 large red onion, cut into
    2-inch pieces
2 green bell peppers, seeded and
    cut into 2-inch pieces
2 yellow bell peppers, seeded
    and cut into 2-inch pieces
½ pound small button mushrooms,
    stems trimmed

Needed items
large saucepan
4 6-ounce custard cups or any
   small cups

2 teaspoons olive oil
1 cup Basmati or long grain
   white rice
½ cup frozen corn
1 4-ounce can chopped
   green chiles
2 teaspoons ground cumin
½ teaspoon salt
¼ teaspoon ground black pepper
2 cups chicken broth or water
   non-stick cooking spray

Rice, Corn, and Green Chile Timbales

Timbale (tim-BAL-ay) is the French word for "kettle drum" meaning cooked in a small, high-sided, drum-shaped mold. But, you don't really need a drum-shaped mold, and, for this recipe, you don't actually cook anything in the mold. Just press the rice mixture into small custard cups (the truth is, I pressed the mixture into the 4-ounce chile can once it was empty!) and then invert the molds onto plates. It's easy, quick, and makes a great presentation.

Note: You can prepare the timbales in advance and refrigerate overnight (in the molds). Reheat in the microwave or set them in a large shallow baking dish (in ¼-inch of water) and bake 30 minutes at 350° F. Unmold as directed.

1. Heat oil in a large saucepan over medium heat. Add rice and cook until translucent, about 2-3 minutes, stirring constantly. Add corn, chiles, cumin, salt, and pepper and mix well. Add chicken broth and bring mixture to a boil. Reduce heat, cover, and simmer 20 minutes, or until rice is tender and liquid is absorbed.

2. Coat four 6-ounce custard cups (or any small cups, empty tuna cans, etc.) with non-stick spray. Spoon rice mixture into prepared cups and pack down with the back of a spoon. Invert cups onto dinner plates, tap the bottom with your hand and remove cup.

Preparation and cooking time: 35 minutes   *Serves 4*

Chocolate-Swirled Cheesecake

Note the cooling technique for this recipe. It's important that cheesecake be allowed to cool slowly, to prevent the surface from cracking. Also, you can make the cheesecake up to two days ahead of time. Wrap in plastic and refrigerate until ready to serve.

1. Preheat oven to 300° F.
2. To make the crust, combine graham cracker crumbs, melted butter and sugar in a medium bowl. Mix well with a fork to combine. Press the mixture into the bottom of a 9-inch springform pan that has been coated with non-stick spray. Set aside.
3. To make the filling, melt chocolate in a double boiler or medium bowl over simmering water. Set aside to cool slightly.
4. In a large mixing bowl, combine cream cheese, sour cream, egg, and vanilla. Mix on low speed until smooth and creamy. Fold in sugar and flour. Pour filling into prepared pan.
5. Drizzle melted chocolate over surface of cheesecake. Using a toothpick (or knitting needle) swirl the chocolate into the filling, just until decorative swirls form (don't over-swirl, or you'll lose the effect!).
6. Bake 1 hour, or until center is set. Turn off oven, prop open the oven door (not all the way, just slightly), and allow the cake to cool 15 minutes. Transfer pan to a wire rack and cool completely. Cover with plastic wrap and refrigerate until ready to serve.

Preparation time: 20 minutes
Cooking and cooling time: 1 hour 15 minutes

Makes one 9-inch cheesecake
(12 servings)

Needed items
  medium bowl
  9-inch springform pan
  double boiler or medium bowl
    and medium saucepan
  large mixing bowl
  mixer
  toothpick or knitting needle
  wire rack
  plastic wrap

For the Crust:
  1 cup chocolate graham cracker
    crumbs
  3 tablespoons butter or
    margarine, melted
  2 tablespoons granulated sugar
    non-stick cooking spray

For the Filling:
  1 6-ounce package semi-sweet
    chocolate morsels
  2 8-ounce packages cream
    cheese (regular or nonfat),
    softened
  1¼ cups sour cream (regular
    or nonfat)
  1 egg
  2 teaspoons vanilla extract
  1 cup granulated sugar
  6 tablespoons all-purpose flour

Herbs and Spices

Adobo Seasoning
Mexican blend of spices, usually consisting of cumin, garlic, black pepper, oregano, turmeric, and salt.

Allspice
Brown, rough-textured, dried berries resembling large peppercorns. Also called pimento or Jamaican pepper (one of the main spices in Jamaican "jerk" seasoning). Aroma and flavor of cinnamon, nutmeg, and cloves. Used heavily in the Middle East, West Indies and Central America for seasoning seafood, meat, and vegetables. In Northern and Eastern Europe, whole allspice berries are used mainly for pickling seafood and meat. Can be used to add flavor to all types of marinades, chutneys, puddings, and rice dishes. Frequently paired with nutmeg, cloves, and cinnamon for baking.

Ancho Chile
Ripened and dried poblano chile. Deep reddish-brown in color. Mild to very hot.

A

Anise

Greenish-brown, lightly striped oval seeds with mild, licorice-like flavor. Used to add perfume to tomato sauces and to flavor breads, cakes, candies, chutneys, plum puddings, pastries, biscotti, and rice dishes. Anise also has a particular affinity for shellfish and is frequently added to mayonnaise and served with cooked lobster.

Annatto or Achiote

Fragrant seeds, native to tropical America and the Caribbean, that are frequently ground into a paste and used to color (bright orange) and flavor meats and fish. Important ingredient in Mexican cooking.

B

Basil

Sweet and fragrant. The fresh taste of basil pairs perfectly with tomatoes, egg dishes, fish, and Mediterranean vegetables, such as eggplant, zucchini, and bell peppers. Best added to hot dishes just before serving as fresh herbs often lose flavor when cooked. Leaves should be torn or gently chopped to prevent bruising and preserve flavor.

Bay Leaves

Pungent, complex flavor. Used both fresh and dried in bouquet garnis, stews, soups, stocks, and marinades. When dried and crumbled, leaves infuse distinct flowery taste to oils. Usually associated with French and Mediterranean cooking.

Bouquet Garnis

Bundle of fresh herbs, typically bay leaves, parsley, and thyme, tied together with string and used to season soups, stews, and stocks. May also contain rosemary, oregano, and black peppercorns.

Caraway Seeds

Skinny, hard, and ridged chestnut-brown seeds with slight licorice, mildly bitter flavor. The distinct smoky and nutty character is used widely in Northern and Central European and Jewish cookery to season fruit and pork dishes, cakes, breads, cheese, and sausage. Synonymous with the flavor of rye bread.

Cardamom

A member of the ginger family. Small green, white, or brown pods hold tiny irregular-shaped dark brown seeds. Green pods are natural, white are bleached, and brown have delicate smoky flavor. All have a strong floral-citrus taste and aroma with a hint of pepper and ginger. Essential ingredient in Indian curries, the spice mix garam masala and bean and vegetable dishes. Used in Northern and Eastern Europe for pickling and to season cakes and pastries. Pairs well with cooked fruits, especially peaches.

Cayenne Pepper

Reddish-orange powder made from dried cayenne peppers. Extremely hot, with a sharp taste and bitter smell. Adds zest to cheese and egg dishes when used sparingly. Pairs well with fish and shellfish and is frequently used as a condiment with oysters, crab, and lobster.

Celery Seed

Tiny, green-brown dried seeds of wild celery. Intense celery flavor is used to season salad dressings, dips, egg dishes, pickles, soups, stews, breads, crackers, and tomato juice. Excellent rubbed on beef before roasting. Seeds can be bitter when used to excess.

Chervil

Similar flavor to parsley with a sweet and mild anise taste. Used to flavor poultry, fish, and vegetable dishes.

Chili Powder

Dried and ground chiles, sometimes mixed with other ground spices and herbs, such as cumin, curry, and coriander.

C

Chinese 5-Spice

A licorice-scented powder made with star anise, Szechwan peppercorns, fennel, cinnamon, and cloves. Used in soups and stews, and to season meat and poultry.

Chipotle Chile

Light brown, dried smoked jalapeño, often packed in adobo sauce. Mild to very hot.

Chives

A member of the onion family with a similar, more delicate flavor. Frequently chopped and used to garnish egg dishes, sauces and soups, salads, and mixed vegetable dishes. Can be cut up and frozen until ready to use.

Cilantro

Fresh, sharp flavor and similar shape to flat-leaf parsley. Important component of Asian and South/Central American dishes, salsas, and uncooked sauces for vegetables, meat, fish, and poultry.

Cinnamon

Dried inner bark of the low-growing evergreen bush. The peeled bark is cut into thin strips and then dried in the sun. As the strips dry, they curl inside each other, making the familiar quill-shape we see at the market. Sweet, fragrant spice is used extensively to flavor meat dishes in the Middle East and to add a distinct flavor to the curry and rice dishes of India and Asia. Pairs well with chocolate and coffee and is used heavily in cakes, cookies, custards, and spiced wines. Whole cinnamon sticks infuse flavor into teas, ciders, and stews.

Cloves

Young, unopened flower bud of the clove tree. When dried, this reddish-brown, nail-shaped spice becomes one of the strongest spices (in fact, it can overpower a dish if used too heavily). Used in curries, sauces and stocks, apple dishes, pickles, spiced wine, and pickled fish. Adds depth and warmth to long-simmered red meat stews. Pairs well with salty foods, such as baked ham.

Coriander

Tan, round, papery seeds of the fresh cilantro plant. Seeds are milder than cilantro leaves, and have a sweet, light citrus taste with a hint of caraway. Used with fish, in sausages, chutneys, breads, cakes, and as a pickling spice. Can also be used to flavor roasted meat and to season curry dishes. In India, coriander is often lightly roasted and ground before using in order to extract more flavor.

Cream of Tartar

White crystalline form of salt. Used to prevent sugar from crystallizing in candies, frostings, and sweet desserts. Also used to control the rise of dough in baking.

Cumin

Small, dried, slender, light-brown ribbed seeds, similar in looks to caraway. Deep, pungent, and smoky spice with an earthy aroma. Frequently used in the blending of curry and chili powders in Indian, North African, and Mexican cooking. Works well as a spice rub before grilling or roasting. Ground cumin is often added to salsas, dips, vinaigrettes, and yogurt-based dressings.

Curry Paste

A thick paste consisting of chiles, garlic and seasonings. Used as the basis for classic curries and available in four varieties - red, green, Massaman, and Panaeng.

Curry Powder

A mixture of spices used in Indian cooking. Traditionally comprised of turmeric, coriander, cumin, cayenne, cardamom, cinnamon, cloves, fennel, fenugreek, ginger, and garlic.

D

Dill
Feathery leaves with a flavor similar to parsley and fennel. Perfect partner for fish.

Dill Seed
Flat, oval, yellowish-brown seeds of the dill plant. Sharp, piquant, slightly bitter flavor reminiscent of caraway and anise. Used to season the brine for dill pickles. Excellent partner for fish and pairs well with cauliflower, green beans, cabbage, and root vegetables. Popular in salad dressings, cole slaw, and egg and potato-based dishes. Occasionally used in breads and muffins.

F

Fennel
Three great parts—a feathery herb, an aromatic seed and a bulbous vegetable. The herb and seeds have strong anise flavors. Italian cooks use fresh leaves with pork, veal, and fish and in soups and salads. The seeds are often lightly crushed or ground and used in Mediterranean seafood dishes and tomato sauce, as a rub for seafood, pork, lamb, and beef, and in curries, Italian sausages, breads, cakes, fruit tarts, and sweet pickling spices.

Filé Powder (Gumbo Filé)
Olive-green powder from dried, ground sassafras. Woodsy and earthy flavor with slightly sweet note, suggestive of root beer. Added at the end of cooking as a thickener and flavoring in gumbos, spicy soups, and stews.

Fines Herbes
A mixture of fresh parsley, chervil, tarragon, and chives.

G

Garam Masala
An Indian spice blend of cardamom, coriander, cumin, cinnamon, cloves, black pepper, and nutmeg.

Garlic Powder
Dried, ground garlic cloves. ⅛ teaspoon equals 1 clove.

Ginger
Fine, buff-colored powder from dried, ground ginger rhizome. Sweet-hot flavor with a refreshing, sharp, almost lemony, pungency. Used predominantly in sweet dishes, such as breads, cakes, cookies, sauces, custards, fruit dishes, and pickles, as well as in ginger beer and wine. Also used heavily in Indian, Asian, and Moroccan savory dishes and curries. Ground ginger is not interchangeable with fresh.

J

Juniper Berries
Purple-black, leathery, dried berries the size of peas. Strongly aromatic and sweet with a hint of pine. Because of its strong flavor, juniper pairs well with venison, dark-meat game birds, and other robust game meats. Also used in stuffings, sauces, patés, meat stews, red wine marinades, sauerkraut, apple and pear dishes, and with pork and chicken. Berries should be crushed before using to bring out their inherent taste and aroma.

L

Lemongrass
A tough, reed-like plant with a strong lemon flavor and aroma. The tough outer stalks and roots should be removed before chopping the softer, inner stalks. Used heavily in Asian cooking.

Lemon Peel
Thinly pared outer rind (yellow portion only) of a mature lemon that is dried and milled. Used in place of fresh lemons and fresh lemon peel in breads, cakes, cookies, custards, and cream sauces for chicken, lamb, and pork.

Lemon Pepper
Citrus-flavored seasoning made from salt, coarse black pepper, red and green bell peppers, garlic, onion, and lemon flavoring. An all-purpose seasoning that can be used to season roasted and baked meat, poultry, and fish.

M

Mace
The thin, lacy seed covering of nutmeg with similar warm, sweet, and rich flavor. Unique, musty quality used to season stews and sauces, fish, meat (particularly veal and chicken), and vegetables. Also adds flavor to cream sauces, poaching liquids, and clear stocks.

Marjoram
Sweet-scented herb similar in flavor to oregano. Used extensively with grilled meat and poultry, stuffings, sausages, garlic-flavored dishes, and pizzas. Has a great affinity with thyme and the two herbs are often mixed together or substituted for one another.

Mexican Oregano
A dried variety of oregano with a more complex, aromatic flavor.

Mint
Refreshing menthol flavor and aroma. There are three varieties of mint—spearmint, peppermint, and Apple or Bowles mint. Spearmint is the variety most commonly used in cooking and it is often paired with strong meats, such as lamb, mutton, and duck. Its distinctive summer taste goes well with summer fruits and vegetables, such as tomatoes, cucumbers, eggplant, zucchini, and fresh summer berries. Spearmint is also used in fruit salads, punches, and iced teas. Apple mint combines the taste of mint with that of apples. Peppermint is the strongest mint variety, and often too strong for cooking. The oil from the leaves is used to flavor liqueurs, peppermint candy, and chocolate.

Mustard (dried)
Found either as whole seeds or ground seeds that have been passed through a fine sieve. Pungent, sharp, and full-flavored. For best results, mix dried mustard in cold water and let stand 10 minutes, allowing the flavor to develop, before using. Main ingredient in prepared mustard. Often used to add flavor to spice rubs, roast beef, ham, sausages, and cream sauces. Whole seeds used in pickling brines and poaching liquids.

Nutmeg

Solid brown, olive-sized, hard seed of the fruit from the Indonesian evergreen tree. Warm, sweet, and rich flavor used frequently by Italian and Middle Eastern cooks to season puddings, custards, eggnog, quiche, meats, vegetables, cheese, and sausage. Often paired with cinnamon and cloves for pies, cakes, and cookies. A dash of nutmeg brings out the cheese taste in mixed dishes, such as lasagna and stuffed shells, and intensifies the flavor of spinach, pumpkin and squash dishes, terrines, and patés. Freshly grinding the hard, brown seed yields a fresher taste than the bottled, powdered variety.

Old Bay Seasoning

Highly seasoned blend of spices, including celery seeds, mustard, red pepper, bay leaves, cloves, allspice, ginger, mace, cardamom, cinnamon, paprika, and salt. Used to season seafood, poultry, meat, and salads.

Oregano

Member of the marjoram family. Strong pungent flavor and aroma. Important ingredient in Italian cooking, frequently used to flavor pizzas, meat, fish, and vegetables.

Paprika

Finely ground powder made from mild to medium pimiento chiles. The intensity of flavors depends on the ratio of flesh to seeds, but much of the paprika sold outside of Hungary is fairly bland. Used extensively in Hungary to season soups, stews and meat, chicken, fish, and vegetable dishes. Makes a colorful garnish when sprinkled over egg and cheese dishes or used in cream sauces. Available hot and sweet.

Parsley

Probably the world's most widely used herb. Two main varieties include curly-leafed and flat-leafed, often referred to as Italian parsley. Curly leaves make a nice garnish, while flat leaves are frequently preferred in cooking. Parsley brings out the flavor of other herbs and is always included

N

O

P

in herb mixtures such as bouquet garnis and fines herbes. Used with all types of fish, shellfish, meat, poultry, game, and vegetables. Fresh parsley is best added at the end of cooking, as cooking diminishes flavor.

Peppercorns
Small, round, dried berries from a tropical vine that come in three varieties—black, white and green—depending on their ripeness and processing. Sharp bite with bold flavor. Black is most familiar, white is hotter and more floral, and green is mild and fresh. Black pepper, cracked or coarsely ground, is excellent pressed onto meats and fish before grilling or sautéing. White pepper is particularly good in white sauces and cream-based dishes. Green peppercorns pair well with fresh vegetables, chicken, and fish.

Pink Peppercorns
Small, bright pink-red berries with a paper-like skin. Mild, floral, and slightly sharp taste. Not a true peppercorn, and delicate, sweet flavor is often used as a colorful garnish for salads and seafood and vegetable dishes.

Poppy Seeds
Nutty-flavored, ripe seeds of the opium poppy. Used extensively in European and Middle Eastern cooking, mainly in sweet dishes such as cakes, strudels, and breads. Can also be used to add flavor to vegetable and pasta dishes.

Poultry Seasoning
Prepared mixture of dried spices, usually some combination of thyme, sage, marjoram, rosemary, black pepper, and nutmeg. Used to season poultry, game, and stuffings.

R

Rosemary
Strong herb with a sweet, floral flavor. Used extensively in Italy to flavor roasted meats and poultry, vegetables, fish, and breads. The stems and leaves of rosemary add wonderful flavor to vinegars and olive oil.

Saffron

Slightly bitter, mildly sweet saffron threads are the whole dried stigmas of the autumn crocus, a beautiful, violet-colored flower. Known as the world's most expensive spice, it takes about seventy-five thousand flowers to produce just one pound of saffron. Steeping the dark orange threads in hot liquid (such as broth or cream) releases and intensifies the characteristic aroma and flavor. Saffron's floral character is used as an essential ingredient in bouillabaisse and paella, and used to flavor fish, shellfish, sauces, soups, and steamed rice, couscous, and pasta dishes. Natural affinity to fennel, garlic, and tomatoes.

Sage

Powerful flavor, pungent and aromatic with a slight camphor taste. Used heavily by Italian cooks in meat dishes (particularly calf's liver and veal) and butter sauces for pasta. Also used throughout the world to flavor cheeses, sausages, and stuffings.

Savory

Similar flavor to thyme, with added peppery taste. Available in two types, summer and winter. Summer savory is excellent in fresh green salads, while winter savory, with its pungent flavor, is better suited to hearty soups and stews. Both are frequently used in fish and meat dishes, sausages, and stuffings, and fresh summer savory is a nice addition to vegetable juices.

Seasoned Salt

Prepared mixture of salt and various spices. Used on grilled and roasted poultry, fish, and vegetables.

Sorrel

Leaves resemble baby spinach and share a similar taste. Widely used in Europe and the Mediterranean to flavor soups, tarts, fish sauces, omelets, meat stews, vegetable dishes, and salads.

S

Star Anise

Dried, star-shaped fruit from the evergreen tree of the magnolia family. Intense licorice aroma and taste, yet sweeter and richer than anise or fennel. Essential ingredient in Chinese 5-Spice and adds a sweet, warm flavor to meat stews and Chinese pork and duck dishes. Pairs well with cinnamon and ginger in savory Asian dishes. The sweet taste can be added to fruit poaching liquids, hot spiced wine, or ground and used in cakes and cookies.

Szechwan (or Sichuan) Peppercorns

Dried, reddish-brown berries from a Chinese tree. Woodsy-spicy flavor. Not related to black peppercorns or chile peppers. Essential ingredient in Chinese 5-Spice and adds exotic flavor to poultry, pork, and red meat dishes. Often combined with fresh ginger and hot chiles, or toasted with salt and used as a condiment.

T

Tandoori Spice Mix

An Indian spice combination consisting of garlic, ginger, coriander, cumin, red pepper, cinnamon, and turmeric.

Tarragon

Pungent, slight anise flavor. One of the four herbs in fines herbes and frequently associated with French cooking. Pairs particularly well with chicken, roasted meat and fish, cream sauces (it's an essential ingredient in Béarnaise sauce), and egg dishes. Fresh leaves can be steeped in wine vinegar and the mixture can be added to salad dressings, vinaigrettes, and mayonnaise-based sauces.

Thyme

Powerful aromatic herb with a slightly bitter flavor. Member of the mint family. One of the herbs of bouquet garnis and used extensively in Mediterranean and French cooking. Used to flavor stocks, stuffings, soups, vegetables, fish, poultry, game, and herb butters. Lemon thyme, with a slight citrus taste and more subtle thyme flavor, is often used in fish, egg, and fruit dishes.

Turmeric
Member of the ginger family, fragrant, curry-like, and slightly bitter. Used to add bright orange-yellow color and mild seasoning to curries, stews, soups, sauces, pickles, chutneys, relishes, drinks, and sweet desserts. Pairs well with meat, seafood, and vegetables and is often used with other spices in North African couscous and Middle Eastern rice dishes. Used commercially to impart yellow color to mustards, butter, and cheese.

Vanilla Extract
Sweet, intense vanilla flavor. Used extensively in cakes, cookies, muffins, custards, puddings, soufflés, meringues, mousses, and candies.

V

Cooking Terms

Aioli
Garlic mayonnaise.

A

Al Dente
Literally, "to the tooth." To cook (usually pasta or rice) until tender but still firm, not soft or mushy.

Aromatics
Plants, such as herbs and spices, used to enhance the flavor and fragrance of a dish.

Aspic
A clear jelly made from stock or fruit and vegetable juices. Can be used to coat foods or can be cut into cubes and served as a garnish.

Bain-Marie
A water bath used to gently cook foods (almost like a double boiler, one pot nestled into another pot of simmering water).

B

Baste
To moisten the surface food with drippings or marinades during cooking.

Blanch
To briefly cook in boiling water or oil before finishing by another cooking method or storing for later use.

Blind Baking
To partially or completely bake an unfilled pie or pastry crust.

Braise
To sear the surface of meat or vegetables in a hot pan, and then simmer in liquid until tender.

Butterfly
To cut meat or seafood through the center and open it out, like butterfly wings (i.e., butterflied shrimp).

C

Caramelize
To sauté in sugar and fat (usually butter or oil) until golden brown.

Chiffonade
To cut into fine shreds, usually refers to vegetables or fresh herbs.

Clarify
To remove solids from a liquid (such as butter or stock). To make clarified butter, simmer stick butter over low heat until the butterfat, water, and milk separate, forming two distinct layers (about 10 minutes). Using a spoon, remove and discard the solids from the clear yellow liquid. Refrigerate the yellow liquid until solid and use as needed in recipes calling for butter or clarified butter.

Compote
Fresh or dried fruit cooked in syrup or liqueur.

Confit
Meat or poultry that has been cooked and stored in its own fat.

Coulis
A thick purée, often made with vegetables or fruit.

Cure
To preserve food by salting, smoking, or drying (or a combination of these processes).

Deglaze
To dissolve pan drippings and cooked food particles by adding liquid (wine, water, or stock) and simmering until blended.

D

Dice
To cut into small cubes (¼-inch to ¾-inch in diameter).

Dredge
To coat with dry ingredients, usually flour or bread crumbs.

Egg Wash
A mixture of eggs (or egg yolks or whites) and milk or water. Brushed on baked foods to produce a shiny surface.

E

Emulsion
A mixture of liquids, one of which is fat or oil and the other which is water-based. Tiny droplets of one or the other (fat or liquid) are suspended in the other in the presence of emulsifiers, such as eggs or mustard (i.e., salad dressings, mayonnaise). Emulsions may be temporary or permanent, depending on the mixture.

Fondant
An icing made with sugar and water used primarily on candies and pastries.

F

G

Ganache
A filling or glaze made of heavy cream and chocolate.

Génoise
A sponge cake made with eggs. Used frequently in layered cakes and petits fours.

Giblets
Poultry organs and other parts, including the liver, heart, gizzard, and neck.

Glaze
To give food a shiny surface by brushing with sauce, fruit preserves, or icing.

I

Infuse
To blend flavors, such as steeping herbs and spices in liquid.

J

Julienne
To cut into thin strips (⅛-inch square by 1-2 inches long). Fine julienne is 1/16-inch square.

M

Mince
To chop into tiny pieces.

Mirepoix
Combination of chopped or minced vegetables, usually onion, carrots, and celery. Used to flavor soups, stocks, and stews.

Mise en place
To have all ingredients "in place" and ready to use.

Napoleon
Layered pastry rectangles with a variety of fillings (traditionally a pastry cream filling and fondant glaze).

Parboil
Similar to blanching, to briefly cook in boiling water before finishing by another cooking method or storing for later use.

Pare
To peel or trim the outer skin from fruits and vegetables.

Pesto
A thick purée traditionally made with basil, olive oil, pine nuts, and Parmesan cheese. Variations can be made using cilantro, parsley, and a host of other ingredients, including sundried tomatoes and roasted red peppers.

Phyllo Dough
Pastry made with thin sheets of flour and water and layered with butter. Used for both sweet and savory dishes. Also known as filo dough.

Pilaf
A technique for sautéing grains in butter or oil and then simmering in stock or water until tender.

Poach
To cook gently in simmering liquid.

Proof
To allow yeast to rise once warm water and salt are added.

Purée
To process food into a smooth paste. Can be done with a fine sieve, food processor, blender, or food mill.

Q

Quick Bread
Bread made with chemical leaveners, such as baking powder, instead of yeast. Quick breads require no rising time before baking.

R

Reduce
To decrease the liquid volume by simmering or boiling. Used to make a thicker or more concentrated sauce.

Render
To cook high-fat foods, such as bacon, in order to release the fat. The fat is then typically used in sautéing or pan-frying.

Roast
Dry heat method of cooking food, typically in the oven, over longer periods of time.

Roux
An equal mixture of flour and fat (butter or oil) used to thicken liquids.

S

Sauté
To cook foods quickly in a small amount of fat.

Savory
Not sweet.

Scald
To heat liquid (usually milk or cream) just below the boiling point, when small bubbles just appear around the edges.

Score
To make several small cuts into the surface of food, usually meat, to promote even cooking.

Sear
To brown the surface of a food (typically meat, fish, and poultry). Frequently followed by another cooking method, such as braising.

Simmer
To cook just below the boiling point.

Skim
To remove surface material, such as fat, from a liquid during cooking.

Slurry
Starch dissolved in a cold liquid (such as cornstarch in water) before adding to a hot liquid. A slurry prevents lumps in the final product.

Sweat
To cook vegetables or fruit in a small amount of fat until tender but not golden (unlike sautéing, where food is often cooked until golden).

Truss
To tie up meat or poultry with string before cooking. Trussing promotes even cooking and yields a better presentation.

T

Zest
Thin outer portion of citrus rind (colored portion only) used for flavoring.

Z

Equipment

Baking Sheet (Sheet Pan)
Flat or shallow rectangular pan used for baking.

Bread Pan
Loaf-shaped pans available in 8- or 9-inch lengths. Miniature bread pans are also available in various sizes.

Bundt Pan
Large, fluted pan with a central tube used for making decorative, dense cakes.

Cake Pan
Round or square pan (8 or 9 inches in diameter) used for unfilled cakes and bars.

Casserole Dish
Baking dishes, varying in size from 1 pint to 10 quarts, designed for slow cooking in the oven.

B

C

Cheesecloth

Fine mesh gauze used in place of fine sieves to strain some sauces. Also used to bundle herbs and spices, as in bouquet garnis.

Clay Pots

Unglazed clay casserole that is first soaked in water and then filled with food (usually chicken or meat). The casserole is covered, placed in a cold oven and oven temperature is then set to a very high heat. Hot steam from the wet clay cooks the food with a "brick oven" effect and helps tenderize the food. Available in various shapes and sizes.

Colander

Stainless-steel sieve used for straining food.

Custard Cups

Taller than ramekins, baking cups that hold 4 to 5 ounces. Used for puddings, desserts, and molds for rice and other dishes.

D

Deep Fat Fryer

Deep, two-handled pot with gently curved or sloping sides and wide surface area. Wire mesh basket that fits inside is used to drain fried foods.

Double Boiler (Bain-Marie)

Nesting pots with single, long handles. Simmering water in the bottom pot is used to gently cook, warm, or melt food in the upper pot.

Dutch Oven

A large stockpot (usually cast iron or enameled cast iron) with a lid. Used for stewing or braising on the stovetop or in the oven.

F

Food Mill

Strainer with a hand-operated curved blade used to purée soft foods, such as mashed potatoes and applesauce.

Gratin Dish
Shallow, oval baking dish made of ceramic, enameled cast iron, or enameled steel.

Grill Pan
Skillet with ridges used for stove-top grilling. Available with non-stick surface.

Jellyroll Pan
Large, shallow baking sheet with short sides.

Mandoline
A slicer with steel blades used to make various cuts.

Muffin Pan
Pan with 6 or 12 muffin cups used to make muffins and cupcakes. Miniature muffin pans are also available.

Non-Reactive Pots and Pans
Glass, ceramic, and porcelain cookware that does not react with food (especially acidic foods such as tomatoes) or impart any flavor to the dish. Used both on the stove-top and in oven cooking. Glass and porcelain cookware should not be subjected to extreme temperature changes, although modern glass ceramic bakeware has been developed to go from the freezer to the oven without the risk of cracking or breaking. Read the manufacturer's directions before use.

Omelet or Crepe Pan
Shallow skillet with very short, slightly sloping sides.

P

Paella Pan
A wide, shallow pan designed for cooking Paella, a traditional Spanish, rice-based dish.

Pie Pan
Shallow, round baking pans that are 8, 9, or 10 inches in diameter and 1-1 ¼ inches deep. Deep-dish pie pans are also available and are ideal for pot pies and deep, double-crusted, fruit pies.

Pizza Stone
Dense stoneware, either round or rectangular, that conducts heat like the floor of a brick oven. Used for baking pizzas and breads.

Pressure Cooker
Pot with a pressure lid that allows food to cook and tenderize under steam pressure. Safety valves in the lid dissipate the steam safely. Pressure cooking greatly decreases standard cooking times.

Q

Quiche or Tart Pan
Round baking pans with low fluted sides and solid or removable bottoms. Miniature tart pans are also available.

R

Ramekin
Miniature soufflé molds (usually 4-ounce capacity) used for egg dishes, custards, and mousses.

Ring Mold
Deep, large, round pan with a central tube, used for cakes, breads, rice molds, and gelatins.

Roasting Pan
Rectangular or oval pan with medium-high sides used for both roasting and baking. Available in various sizes.

Rondeau
Stockpot that is wider than it is tall, with two loop handles.

Saucepan
Pan with straight or slightly flared sides and a single, long handle.

Saucepot
Smaller version of a stockpot with straight sides and two loop handles for lifting.

Sauté Pan
A shallow skillet with sloping sides and a single, long handle. Also referred to as a Sauteuse.

Sieve
Wire mesh strainer used to strain or purée foods.

Skillet
Shallow pan with slightly sloping or straight sides and a single, long handle.

Soufflé Dish
Round, straight-edged ceramic dish. Available in various sizes.

Springform Pan
High-sided, round pan with removable bottom and a clamp that releases the sides. Used for baking tortes and cheesecakes that are otherwise difficult to unmold.

Steamer
Set of stacked pots. Upper pot with a perforated bottom nestled into a larger pot of simmering or boiling water. Steam from simmering water in the bottom pot is used to gently cook food in the upper pot.

S

Stockpot
Large, straight-sided pot that is taller than it is wide.

T **Tube Pan**
High-sided pan, wider at the top than the bottom, with a central tube that promotes rapid rising and even baking. Traditionally used for angel food cake.

W **Wok**
Large, round-bottomed pot used to cook food as quickly as possible.

Index

achiote. *See* annatto
adobo seasoning, definition of, 179
aioli, definition of, 193
al dente, definition of, 193
allspice, definition of, 179
almonds
    almond-crusted drumsticks, 49
    almond-raisin oatmeal bars, 167
    apricot-almond bars, 122
    basmati pilaf with toasted almonds and cumin seeds, 141
    parmesan-almond crusted broccoli, 109
    pasta salad with almonds and grapes, 169
ancho chile, definition of, 179
andouille penne with andouille and parmesan, 21
anise, definition of, 180
annatto (or achiote), definition of, 180
apple
    apple-cinnamon coffee cake, 161
    apple-oat muffins with mixed fruit, 112
    pie, 117
    roast chicken with apples, sweet onions, and dried fruit, 45
    spice bread, 10
    strudel, 118
apricot-almond bars, 122
aromatics, definition of, 193
artichokes
    Italian-style stuffed, 101
    new potato salad with string beans and artichokes, 102
asparagus
    Dijon chicken with asparagus, 40
    steamed, with tomato vinaigrette, 140
aspic, definition of, 193

A

B

bain-marie, definition of, 193
baking sheet (sheet pan), definition of, 201
bananas
    banana-nut scones, 111
    super moist bread, 7
bars
    almond-raisin oatmeal, 167
    apricot-almond, 122
    carrot cake, 125
basil
    definition of, 180
    linguine with roasted garlic basil pesto, 17
    rolled basil-pesto bread, 4
baste, definition of, 194
bay leaves, definition of, 180
beef, 63-73
biscuits, buttermilk-chive, 11
black beans
    and rice, 100
    chicken and black bean enchiladas, 37
    crispy broiled scallops with spicy black beans, 154
blanch, definition of, 194
blind baking, definition of, 194
blueberry muffins, 113
bouquet garnis, definition of, 180
braise, definition of, 194
bread, 2-11
    pan, definition of, 201
    pizza dough, 1
    sticks, parmesan-sesame, 166
broccoli, parmesan-almond crusted, 109
brownies, super-rocky, rocky road, 127
bundt pan, definition of, 201
burritos, beef and bean, 73
butterfly, definition of, 194
buttermilk

C

D

desserts, 111-32
    almond-raisin oatmeal bars, 167
    apple-cinnamon coffee cake, 161
    chocolate-hazelnut cookies with white chocolate chips, 170
    chocolate-swirled cheesecake, 177
    mixed berry sweetheart shortcake, 141
    orange-pecan pie, 138
    passion fruit sherbet, 155
    pecan-raisin sticky buns, 160
    pumpkin pie with hazelnut crust, 146
    smoothie, strawberry, 172
    swirled pumpkin cake, 159
    walnut-fudge torte, 150
dice, definition of, 195
dill, definition of, 184
dill seed, definition of, 184
double boiler (bain-marie), definition of, 202
dredge, definition of, 195
dressing, cranberry cornbread, 149
duck, Peking, 60
dumplings, Chinese, with soy-ginger dipping sauce, 78
Dutch oven, definition of, 202

E

eggplant parmesan casserole, 26
egg wash, definition of, 195
emulsion, definition of, 195
enchiladas, chicken and black bean, 37
equipment, definitions of, 201-206

F

fajitas, chicken, 46
fennel
    bowties with roasted sweet potatoes and caramelized fennel, 19
    definition of, 184
    seared tuna with anchovy-olive crust and roasted fennel, 85
fettucine, spinach, with fresh tomatoes, 22
filé powder (gumbo filé), definition of, 184

G

H

lobster
    broiled lobster tails, 140
    lobster-corn risotto, 34
lo mein, chicken, 51

mace, definition of, 186
mandoline, definition of, 203
marjoram, definition of, 186
marsala, chicken, with jack cheese, 42
meatballs, with five different sauces, 72
meatloaf, 68
Mexican food
    beef and bean burritos, 73
    black beans and rice, 100
    breakfast quesadillas, 172
    chicken and black bean enchiladas, 37
    chicken fajitas, 46
    crab and shrimp enchiladas, 92
    goat cheese quesadillas with green chile salsa, 166
    layered Mexican chicken with corn tortillas, 39
Mexican oregano, definition of, 186
mince, definition of, 196
mint, definition of, 186
mirepoix, definition of, 196
mise en place, definition of, 196
muffin pan, definition of, 203
muffins, blueberry, 113
mushrooms
    chicken and wild mushrooms in champagne cream, 136
    gravy, 145
    rigatoni, 27
    risotto, 33
    sauté, 108
    stuffed steaks, 63
mussels, roasted, in garlic-shallot broth, 95
mustard (dried), definition of, 186

M

pan, definition of, 204
pumpkin, with hazelnut crust, 146
pilaf
basmati, with toasted almonds and cumin seeds, 141
definition of, 197
pink peppercorns, definition of, 188
pizza,
deep dish, 1
stone, definition of, 204
poach, definition of, 197
poblano chiles, crab-stuffed, with mango salsa, 91
polenta
baked, with spicy vegetable ragout, 107
creamy, with smoked gouda, 108
poppy seeds, definition of, 188
pork, 75-79
potatoes, 102-5
bowties with roasted sweet potatoes and caramelized fennel, 19
corn and red potato hash, 173
maple-orange sweet potatoes, 144
pot pies
beef, 70
chicken, 56
poultry, 35-61
chicken and wild mushrooms in champagne cream, 136
Christmas goose, 148
roast turkey with fresh herbs, 143
seasoning, definition of, 188
pressure cooker, definition of, 204
proof, definition of, 197
pumpkin
pie with hazelnut crust, 146
pumpkin-orange spice loaf, 9
swirled pumpkin cake, 159
purée, definition of, 197

Q

R

slurry, definition of, 199
smoothie, strawberry, 172
sorrel, definition of, 189
soufflé dish, definition of, 205
soup, pasta e fagioli, 17
spaetzle, 149
spaghetti
   bolognese, 24
   carbonara, 29
spareribs, barbecued, 79
spices, definitions of, 179-91
spinach
   coriander shrimp with garlic spinach, 93
   fettucine with fresh tomatoes, 22
   lasagna, 13
   quiche with caramelized shallots, 157
   rolled chicken with spinach and blue cheese, 53
   sautéed, with garlic and pine nuts, 100
springform pan, definition of, 205
star anise, definition of, 190
steak
   cheese, with fried onions, 68
   grilled flank, with peppercorn mélange, 64
   sure-fire shish kebabs, 175
   wild mushroom stuffed, 63
steamer, definition of, 205
sticky buns, pecan-raisin, 160
stockpot, definition of, 206
strawberry smoothie, 172
string beans, roasted red peppers and string beans, 106
strudel, apple, 118
stuffing, sourdough, with sweet Italian sausage, 144
sweat, definition of, 199
sweet potatoes
   bay fries, 103

bowties with roasted sweet potatoes and caramelized fennel, 19
   maple-orange, 144
   whipped candied, 105
swordfish, caper-crusted, with black olives, 86
Szechwan (or Sichuan) peppercorns, definition of, 190

About the Author

Robin Vitetta-Miller has a master's degree in food and nutrition and is a contributing editor for *Cooking Light Magazine*. Her regular columns appear in *Shape*, *Health*, *Natural Health*, *Men's Fitness*, and *Jump*. She has also written articles on food and health for *Family Circle*, *Mademoiselle*, *Woman's Day*, and *First for Women*.

Acting as a spokesperson, Robin has appeared on local and national television, hosted home videos and cable television segments, spoken at media events, and written recipes for Campbell's Soup Company, Weight Watcher's Food Company, *Cooking Light Magazine*, *Health Magazine*, *Men's Fitness Magazine*, Quaker, Uncle Ben's Rice, Del Monte Foods, SlimFast, California Prunes, Hamilton Beach, Equal/Nutrasweet, Bisquick, *Family Circle Magazine*, Nathalie Dupree, Mr. Coffee, T-Fal, and Braun. Currently, she appears regularly on network and cable television.

Robin and her new (handsome) husband Darrin, reside in Princeton, New Jersey.